CW00968414

THE FAST SET

THE FAST SET

*Three Extraordinary Men
and Their Race for the Land Speed Record*

C H A R L E S J E N N I N G S

LITTLE, BROWN

A *Little, Brown* Book

First published in Great Britain in 2004
by Little, Brown

Copyright © Charles Jennings 2004

The moral right of the author has been asserted.

A CIP catalogue record for this book
is available from the British Library.

ISBN 0 316 86190 1

Printed and bound in Great Britain by
Clays Ltd, St Ives plc

Little, Brown
An imprint of
Time Warner Book Group UK
Brettenham House
Lancaster Place
London WC2E 7EN

www.twbg.co.uk

CONTENTS

Acknowledgements

The idea for *The Fast Set* first came to me while I was writing a book about Scotland and came across John Cobb's memorial by Loch Ness. Cobb, like Campbell, Eyston and Segrave, was part of the background noise provided by an earlier generation, both mysterious and quaint. But a profile of Cobb by David Tremayne – indefatigable chronicler of the World Land Speed Record – got me thinking about Cobb, the forgotten hero, exemplar of a lost breed. And originally I was going to write only about him.

But Campbell, in death as in life, muscled his way in soon after. And Segrave made his presence felt not long after Campbell. So I now had three 'speed kings' to contend with, rather than one. I decided, shortly after finding myself trying to get to grips with a fourth – Parry Thomas, Segrave's precursor – that the book should attempt to describe the history of a phenomenon first and offer a multiple biography of the personalities second. The world's reactions are as important as those of the main players. I only hope this account manages to be reasonably coherent.

In all this, my biggest thanks must go to John Pulford, Curator of Collections at the Brooklands Museum in Weybridge. Astonishingly patient and helpful, he and his team of assistants put up with me for weeks on end as I churned through the material in the library and archives. I was, of course, eager to return there as often as I could – not least because the Brooklands Museum, as well as its library, contains a remarkable collection of period motor cars, memorabilia, bits of aviation history, plus many complete and enormous aeroplanes. It also has what is left of the legendary Members' Banking from the old Brooklands racetrack, this alone giving it a magical and, at times, positively eerie atmosphere.

Other people and institutions have helped too: Dr Jim Andrew at the Birmingham Museum of Science and Technology; Vanna Skelley at Castrol International; Stuart Wyss at Dunlop Tyres; Trevor Dunmore at the Royal Automobile Club; Penny Hatfield at Eton College; Jacqueline Cox at Cambridge University Archives. My thanks are due to all of them, as well as to the late John Granger, archivist and historian, who died before this book was finished.

Personal reminiscences and observations were provided most generously by Ronnie Pook (lunch too, as it happened), Frankie Sculthorpe, Michael Radford and Paul Foulkes-Halbard. Dr Tim Reilly got me pointing in the right direction for the history of tuberculosis; Alison Gough gave me some essential Brooklands pointers. Thanks also to Richard Hymans; to the library staff at the National Motor Museum at Beaulieu – home, incidentally, to an early Campbell Land Speed Record racer, plus Segrave's two extraordinary record breakers; to the Surrey History Centre; and to the online Pathé Newsreel resource – a marvellously democratic research tool.

A good deal of the material and many of the quotes derive from contemporary sources: newspapers, magazines, newsreels, radio. Although plenty of books have been written about the speed kings, I found the most useful to be *The Record Breakers* and *Life with the Speed King*, both by Leo Villa. Dorothy Lady Campbell's highly partial memoir *Malcolm Campbell: The Man as I Knew Him* is a fascinating read, in which her natural gentility struggles with a fierce desire to take revenge on her ex-husband. I have quoted from all three books. I would also recommend to anyone with an interest in John Cobb, Thomson & Taylor and the Brooklands story *25 Years at Brooklands Track* by R.H. Beauchamp. *The Locke Kings of Weybridge* is an invaluable brief history of the track and the family behind it, written by J.S. Pulford, John's father. William Boddy's *The History of Brooklands Motor Course* is the standard reference work.

Needless to say, any mistakes in *The Fast Set* are entirely the result of my own incompetence and/or inattention. From the moment Campbell barged in on what was once going to be Cobb's story, the material started to expand exponentially. My apologies to the reader if, as a consequence, I've failed to keep control of all the details. But then, control, as the speed kings knew, was always the biggest problem.

1

Brooklands

((☾ ☽))

Feelings in Edwardian society were mixed, and essentially lopsided, when it came to the subject of motor racing. In 1903 the *Autocar* – the British automobilist's friend and champion – saw it as an elemental struggle, worthy of the highest. 'At racing speeds,' the magazine claimed, 'titanic forces are played with, and if one of the laws they recognize is broken but for the fraction of a second an accident must occur.' This was good, because it was 'The sense of controlling power while all goes well, and the ever-present risk, which constitute the attraction of motor racing to its votaries. It is a pastime for strong men, and only those exceptionally gifted by nature with nerves of steel can shine in the strife.'

Set against this view was that held by the larger part of humanity, the non-racing crowd. At the same time as the *Autocar* was hymning titanic forces and nerves of steel, one of the magazine's correspondents, a Mr H.A. Evans, was complaining that 'No worse specimen of the road hog has come under my notice than the well-to-do gentleman who drives a powerful car at high speeds on the present highways, utterly unsuited for such a purpose.' Moreover, Mr Evans wished to enter 'a strong protest against this frenzy for speed, this utter lack of consideration for others, this contempt for the poorer portion of the community. It was a similar feeling carried to greater extremes which produced the French Revolution.' Even Henry Sturmey, an engineer and notionally susceptible to the charms of motoring, growled that 'At fifty miles an hour, or anything near it, the driver is not really master of his machine, and is but an atom at the mercy of the gigantic forces he has called into being.' Times were changing; the car – worse, the racing car – had arrived. And, as at any time of change, there was a good deal of mutual incomprehension, shouting and general disquiet.

Until about 1905 the French had had things pretty much their own way when it came to organising motor races. The Germans – Karl Benz of Mannheim and Gottlieb Daimler of Cannstatt – may have invented the rickety, teetering horseless carriage in the 1880s, but the progressively minded French had instantly become its most ardent supporters. Indeed, the first recorded sale of a car was to a Frenchman in 1888: a Benz, to M. Emile Rogers, in Paris. Months later, and the manufacturers Peugeot, Renault, Panhard et Levassor and Serpollet had all sprung up like weeds, mostly around the capital.

As a consequence, the very first formally organised motoring contest was the Paris–Rouen Trial of 1894. Initiated by *Le Petit Journal*, this offered a prize of 5000 francs to whichever automobile performed best over the 78 miles separating the two cities. Over a hundred vehicles entered. After much pruning of numbers, twenty-one starters were drawn up, thirteen of which were petrol-driven; the remaining eight steam-powered. The racing was less against the clock and more against the prejudices of *Le Petit Journal*'s specially appointed jury. This team of experts was concerned not only with the absolute speed made by the vehicles, but with their practicality and their theoretical rightness. This meant that when an enormous De

Dion steam tractor came in first, fuelled by a stoker, steered by a driver and drawing its passengers behind it in a separately articulated carriage like a railway train, it was immediately demoted to second place for being ideologically impure. First prize instead went jointly to a Peugeot, which had managed an average speed of 11.5 mph, and a Panhard.

The first true race took place the following year. The object was simply to get from Paris to Bordeaux and back again as fast as possible: a distance of 732 miles on unmade roads, four days being allowed for the competition. This time there were twenty-two starters. Emile Levassor, a director of the Panhard et Levassor motor company, staggered everyone by driving one of his own products almost continually for forty-eight hours, arriving back in Paris on 13 June 1895, to be greeted by a huge and passionate crowd. To his – and the crowd's – rage, he was then denied the first prize of 31,000 francs because of a technical infringement. His car had only two seats instead of the required four. The eventual winner, a Monsieur Koechlin, driving a Peugeot, came in eleven hours later. But it is Levassor who is commemorated in a fine baroque bas-relief overlooking the original finish line at the Porte Maillot.

After that, races happened all over the place, but almost invariably started at Paris. In 1896 they ran from Paris to Marseilles and back. Eighteen ninety-eight saw Paris–Amsterdam–Paris. Eighteen ninety-nine saw a Paris–Bordeaux one-way, plus a Tour de France. Nineteen hundred had Paris–Lyons, 1901 Paris–Berlin and 1902 Paris–Vienna. And for 1903 they announced a sprint from Paris to Madrid, to be undertaken by more than 270 cars.

By now Benz and Daimler's original invention – once so fragile and impermanent, a buggy to which someone had forgotten to attach a horse – had mutated into something genuinely terrible. Eighteen years of engineering progress had seen to it that the racing cars of the new century – the Renault 30, the Mors 70, the Mercedes 90 – weighed as much as a gun carriage and could reach 100 mph on the open road. Even stationary, they intimidated: the driver and his mechanic were seated up at shoulder height, swathed in leather jerkins and monstrous face masks, the vehicle shuddering and stinking beneath them, hideous begrimed radiator coils shimmering with heat, smoke pouring out at the rear, the whole machine apparently innocent of brakes. The French Government was deeply apprehensive and wanted to ban the Paris–Madrid race. There was never any crowd control at these events and spectators simply swarmed on to the road, parting hysterically at the last minute to let the racers through. It was an invitation to disaster. But public pressure overwhelmed state nervousness and the race was allowed to go ahead, on 24 May 1903. The first day's racing would take the drivers from Paris as far as Bordeaux. Around two million spectators were reported to be lining the roadside.

It was carnage. In the smoke and dust, no one could see where they were going. Tyres burst and cars exploded and flew off the course. Vehicles that were moving smashed into others that had stopped. Whole cars were flung upside down into fields. By the end of the first day two drivers, one riding mechanic and five spectators had been killed, while scores more were injured and were lying in hospital or bloodied in the dust at the track's edge. The race was stopped at Bordeaux and the cars summarily halted, before being towed off in shame to the railway station by teams of horses. It was named 'the Race of Death'. The authorities at once banned open-road, point-to-point races in France.

But the members of the Edwardian motoring fraternity were only marginally abashed. After all, they now had the Vanderbilt Cup to look forward to – an annual international event, first run in 1904 and sponsored by US millionaire William K. Vanderbilt Jr – plus the expectation of the first Grand Prix, to be run on a specially modified sixty-four-mile road circuit at Le Mans in 1906. And in the meantime there was the Coppa Florio of 4 September 1905.

The Coppa Florio was big news: Italy's longest, most arduous and most demented motor race. By the end of August that year wealthy enthusiasts were struggling across Europe to get to the start of this event, organised by Count Vincenzo Florio, son of a rich Palerman businessman, as a reply to the French and their near-monopoly on prestige automobile races. It was to be a 231-mile, three-lap dash through Brescia, on to Cremona and back through Mantua, thundering down from the foothills of the Italian Alps and across the plains, covering the vineyards in dust, scaring livestock. All the key motor manufacturers would be there, along with tens of thousands of spectators.

Over twenty huge cars made it to the Coppa's start line, ready for three laps of the triangular road course, each lap taking well over an hour and a half. Florio, who had participated in 'the Race of Death', was one of the competitors, roaring with them through the stuccoed streets of Brescia and off into the dirt and heat of the baking countryside. Four and three-quarter hours later Carlo Raggio, driving a gigantic Itala, came in first. Arthur Duray was second in a de Dietrich, ten minutes behind. Vincenzo Lancia was third in a FIAT and, flushed with triumph, went off to start his own car business. Florio himself came in seventh, driving a Mercedes. No one was killed and the celebrations went on well into the night

Among the British devotees in this eager crowd was one Hugh Locke King: fifty-six years old, rich, car-mad, sandy-haired, with high cheek-bones and a penetrating gaze. He was lucky to be there at all. Displaying his usual level of incompetence, he had got to Brescia so late that he missed the entire race and had to make do with the aftermath. This was bad enough: it had taken him days to get there from Surrey. It would take days to get back; and he had seen nothing. But his annoyance at failing to see the Coppa Florio turned to horror when he discovered that even had he seen every second of the competition, he would have had no one to cheer on. There was not a single British car entered in a field packed with

Mercedes, FIATs, Italas, de Dietrichs, Isotta-Fraschinis and Darracqs. This was because – he was laughingly told – there were no British cars fast enough to compete and anyway no British drivers with any experience of racing. Britain was a slow country with slow cars and slow drivers.

Well, this point was specifically inaccurate: S.F. Edge had won the Gordon Bennett race of 1902, from Paris to Innsbruck, in a British-built Napier. But Locke King could hardly dispute the rest. It wasn't until 1895 that the British Government had lifted the requirement for motor cars to be preceded by a man with a red flag; while the national speed limit had been raised to a scant 20 mph in 1903 and was to stay at that level until 1930. There were no enclosed racing circuits in mainland Britain and racing on the public highway was banned. Indeed, there were barely forty miles of tarmacked road in the whole country.

Admittedly, Sir Henry Norman had recently enjoyed a rally through the centre of Mansfield – 'There was no nonsense about strict limits of speed and no ridiculous traps, but careful protection of narrow streets and dangerous corners; with the result that for a couple of hours a stream of motor cars and motor bicycles went sweeping through the town at speed' – but his glee at being able to tear through the Midlands was predicated on the stern fact that, most of the time, he couldn't. The motor car was an affront to the paradigmatic calm of the British way of life. Consequently, any Continental motor race was an implicit gesture of contempt towards Britain's small, hobbled car industry and its slow-witted products.

Locke King returned home to Brooklands House, the mansion at the heart of his Surrey estate, to sulk. Days went by; the germ of an idea crept into his head. He took stock of the acreage surrounding him, and decided that the great flat area of pines, rhododendrons and damp pasturage half a mile to the south of the house was the ideal place for the world's first purpose-built motor test track: an enclosed space where the manufacturers of British Napiers, Wolseleys and Lanchesters could test their products to destruction and thereby develop machines to surpass those from abroad.

At the same time as he brooded on this vision, he realised that not only would a big, fast circuit make the perfect automobile testing-ground, it would also make a perfect commercial racetrack. Convenient for London – a railway station less than a mile away, good road access – it would bring in huge numbers of people. He did some casual arithmetic and concluded that anything from 100,000 to 200,000 spectators could fit in to the natural three-hundred-acre arena he was about to develop. Ticket prices would reflect the novelty and exclusivity of what was on offer and go from 1/- to a provocative £1. What was more, the land adjoining the track (which he also owned) would be bound to increase in value as the area's prestige rose.

He roughed out a plan for the course, which was to be 100 feet wide and nearly three miles long. It would have a clubhouse, seating for thousands, a paddock in which competitors could tend to their cars, and food and drink concessions. Unlike the long, straggling, improvised circuits on the Continent, it would be compact and shapely enough for most of the racing to be visible from the spectator stands at all times. And fencing, plus the natural civility of the British, would ensure that there would be no problem with crowd control.

There were some constraints: the London and South Western main railway line ran along the north-western edge, the River Wey flowed across the site from south to north, the Itala motor works (which Locke King, an Itala fan, had encouraged on to his property in early 1906) lay to the east, and the Weybridge Urban District Council had a sewage farm just off-centre. So the track would have to make its way around these obstacles, unless he was prepared to pay £65,000 – which he wasn't – to move the sewage farm; the resultant shape being somewhere between that of a kidney and a deformed pear. But then, once he had cleared the expenses of construction – which he put at

around £22,000 – he could sit back and negligently amass a
new fortune to replace the old one which he would have by
now spent.

Hugh Locke King's relationship with money was predictable
enough in a Victorian gentleman with no exceptional talents
or energies who, on the death of his father in 1885, had inherited an estate worth nearly £500,000. He spent much of his
life alternately squandering his colossal inheritance and pitching himself into unstable entrepreneurial ventures in order to
make back the money he had just lost. His father, the Hon.
Peter Locke King, had inherited a good deal of property from
his father, the 7th Lord King, comprising estates all over Devon,
Dorset, Somerset and Surrey. Peter Locke King was dynamic
enough to add to this already substantial portfolio, acquiring
possessions in Byfleet, Chertsey and Weybridge, before becoming a Liberal MP for East Surrey, which post he went on to
hold for a quarter of a century.

But when, in 1848, Hugh Locke King was born to the Hon.
Peter and his wife, Louisa Elizabeth Hoare (of the banking
family), it became clear that the family fortunes were set to
change. Never robust, as a child young Hugh was 'not very
strong', according to his sister Clementina, and not 'strong
enough to go to school or college'. He roused himself sufficiently to be called to the Bar in 1873, but never got round
actually to practising as a barrister. Time went by; he became
a keen member of the National Rifle Association. Then, in
1884, he married Ethel Gore Browne, a young woman whose
natural steeliness filled in the gaps in Hugh's threadbare personality. And from that point on they found plenty of ways to get
through the wealth left him by his father.

They built, for instance, the Mena House Hotel, just outside
Cairo. The couple bought this in the late 1880s, partly to make
money, partly to furnish themselves with a winter bolt hole,
necessitated by Hugh's chronic ill health. Brass-embossed doors,
mother-of-pearl mosaics, blue tiles and Mashrabia pierced

windows were put in. Rooms were added. Log fires and a full English breakfast mitigated the Egyptian cold for those staying over Christmas. It never made a penny and they got rid of it within a few years.

In 1892 the family seat, Brooklands House – built in 1862 by Hugh's father in a beefy mixture of Queen Anne and High Victorian – very nearly burned down, and had to be thoroughly and expensively remodelled. As soon as these remodellings were finished, Hugh Locke King built a golf club, at neighbouring Byfleet. This was called the New Zealand Golf Course and came about as the result of a wager that no one could sensibly landscape a course on the ground in question. The club opened in 1895 and actually ran at a profit, but Locke King never made back his original capital investment.

Then there was the food treatment scheme of 1897. This required Locke King to pour yet more of his fortune into developing a process invented by a Mr Lionel Gye, 'For the purpose of arresting decay in and preserving fresh meat, vegetables and other substances'. Food treatment turned out to be no more profitable than the Mena House Hotel. Within four years Gye, 'the first and true inventor' of the process, was pleading bankruptcy and begging subventions off his friends, having taken Locke King's money down with him. Locke King attempted to pursue Gye through the law courts in order to recover his original investment. But Gye was broke and Locke King was forced to retire and consider his options. This meant that, when the plan came into his head to construct a new kind of motor-racing course in, more or less, his own back garden, he had spent nearly a decade without going after some kind of fruitless commercial undertaking. He had a good deal of pent-up enthusiasm to work off.

He started on the new project in the summer of 1906. Within months his fatal commercial wooziness was infecting every part of the scheme. Originally the racetrack was meant to be perfectly flat. Then Colonel Henry Holden, Superintendent of the Royal Gun and Carriage Factories at Woolwich – an authority on mechanised vehicles, who had been drafted in by Locke King – pointed out that it needed banked curves so that cars could travel at 90 mph without slowing down. Railway engineers had been using this technique for years: it was known as super-elevation. Plainly, super-elevation would put up the costs. But if Brooklands was to be at the leading edge of technology, it had to have banked corners. Locke King limply agreed with Holden and a railway engineer named Alexander Donaldson came in to oversee the project.

Donaldson's first contribution was effectively to double the estimate for building the circuit, raising it from £22,000 to £43,000. A few months later Price & Reeves, the contractors whom Donaldson had brought in to do the actual spadework, raised the estimate to £60,750. Unable to face the prospect of sanctioning so much expenditure on a whim, but equally incapable of giving up the idea which had seemed so irresistible a year earlier, Locke King resigned from the heat of the action and let his wife take charge. Ethel Locke King's solicitor warned her that if she couldn't find the money to finish the track, or if it failed to make a profit, 'Then your situation will hardly bear thinking about.' Another estimate came in: it would now cost almost £97,000 to complete the track and put up the necessary buildings and grandstands.

Ethel gritted her teeth, approved the latest batch of figures, and in January 1907 ten steam cranes, a hundred handcarts, sixty-eight tip wagons and seven miles of railway line were moved on to the Brooklands site. Work to clear the ground had been going on since the previous autumn, but this was the point of no return. To an increasingly frail Hugh Locke King (as his distant relation the Earl of Portsmouth observed, Locke King 'had a weak heart which might kill him at any moment'), it was now clear that not only was all his available capital being used up before his eyes, but he would have to borrow massively to see the job through. Before long he was in debt for the sum of £159,000 and had no way to pay his creditors back, or even keep them at bay. Worse, while he had suffered previous business reversals, these had been at least bearable and relatively private; but Brooklands was vast and it was public. Indeed, the project was being supported by a gallery of astonishingly prominent figures.

The first committee meeting of the Brooklands Automobile Racing Club had been held in December 1906 and involved, among others, Lord Montagu of Beaulieu, Prince Francis of Teck, the Duke of Beaufort, the Duke of Westminster, Lord Dudley, Lord Churchill, Lord Essex, Lord Tollemache, Lord Northcliffe, Lord Sefton and Lord Lonsdale (President). This attendance register from Debrett indicates how keen Britain's titled classes were for Brooklands to succeed. If Locke King went bust, however, the same collection of names would have generated intense public attention, humiliation for him and his friends and an almost certain ostracism by the same smart crowd which up until that point had been lending its eager co-operation.

The only way out was to go forward and complete the project. Eighty truck loads of gravel and cement were arriving every day and half a million tons of earth were being shifted to make up the banked sections of the circuit. An army of horses, wagons and two thousand navvies trudged across the pancake of mud in the centre. An impressive banked bridge was built out of reinforced concrete on the revolutionary new Hennebique principle, to carry the track over the meandering River Wey. The racetrack was set to open in June 1907, but by April the place still resembled a vast archaeological dig punctuated by splintered pine trees and piles of horse manure. A last, tremendous push between May and June saw the track incomplete but sufficiently whole to be presented to its titled supporters on 17 June, the advertised day of opening.

A shattered Hugh Locke King fumbled through his inaugural speech. He was just able to thank Colonel Holden, without whom 'the course could not have been made', and to applaud the work of Messrs Price & Reeves. He also recommended them to anyone else thinking of constructing a motor-racing track. Exhausted by this performance, the tremulous owner and begetter of Brooklands was then loaded into the passenger seat of his wife's Itala tourer and driven off round the circuit at the head of a forty-strong procession of cars.

Pretty soon the more ambitious motorists in the procession broke ranks. A Darracq was seen to run at 90 mph up on the banking; cement dust flew everywhere. The neighbours began to contemplate litigation. No sooner had the course opened than Mr Dams, Mr Cox and Mr Meares applied for a court injunction to restrain Locke King from using the track in such a way as to cause a nuisance. Locke King called thirty witnesses in his defence and argued that, far from intending to poison the tranquillity of Weybridge with his racetrack, he thought that it might provide an added attraction, as it would give his neighbours something to see. The case, heard in 1908, went against him and he was ordered to build a new entrance road to Brooklands as well as to pay the £7000 costs of the hearing.

Noise restrictions were also introduced. Small comfort that it was the first purpose-built motor-racing track in the world; or that news had reached England that the German Kaiser had been so impressed by accounts of the building of Brooklands that he had ordered the construction of a similar track in Germany. The opening was not a success.

A few days after the ceremonial drive-past, Lady Monkswell, a friend of the Locke Kings, noted in her journal that 'They have been building this awful motor track and are so hated by their neighbours . . . that hardly anyone will speak to them.' Stimulated by the prospect of her friends' suffering, she accepted an invitation to Weybridge, where she found that 'The motor track is a perfect nightmare . . . within it stands a ruined farm and cut down trees, mere desolation. A more unenjoyable place to come to on a hot Sunday afternoon I cannot imagine. The beautiful Surrey landscape looks down into this purgatory of motor stables and everything that motors require, seats for thousands of spectators out in the side of the hill.' Mr and Mrs Locke King 'were there looking most depressed'.

Competitors and paying spectators, too, were dismayed by the look of the place and the procedures used during the first public race meeting, three weeks after the opening, on 6 July 1907. A crowd of around twenty thousand turned up for the event and the prize money was lavish. Nearly £5000 had been put up in total; there were six races; and the winner of the Montagu Cup, the big race of the afternoon, stood to take away a massive £1400, plus a trophy worth £200.

Yet there was something ludicrous about the afternoon's entertainments. It wasn't just the lack of viewing points or refreshment facilities – still waiting to be installed – or the bare and blasted landscape stretching off towards Byfleet, which pointed this fact up. The track itself was to blame, being no more than naked concrete, laid in fairly brutal shuttered sections and plainly awaiting some slinkier final finish. Indeed, the plan had initially been to lay a sturdy base of tar concrete, topped off with a half-inch of smooth black Tarfaalt, as used on the promenade at Westcliff-on-Sea.

Then, as the costs ran out of control, the tar concrete base was changed to a cheaper gravel concrete. Tarfaalt was still meant to be applied like icing on top, but what Price & Reeves eventually laid was gravel concrete alone, which was lumpy, ridged, apt to crack, threw up a storm of powder and grit and lacerated car tyres and the drivers' faces. In addition it had escaped no one's attention that some of the banking on the corners was so steep – almost vertical in places – that it would anyway have been physically impossible to apply a layer of Tarfaalt, which, unlike plaster on a wall, needed a road roller to go over it.

This same monumental, hundred-foot-wide track reduced

Edwardian racing cars to the size of toys as they roared off
uncertainly into the distance. Even inside the machines there
could be a sense of dislocation, as an early volunteer from the
Autocar claimed: 'It is more like being at sea than anything
else. There is nothing but the interminable expanse of track in
front; cars overtake as ship overtakes ship. The fact that they
are proceeding at speeds from five to sixty miles an hour is
forgotten. Nothing but the rush of the wind and the bite of
the concrete dust indicates speed at all.'

The competitors had no numbers painted on their cars and
could only be told apart by the colours of the shirts they wore,
following the conventions of horse racing. Lady Monkswell
had grudgingly confessed that 'The controlled strength of the
motors prevents this great horrid place from being vulgar.' But,
for a spectator perched distantly on the hill where the Members'
enclosure stood, it was the greatness of the place which effectively emasculated the controlled strength of the motors and
made it impossible to tell one driver's shirt from another at a
distance of much more than a hundred yards.

That Brooklands stayed this way – oversized, incomplete
and fundamentally wrong – until its demise, thirty-two years
later, was telling. It was never quite finished and was never
going to be. Just as Hugh Locke King and his wife stumbled
into the scheme, improvising their way through an obstacle
course of financial and engineering crises, so the Brooklands
circuit was subjected in its life to a fever of experimentation
– adding, changing, tinkering and discarding – in an effort to
get the track to work, to come good. Its enclosing, organic
shape suggested a kind of completeness. Its grandeur and its
architectural massiveness made it seem 'like a great Roman
work'; presumably with the same virtues of longevity and
imperial masterfulness. It was a kind of Coliseum, complete
unto itself and unbreachable. But its form flattered to deceive.
It was at root flawed, reactive and always on the lookout for
a fix that might stick.

The surprise was that, even though it bore Hugh Locke King's personality like an unsatisfactory child, it was a success despite itself – for a time the first and then *the* motor-racing venue in England – and a place whose garbled values were ultimately perpetuated by those national and international prodigies of daring and fame Sir Henry Segrave, Sir Malcolm Campbell and Mr John Cobb. It was the *fons et origo* of their quest for speed; the birthplace of the speed kings.

Thus Brooklands opened as the first purpose-built motor-racing track anywhere in the world and had its first race a year before even the circuit at Indianapolis, Indiana. Soon it was being used for record-breaking attempts, primitive motor industry stunts (such as a Royal Automobile Club-organised trial to discover which type of tyre raised the least dust), motor races, and the job for which it was originally conceived, testing British production cars. Indeed, the competition among car makers using Brooklands was for a while so keen that as well as dressing up test models to conceal their true origins from industry spies, they would glue false beards to the drivers.

It quickly gained a reputation as a smart place to be. As *The Social Guide* of 1911 explained, 'While in the first season the races were merely contested by trade rivals, competitors are now, to a great extent, amateurs, with the result that good sport is seen, and a fashionable crowd is generally found at Brooklands.' Not just, it should be said, because of the races – but because of the aeroplanes. Significantly, *The Social Guide*, having listed the eight forthcoming main race meetings at Brooklands for that year, closed its announcement with the news that 'There will be Flying Competitions on each of the above dates.' This meant more than a few fly-pasts and some dogged aerobatics in a Farman biplane. It indicated that Brooklands was not just a centre of motoring activity: it was somewhere where the even more innovative businesses of flying and aircraft manufacture were being conducted, in the great empty space south of its clubhouse and spectators' stands.

Britain's first great aviator, A.V. Roe, had established the trend by setting up in a shed opposite the Brooklands' clubhouse and building a little string-and-fabric biplane in 1907. The Clerk of the Course, Major Ernst de Rodakowski – who had been instrumental in the building of the track, and indeed in the running of the Mena House Hotel all those years ago – had a highly sectarian view of the world. He loathed Roe and struggled to be rid of his tone-lowering presence. He persistently harassed the penniless engineer, who was not only forced to take out his plane and test it when de Rodakowski wasn't looking, but had to subsist on a diet of dates and kippers while sleeping rough in his shed, inside a wooden crate. Roe claimed that for days on end his only companion was a robin. Nonetheless, in 1908 he became the first Briton to leave the ground in a heavier-than-air machine, successfully achieving take-off at Brooklands. Then de Rodakowski had his way and finally ejected him, his flying machine and his shed from the track.

In 1910 Roe founded the famous AVRO aircraft company (along with his brother, H.V. Roe, the husband of Dr Marie Stopes) and claimed his knighthood; while de Rodakowski lost his job.

It was de Rodakowski's successor, Major J. Lindsay Lloyd, who understood the way things were going. He also spotted the financial benefits of diversification, and in 1909 started to promote the far end of the Brooklands site as a little aerodrome. Within two years there were six flying schools, a clutch of constructors (Martinsyde, Sopwith) and numerous private enthusiasts infesting the sheds which the Brooklands Automobile Racing Club had erected down near the sewage farm. The Keith Prowse ticket agency opened the world's first aviation booking office in 1911, in a tiny brick building the size of a bus shelter. Four guineas bought a flight of three circuits round the Brooklands aerodrome, or you could go across country for ten guineas.

In September 1913 a French pilot named Celestin-Adolphe Pegoud gave the first British demonstration of looping the loop. Members of the public could visit the flying ground on payment of a 1/- admission fee. Twenty years later Brooklands was one of the south-east's centres of aviation and the Brooklands School of Flying ('For really expert instruction on really modern lines you must come to Brooklands') was an adjunct of modern life. Pupils sat in an open-sided wooden box out on the grass while an instructor familiarised them with hypothetical controls.

It also emphasised that the Brooklands vision, the Brooklands concept, was now more or less illimitable – a vision which in thirty-two years helplessly embraced motor racing, lawn tennis, motorcycling, bicycling, a bijou golf course, flying, on-course betting, hill climbs, speed record breaking, billiards in the club-house and *thés dansants* in the hilltop restaurant. In the early days there was the opportunity to shoot rabbits on summer nights, when sportsmen with shotguns would drive round the track, catching the animals in the glare of their acetylene head-lamps. In 1931 the owners entertained the idea of building a swimming pool, but later abandoned it. The flying was just the biggest and most visible of the schisms from Locke King's original scheme; and it was, in the end, to overwhelm it entirely.

At the northern end of the site, Locke King's more consciously realised end, the Brooklands staff hit upon the idea of making the motor races interesting by putting legible numbers on the cars and handicapping them. A short, stout man named A.V. 'Ebby' Ebblewhite – car-obsessed but a musical-instrument maker by profession – worked out a way to handicap the faster cars in any given race by letting the slower ones start first. A single starting line was marked out on the concrete, along which all the competitors would range themselves. Ebblewhite, clutching a miniature Union Jack, would stand in front of each car in turn, gazing at his stopwatch. When the time was right he would skip out of the way, drop the flag to signal that the competitor could go, and turn his attention to the next machine. Ideally, the faster cars then spent the next five or so laps catching the slower ones, with the result that every race would be run as a kind of fugue, ending in a breathless dead heat.

The racing cars themselves were mostly Continental in origin. It took time for Locke King's dream of more, faster British cars to burgeon into reality. Yes, Vauxhall, Sunbeam and Austin were there; but so were Mercedes, Peugeot, Bugatti, as well as the now-vanished patrician order of Lorraine-Dietrich, Le Gui, Chenard-Walcker, Brenna, de Dion Bouton, Itala, Darracq, Sizaire-Naudin and Piccard-Pictet. Whatever their nationality, they were a bewildering mishmash of stripped-down, lashed-up, mangled semi-specials, lumbering Edwardian four-wheelers resembling huge pieces of furniture or military hardware, their doors, bonnets, mudguards and carriage lamps torn off, and sometimes with grotesque submarine sports bodies bolted in place.

Their vastness was a functional necessity. In these early days the way to make an engine more powerful was to make it bigger. The Renault racer of 1906 had four cylinders but a capacity of over thirteen litres. The Benz of 1909 also had four cylinders but a capacity of twenty-one litres. The Fiat 300 CV of 1911 (FIAT had evolved into the lower-case Fiat in 1906) had four cylinders and a capacity of twenty-eight litres – equivalent to about sixteen modern car engines. The towering cylinder blocks and vast flywheels of such motors imposed their own aesthetic on the rest of the vehicle, preventing any serious Edwardian contender from being anything other than a rolling misshapen giant. A notional connection with horse racing remained insofar as the owners liked to give their machines names, in order to civilise their dwarfing ugliness: *Billy, Ettie, Golliwog, Nautilus, Dolly Varden, Vieux Charles Trois.*

And so a routine grew up: racing throughout the season; flying and motoring stunts and tests all year round. The facilities improved. The Royal Automobile Club (RAC) held Gala Meetings in which entrants were blindfolded: an observer sat beside each driver and rang a bell if danger loomed. There was a race for London taxicabs in 1909. Hugh Locke King didn't make any money, but at least his finances regularised themselves a year after the opening of Brooklands – no thanks to the track, which, predictably, failed to generate an income. The answer came in the time-honoured form of loans from sympathetic friends and family, along with the sale of some of the remaining bits of his inheritance. And Locke King survived. In the first six years of its life Brooklands began to develop an identity, to consolidate. Then the First World War broke out.

2

The Smart Set

During the Great War Brooklands was commandeered by the military, becoming Britain's largest aircraft manufacturing centre. The War Office took over the aerodrome in August 1914; by October the racetrack had also been closed to the public. The Army Flying Corps established an HQ there soon after; its lorries ploughed across the infield and broke up the concrete track far more thoroughly than the racing cars had ever done. In 1915 the Itala car factory went broke and sold its premises to the Vickers aviation company. Vickers promptly painted its name in enormous letters on the side of the works and dedicated itself to turning out BE2c biplanes, SE5a fighters and the Vickers Vimy bomber. So much inadvertent damage was done to the fabric of Brooklands that it took until 1920 to repair itself and reopen. But this discontinuity served it well. The twenties were just about right: a nervously fortuitous arrival that enabled Brooklands properly to create its own myth.

Speed had become intrinsically fascinating. Motor transport, air transport, wireless communication: these were fashionable, challenging ways to abbreviate time and space, to escape the past, to anaesthetise the present. At the end of 1919 there were still only about 200,000 motor cars in the UK, for a total population of over forty million. And there were around a hundred different makes of car, all being assembled piecemeal around Britain, in little factories and lock-ups. It was still barely an industry. But the historical dynamic was working in its favour.

By 1930 over a million private cars would be registered in the UK. And in the intervening years many people got their first true taste of speed as the result of driving, or at least sitting in, a moving, open-topped car. For a generation whose most daring adventures through space and time would have been in the closed compartment of a railway train travelling at 60 mph, the unmediated experience of wind, noise, the smell of petroleum spirit and burnt engine oil, the suppressed awareness that cars crashed every day with bleak regularity, would have been intoxicating and appalling. For the owner of a sporting Delage or a sophisticated Cadillac, the sensual excitement of travel was heightened by the knowledge that his car shamelessly advertised his social position at the same time as it kept him apart from the rest of the commonalty.

Motoring was a pleasure still largely confined to the rich, or at least, the well-heeled: a Vauxhall tourer cost £895 in the mid-1920s, while a Bentley chassis alone came in at £1450. A newly built three-bedroomed suburban home, on the other hand, could be bought outright for £900. In pre-war days owning a motor car had entailed nearly the same level of financial commitment and fervid eccentricity as keeping a yacht. Since then, advances in production techniques had helped to rebalance the equation between what you paid and what you got. But even a drab vehicle such as a Bean 5-Seater cost a provocative £395. About the cheapest car you could buy was a two-stroke Trojan, at £125; much favoured by poor clergymen. Still, that was inflammatory enough at its top speed of 30 mph, thanks in part to its solid tyres and non-conformist suspension; even the Trojan shared something with its grander relations.

Moreover, although plenty of twenties vehicles still had the same visual impact as the flying wardrobes and modified hearses of the Edwardian era, others were just starting to enter a golden age of car design. The Kaiser's War, the first thoroughly mechanised mass conflict, had taught engineers much about the internal combustion engine. Consequently, the Hispano-Suiza, Bugatti, Bentley and Mercedes (soon to become Mercedes-Benz) marques were moving towards more sophisticated creations, cars whose engineering promised masculine thrills and whose increasingly sculpted forms not only made them look more the way cars should look, but, in the case of the Bugatti, even crossed the line between expressive utility and autonomous beauty.

Excitable Italian Futurists had been on to this since before the war. Marinetti's 1909 *Futurist Manifesto* ('We declare that the world's wonder has been enriched by a fresh beauty: the beauty of speed. A racing car with its trunk adorned by great exhaust pipes like snakes with an explosive breath . . . a roaring car that seems to be driving under shrapnel, is more beautiful than the *Victory of Samothrace*') was one instance; Giacomo Balla's 1913 painting *Speed of a Motorcycle* another. For them the world was moribund; it could only be reinvigorated by the annihilation of the past and the constitution of a new present based on steel, oil and rubber.

Quieter post-war converts varied from René Lalique, whose delectable glass radiator mascots could be lit from inside, glowing more intensely as the car's speed increased, to Evelyn Waugh. Rather, Waugh didn't endorse speed as an end in itself; but he did accept its fashionability. His critique of it fills the concluding quarter of his late-twenties satire *Vile Bodies*. One of his characters, Agatha Runcible, turns up for a round-the-houses motor race: 'There were Speed Kings of all nationalities, unimposing men mostly with small moustaches and apprehensive eyes; they were reading the forecasts in the morning papers and eating what might (and in some cases did) prove to be their last meal on earth.' In the course of the story Agatha gets drunk, nearly blows up the pits and ends up competing in car number 13 before wrecking it 'on the market cross of a large village'. We last see her in a Wimpole Street nursing home: '"All friends here," said Miss Runcible, smiling radiantly. "Faster . . . Faster . . . it'll stop all right when the time comes . . ."'

Back in the real world, the Duke of Leinster won a £3000 bet by driving his Rolls-Royce from London to Aberdeen in fourteen and a half hours, prompting enquiries as to whether he would be prosecuted for speeding. As Sinclair Lewis wrote of Babbitt in his 1922 novel of that title, 'His motor car was poetry and tragedy, love and heroism.' Kathleen, Countess of Drogheda, *was* fined twenty shillings for driving her car through London in a dangerous manner. 'I can't stop, I'm in a hurry,' she told the police. Mrs Barbara Innes, daughter of the Hon. Lancelot Lowther, took a job in 1924 selling motor cars at a Bond Street showroom. 'I intend to specialise in salesmanship,' she said. 'I shall drive for the firm as well as demonstrating to customers. I shall miss a certain amount of hunting but foot-and-mouth disease has stopped most of that so I really cannot grumble.'

The Hon. Elizabeth Ponsonby – the model for Agatha Runcible – invented the champagne bottle party and the find-the-hidden-clue motor-car race. In 1923 the Marchioness of Queensberry decided to drive herself to Rome in a sports car; in the course of her trip she ran out of money and had to live on buns. Major Forbes-Leith, on the other hand, successfully drove his Wolseley from England to India (8500 miles) in 1925: 'The greatest motor drive in the history of mankind.' In 1927 Isadora Duncan was strangled when her billowing scarf caught in the wheels of her Bugatti.

The bleak, industrial scale of modern motoring and aviation – the purgatorial banality – was all to come. At Brooklands, not only were speed and excitement freely on offer to the jittery survivors of the war, but the distorted concrete oval of the track made an ideal enclosure in which to enjoy them. The banking at either end and the railway line on the western side created a cordon sanitaire with which to exclude the rest of the world. Later on, enthusiasts would wistfully compare it to a country estate: enclosed, semi-formal, green. For the necessarily well-connected and well-off members of the Brooklands Automobile Racing Club – the majority of whom were social members and never raced in their lives – there was, according to Brooklands regular P.J. Wallace, 'a sense of complete freedom to do as one liked'; and, whatever your taste, 'the dominating impression everywhere was one of free and easy friendliness'.

It was not a sporting venue in the sense that one now understands the term. Quite apart from anything else, motor racing at the start of the 1920s was a sport with only vestigial rules and an immature international structure. All the same, the Association Internationale des Automobile-Clubs Reconnus (AIACR), which had been founded in 1910 to act as the governing body for motor sport in Europe, was busying itself inventing regulations concerning engine size and body weight for racing cars (the 'formula') and in stirring up enthusiasm for fresh Continental, and even intercontinental, competition. By 1921 the French Grand Prix at Le Mans had been joined by an Italian Grand Prix near Brescia (the circuit at the Monza Autodrome opened a year later), as well as by a race at Indianapolis, the Targa Florio (successor to the Coppa Florio and held in the mountains of Sicily) and a Gran Premio Gentlemen, again at Brescia.

Nineteen twenty-two was still livelier. Tentative post-war opportunism brought out some of the most serious Continental car makers – Bugatti, Fiat, Ballot, Sunbeam-Talbot-Darracq (STD) – followed later by Alfa Romeo, Delage and Benz. Drivers were either gentleman adventurers or manufacturers' employees who had come up through the ranks. The races themselves were terrifically arduous, lasting from four to six hours – at the end of which the glory of victory accrued first to the car makers, secondly to the filthy and exhausted drivers. Racing abroad was not something to be undertaken trivially.

Brooklands, being so far removed from Continental practice, hardly felt the presence of the AIACR at all. Instead, it was the conviviality of the place that counted more than its competitiveness – along with the oddly sequestered nature of its pleasures, the way it offered asylum from the traffic police and the hand of authority. A mere forty-eight of the 744 drivers listed in the 1907–14 period actually made it back to Brooklands in the 1920s.

The post-war intake was composed, therefore, of young men who had just missed the fighting; and, in greater numbers, of men who had survived the fighting but had been stimulated both by action and the machinery with which they had fought. Either way they tended to come from the same narrow social class and to have money. It was an age characterised by Brooklands' slogan 'The Right Crowd and No Crowding'. For its devotees, the leafy proprieties of Surrey just visible at the edges of the circuit were reassurance that, even outside, everything was all right; and besides, Piccadilly was only twenty miles away.

For much of this time racers (in cars or on motorcycles) simply drove anticlockwise around the distorted oval, the misshapen concrete pear (now known as the Outer circuit), hitting their highest speeds on the long Railway Straight, which ran parallel with the railway line. Occasionally they would lunge down the Finishing Straight. This was a length of track which split off from the end of the Byfleet banking, headed north-west in a straight line (just in front of the clubhouse) and rejoined the track at the Members' Banking, cutting off part of the uppermost corner, where the Members' Hill and grandstands rose over the circuit.

The idea was to race round in the conventional manner,

before peeling off at the bifurcation known as the Fork, ending the last lap on the Finishing Straight and coming to a halt just after the clubhouse. If you didn't stop, or couldn't, you shot back on to the banking on the far side and into the path of other, slower cars which were still completing their last laps. Or, like the late Vincent Hermon, found that your Minerva racer drove straight up on to the steepest part of the Members' Banking, rolled over and crushed you against the parapet of the Hennebique Bridge.

The clubhouse itself was domestic in scale and appearance, like a deformed country hotel. Its red brick, its pitched roof and its eaves and its amusing green-domed belvedere shared the architectural vocabulary of countless well-mannered Edwardian Surrey buildings. As the years went by it would also acquire – to add to the restaurant, bar, administrative offices and weighbridge that were there already – seasidey white clapboard extensions and a promenade balcony, a ladies' lounge, a bathroom and changing rooms for the gentlemen competitors.

The Brooklands Lawn Tennis Club, established in 1911, of which Lady Dorothy D'Oyly Carte was an early member, offered a selection of hard courts round the back of the club-house and play twelve months a year. The neighbouring row of diminutive, open-sided stalls where drivers fixed their cars up before a race had something decently provisional, under-whelming about it; while the paddock stretched between the track and the clubhouse buildings, a parade ground thronged with civilians. On-course betting with Jack Linton, Lionel Pearce, Harry Jay and Long Tom ('For Long Prices') took place in the Members' enclosure. The miniature golf course appeared, as if laid out by pixies. Races took place most weekends during the season, but, like a golf course, the place was open all through the week for whatever a motoring gentleman with time on his hands might feel able to enjoy. Even when the track was being refurbished during the winter months, some motorists would be on hand for testing, or to make record attempts in between the concrete-layers' shifts.

Approaches to fun varied, amid the bark and crackle of the exhausts, the opal-blue smoke. Over here is Captain Alistair Miller, driving a Wolseley Moth round and round and round the track, hour after hour, trying to break long-distance records. 'I believe Mr Miller thought he was a planet,' said an official later. Here is Mr L.C.G.M le Champion, amusing himself by repeatedly skidding his Isotta-Maybach on the aerodrome tarmac in order to burst its tyres; and here is 'Anna' on loan to the *Motor* magazine, commentating on ladies' fashions: 'Possibly it was owing to the influence of Ascot: at any rate, my general impression of the recent rather exciting Brooklands meeting was that the gathering was more smartly dressed than any of its predecessors.'

The lupine, piratical Count Louis Vorow Zborowski, who invariably sports a tasteless check golf cap (specially imported from Palm Beach) and obliges his mechanics to do the same, is endeavouring to start up *Chitty-Chitty-Bang-Bang*, his twenty-three-litre Zeppelin-engined special, with the aid of an aeroplane's half-axle. Can that be the legendary Major 'Shuggar' Cooper with him; or is it Mr C.A. Bird, son of the custard-powder magnate? And will they notice Miss Ivy Cummings, practising for the big race in her Frazer Nash; not, on this occasion, in the company of her mother?

An anonymous motorist has paid his one-day admission fee, filled up at the Shell Petrol Pagoda in front of the clubhouse and is running his new car in: driving round and round for eight hours at 30 mph, while daring bacteriologist Dr J. Dudley 'Benjy' Benjafield thunders past him in a four-and-a-half-litre Bentley at four times that speed. Over there is the Hon. Mrs Victor Bruce, about to start her first flying lesson; while here Mr Walker, first-aid operative and chief lavatory attendant, is taking delivery of another ten-gallon drum of iodine. Here

Mr Charles Mortimer, the popular motorcycling enthusiast, is working out new ways to trick Mr Ebblewhite, the handi-capper, by swapping alcohol fuel for the petrol-benzole mix in his machine and laying the results off with the bookies: without 'a little jiggery-pokery,' he explains, 'you could never make your racing pay as it should.'

And now a woman known only as 'M.L.T.' is being driven round the track for the very first time: 'It was most thrilling. The air became ten times colder, the roar of the exhaust became a shriek, and the song of the engine rose exultantly as the speedometer-needle crept round the blue disc. The gale tore at my hair and my nose became blue, but I wanted to sing or shout or do something completely and gloriously mad.'

At the top end of the fiscal scale was Woolf Barnato, a diamond millionaire from South Africa; a man so breathtakingly rich that at the height of his powers he was spending over £40,000 a year on cars, racehorses and parties. Frivolous yet steely: three times winner of Le Mans, he single-handedly kept the Bentley business alive during the Depression, as well as racing consistently and enthusiastically at Brooklands, putting in a near-record 172 appearances. Eventually he did lose patience with the Bentley concern, allowing Rolls-Royce to snap it up wholesale. 'I know nearly £100,000 went down the drain in Bentley Motors,' he blithely disclosed. 'But in one diamond deal during that time I made £120,000, so I can't grumble.'

Francis Richard Henry Penn Curzon, the 5th Earl Howe, also won at Le Mans, meanwhile moving in remorselessly on Brooklands and British motoring. He wore a cloth cap at a flamboyant angle and carried an oversized golf umbrella as an emblem of potency. So sure was Howe of his centrality to the world of motor sport that he once lobbied – unsuccessfully – to have his personal racing colours of blue and silver adopted as the official racing colours for Great Britain.

The Dunfees – Jack, a 'millionaire', 'irrepressible' and a

'long languid cynic', and his brother, the more introspective
Clive – both competed regularly; until the latter suffered a
dreadful death in 1932 by going over the top of the banking
in his Bentley while overtaking Earl Howe's Bugatti. Dunfee
demolished his car against a tree and was killed instantly. His
corpse then rebounded back on to an unreachably steep part
of the track. It lay there with competitors' cars thrashing past,
until a track official lowered himself on to the concrete with
the help of a fallen branch and dragged the body away. Jack
Dunfee never raced again.

The Duke of Richmond and Gordon won the British Racing
Drivers' Club 500-mile race in 1930, with his co-driver, S.C.H.
'Sammy' Davis. Howe participated in this event, too, allowing one revolutionary-minded newspaper to run the headline
'The Two Earls and Thirty Misters Race'; and to describe the
winning duo as 'An Earl and his minion'. The grandson of
King Chulalongkorn of Siam (the inspiration for King Mongkut
in *The King and I*) left Eton College, abbreviated his name
from Prince Birabongse Bhanuban to B. Bira and raced in a
light-blue ERA christened *Romulus*.

And then there was Commander Glen Kidston. Even by the
standards of between-the-wars Brooklands, the lantern-jawed
Kidston was so dashing as to be almost fantastical. Having
inherited a fortune in his teens, he dedicated his life to both
the deliberate and the unpremeditated pursuit of danger. In the
Great War he survived a German torpedo attack which killed
over 1400 of his comrades. He subsequently lived through the
disintegration of a speedboat at 60 mph and the crashing of
a Bentley at 100 mph. He was nearly burned to death in 1929
when the Lufthansa passenger plane in which he was travelling crashed near Croydon; the seven other occupants were all
killed. But he recovered his equilibrium the next year by winning
Le Mans in a Bentley with Woolf Barnato.

Kidston's final – and possibly greatest – act was in April
1931, when he set a new London–Cape Town air record of

six and a half days, having left his eighteen-year-old girlfriend
with a diamond-encrusted Cartier watch as a farewell gift.
'Millionaire Flier's Record Dash,' yelled the headlines. 'Kidston
Does It.' He claimed that his intention was to 'ginger up'
Imperial Airways, who were, in his opinion, excessively slack
in opening up this vital transcontinental route. In between
times he drove his Hispano-Suiza H6 around London while
dressed in full naval uniform, raced at Brooklands,
photographed big game and conducted an affair with the novelist Barbara Cartland ('Glen was extremely attractive, amusing,
dashing and a wonderful dancer,' she said later). His end came
in May 1931, when, having gingered up Imperial Airways, he
flew his plane straight into South Africa's Drakensberg
Mountains, and Brooklands lost arguably its most glamorous
son.

In the meantime Brooklands made the most of its heyday. On
a warm summer afternoon, what could be nicer than to lounge
in the grass on the Members' Hill, the great bowl of Brooklands
stretching away towards the south-west into the blue Surrey
haze, a picnic hamper handily on the back seat of your tourer,
a sea of smart tailoring and tasteful couture parting around
you, the bookies lined up against the metal railing that edged
the Finishing Straight, your race card reminding you that 'Where
betting takes place, the public are advised to back on the number
of the car and not the driver, as changes of drivers may be
made during the race'; and that 'The public are warned not
to bet with Bookmakers who do not display their official
Brooklands Permit'? Yes, as with all motor races, the place
was sometimes infested with boys wishing they were men; and
men wishing they were more than the men they already were.
And the noise and smell of the cars could be irksome.

But otherwise it was all so ordered, so comfortable, so
spacious. Perhaps you knew someone about to 'take the cement'
and you could watch them compete. Perhaps you might glimpse

a famous driver such as Woolf Barnato or Dr Benjafield or Jack Dunfee. And if a race was boring, why then, it would soon be over and another would take its place. There were a good nine races to get through, after all; but still time after the last one, at five-thirty, to enjoy a drink in the clubhouse.

The downside of all this privileged laxity was that as time went by it became increasingly clear that Brooklands was a terrible circuit on which to hold a motor race. The fun, all along, was a response to an unshirkable difficulty: the track didn't work. Yes, it was fine in the days immediately after the First World War to board your Humber or Salmson or home-made aero-engined leviathan and circulate frantically around the three-mile concrete pear. But by the mid-twenties everyone knew that there was more to motor racing than that. Continental racetracks (now including one at Spa, Belgium, and another at San Sebastián, Spain) had bends, straights, complex challenges. Any driver who wanted to impress had to do so elsewhere: at the very least, in the Isle of Man Tourist Trophy; better, in a Grand Prix or the hair-raising Le Mans 24-Hour endurance race. Compared with what was available abroad, Brooklands was like a slot racer in its simplicity. What could anyone expect? It had been designed in 1906 by an Edwardian amateur, at a time when getting a car to move at all, let alone swiftly and sinuously, was an achievement.

So Brooklands Automobile Racing Club, which ran the place, tried to make the track more intriguing by offering a track within a track, pressing into service the D-shaped loop created by the Finishing Straight and half of the Members' Banking. This could be turned into a little sprint course, which they named the Mountain Circuit as it ran round the hill on which the spectators sat. To enliven the original pear-shaped track, they laid out wicker fences, sandbanks and straw bales, creating chicanes and pseudo-corners. They painted lines over the track surface like motorway lanes, to segregate the very fast cars from the slower ones, to minimise the number of potential crashes, to facilitate the handicapping process and to reduce the chances of cars flying over the top of the banking.

Watching film of the races at Brooklands at this time is often so disorientating as to be quite dreamlike. Little cars scurry along at the bottom of the frame, while at the top, travelling much faster and bouncing passionately up and down on its springs, an absolutely huge car, looking like a bus or a locomotive, thunders by, passing the smaller cars as if they've forgotten to release their handbrakes. The difference in size and speed is dizzying, an affront to perspective: hence the need to marshal the machines by marking the surface of the road. Of course, in the Le Mans 24 Hours, very fast cars have always shared the circuit with relatively slower vehicles. But the circuit is eight and a half miles long, as opposed to three. There is simply more room.

They ran races clockwise and they ran them anticlockwise. They ran races that were handicapped and races which were scratch fixtures. They ran races in which the drivers had to sprint across the track to their waiting cars, jump in and start them up, Le Mans style; races for tourers, in which they put their canvas hoods up for a few laps and then let them down again; races where the cars pelted briefly out of the track altogether and back into it via the Members' Bridge; they ran a race between a supercharged Austin Seven and a Greenbat two-ton electric truck, laden with sacks, in which the truck was given a head start of one hour and twenty-five minutes. There was a 352-foot stretch of tarmac going up the side of the Members' Hill; known as the Test Hill, it was no more than a miniature hill climb in segmented gradients for the proving of brakes and engine power – but even this was commandeered as part of a High Speed Trial Course in 1925.

So, an atmosphere was created in which anything went, provided it submitted itself to the ethos of the circuit, obeyed all the restrictions imposed by the neighbours of Weybridge and didn't demand an interesting track layout. It was inevitable that, for want of anything better and in the absence of any Continental-style races (unless they were prepared to organise a trip abroad), some drivers would put racing to one side and try their hand at record breaking.

Indeed, Brooklands – essentially two huge corners and a straight – could have been built just for this purpose, and drivers had been taking advantage of it from the moment the track was completed. In the brief gap between the invitees' drive-past and the public opening of Brooklands back in 1907, the egomaniacal S.F. Edge had single-handedly driven a Napier for twenty-four hours round the track at an average speed of 65.9 mph.

In February 1913 a driver named Percy Lambert set a world record by driving his Talbot round Brooklands for one hour at just over 100 mph. In June 1914 L.G. 'Cupid' Hornsted broke the World Land Speed Record in a Benz, at 124 mph. In May 1922 Kenelm Lee Guinness, a member of the brewing dynasty, took a new World Land Speed Record at Brooklands in a Sunbeam at just under 134 mph. And in between all these headlining triumphs, hundreds of lesser records were broken, over numerous distances, for different lengths of time, in cars of every possible size and shape.

Such a growth industry was it that by 1925 the RAC had convinced the AIACR that it needed to formalise the engine-size categories in which cars could attempt distance or time records, or both. As a result Class A was for the biggest cars, over 8000 cc; Class H was for minnows whose engines were bigger than 500 cc but no larger than 750 cc. Classes B to G were for everything in between. Measurable distances ranged from a single kilometre to anything the entrant felt like attempting, although 5000 kilometres was usually as much as anyone could manage. Thus, if a two-litre (Class E) car circulated a track for, say, twenty-four hours, it might progressively take the two-litre world speed records for distances of 200 miles, 500 kilometres, 1000 miles, 2000 kilometres and so on, until it stopped. It could also, simultaneously, take the average-speed records for time periods of three hours, six hours, twelve hours and twenty-four. And if a driver wanted to break the same time and distance records in a car with a bigger – or smaller – engine, there was nothing to stop him or her. Nor was there anything to stop another driver, or team of drivers, in a different car of the same capacity from going out the next day and raising the records which had just been set.

By 1930 there were 242 world records on the books, of which seventy-five had been set at the Weybridge circuit. It became an essential part of the track's financial turnover as well as of its sporting character. Fees – which covered the costs of a supervisor, timekeeper and the use of the track – went from thirteen guineas to thirty-six guineas for hand-timing long-distance record attempts; and from eighteen guineas to twenty and a half guineas for electrically timed shorter bids. And when record-breaking activities tailed off at the start of the thirties, Brooklands was quick to try to entice would-be record breakers back with specially reduced prices.

This sub-order of human behaviour now appears hopelessly arcane, obsessional and monotonous. Driving round and round a track at a regular speed for as many hours as either man or machine can stand ought to be nothing less than a judgement on the poverty of one's ambitions. But speed was a sufficient end in itself; even the kind of deglamorised, deracinated speed which expressed itself through solitary laps of Brooklands' concrete on cold murky days in March, away from the world and, indeed, other racers. The fact was that *anything* to do with speed – through space, over time – attracted fanatics, however stupefying the endeavour might be.

More importantly, it was big business, too: a branch of the motor industry which provided copy for thousands of advertisements, formed the constantly shifting base for scores of competing claims among the different manufacturers of cars, car tyres, engine oils, petrol. A car whose suspension stayed

in one piece and whose engine didn't explode in hot fragments
was a car worth crying up. 'At no time did the engine, even
when running at a very high rate of revolutions, appear in any
way to be making heavy weather of it,' said Viscount Curzon
of the 1925 Three-Litre Sunbeam.

Pratts petroleum testified to its own superiority thus: 'Capt.
John F. Duff, driving a 3-Litre Bentley at Montlhéry, established
two world's records (unlimited) covering 1000 Kilos in 6hrs
23min 55s; 1000 Miles in 10hrs 15min 59s. Capt. Duff writes
us as follows – "The uniformity of the spirit you supplied was
evident in the regular running we obtained . . ."' Equally, 'From
June 26th to August 5th this season, Mr J.G.P. Thomas, the
famous racing motorist, has broken no less than FIFTEEN
WORLD'S RECORDS using SHELL.' And, 'On Brooklands
Track – and on every road – DUNLOP Cord Tyres invariably
prove their capacity for supreme endurance and absence of
trouble.'

Aviation was the same. In a world where reliability, consis-
tency and uniformity were still generally aspirations rather
than realities, anything which held together at high speed or
high altitude, or just for a long time, was demonstrably better
than its rivals: 'The engine ran faultlessly for the 57 hours 25
minutes we were in the air,' quoted Napier Engines about
themselves. The de Havilland Aircraft Company pointed out
that 'The 830 Miles Air Race for the King's Cup' was 'won
by Capt. Geoffrey de Havilland, OBE, AFC, flying a *Standard*
Leopard Moth with a *Standard* Gipsy Major engine at an
average speed of 139.51 mph'. Armstrong-Siddeley Cars tried
to have it both ways, drawing attention to the fact that its
motor cars were as dependable as its aero engines – 'For the
experts on motoring matters, the people who *know*, were never
doubtful of the Armstrong-Siddeley. And last year when Sir
Alan Cobham' – the famous aviator – 'with an Armstrong-
Siddeley engine, devoured the great spaces about the world,
the experts were not surprised.'

The blessed tedium of a predictable road journey was generally only available to owners of Rolls-Royces, Mercedes-Benzes,
Hispano-Suizas, and not always then. Rolls-Royce counselled
the drivers of some of its earliest vehicles to 'remember that
when a car is being braked it occupies twice as much road as
when travelling normally'. For the rest of the motoring public,
there evolved a culture of nervous amelioration.

Spark plugs, petrol, carburettors, shock absorbers, oil, safety
glass, tyres and brake liners were all susceptible to improvements and so became promotable commodities in their own
right. This gave sporting motorists their chance. Interested
companies would pay them a bonus every time they competed
successfully in a race, or set an international record, no
matter how small, so long as they used the company's product.
Charles Mortimer noted that after one day's racing at
Brooklands he took home £25 in prize money, £25 from the
bookie, plus a £5 bonus from Dunlop Tyres and £1 from
Champion Spark Plugs. Another day saw him profiting to
the extent of £25 in prize money, a massive £70 from several
bookies, £5 from Dunlop and a total of £8 from Esso for
fuel and oil.

Big-name competitors, meanwhile, were put on full-time
retainers for both racing and record breaking. By the start of
the 1930s the Castrol Oil Company was paying its star driver,
Kaye Don, £2000 a year to stay loyal. Other drivers on the
company's books were paid retainers of anything from £50 to
£1000 per annum. Really well-organised record breakers,
principally in the smaller, less visible classes, were known to
form little consortia for the purposes of milking their backers.
A driver would go out and break some time and distance
records, knowing his car still had something in reserve, and
duly collect the bonuses from his sponsoring companies. His
associate would take to the track a week or so later in a different car, break the freshly broken records and duly collect *his*
bonuses. Then the first driver would go back to the track,

retake the records and receive yet more bonuses. Provided this fraud generated the right kind of publicity headlines, no one objected.

As the twenties went on, however, an obvious truth emerged in this esoteric parallel world of times, distances and numbing endurance. The World Land Speed Record – the LSR – was the Big One, the one with the most promise. To take it, you had to drive your car – of which two or more wheels had to be mechanically propelled – the length of a measured mile in one direction; and then back along the same measured mile in the opposite direction, in order to cancel out any assistance or hindrance the wind or gradient might be giving you. Officials, acting under the aegis of the AIACR, measured the time it took for the car to travel the mile, worked out an average time over the two runs, then converted that time into a speed in miles per hour. That was the record, the headline figure, the emotive 140, 160, 200. How much run-up you took to reach the mile, and how much space you gave yourself to slow down afterwards, was up to you. Rather, it was a matter of whatever terrain you could find to make your attempt in: finding the space was always going to be one of the biggest single problems for Land Speed Record breakers.

But the absolute simplicity of the challenge – to go faster for a mile than anyone else on the face of the earth, in something that resembled a car – was central to its appeal. Like all great sporting endeavours, it was easy to grasp. It also avoided the tedium that encumbered all those tiresomely individuated endurance records by being over with in about forty minutes. At the same time it posed interesting theoretical challenges in all branches of engineering. It also demanded a particular kind of heroism. It was international in scope while keeping something personal, something of the *beau geste* about it. And who knew what commercial possibilities might not arise from it? If you could make £30 in endorsements from an oil company for running a two-litre car for six hours, how much more could you make by driving the biggest, fastest car in the world for a fraction of that time?

But what kind of machines were needed in this battle? The French, again, had shown the greatest initial enthusiasm, with Gaston Chasseloup-Laubat taking the first officially recognised Land Speed Record over the flying kilometre at Achères, just north of Versailles. The year was 1898 and Chasseloup-Laubat drove a Jentaud – which was basically a lightened electric taxi-cab – at just over 39 mph. The Belgian race driver Camille Jenatzy retaliated in 1899 with his electric-powered *La Jamais Contente*, shaped like a double-ended artillery shell. This hit 41 mph; and the struggle went on between the two for the rest of the year, before Jenatzy reached the prodigious speed of 65 mph and Chasseloup-Laubat gave up. Léon Serpollet's 1902 *La Baleine* (also known as *Easter Egg* and *Steam Shoe*) looked like an orthopaedic boot and hit 75 mph using a single, steam-powered piston. Shortly after that the petrol engine took over (saving a moment in 1906, when a Stanley Steamer bid for the record) and the Anglo-Saxons – British and American – joined in. William K. Vanderbilt Jr took the record twice; Henry Ford once.

René Thomas (Delage V12) and Ernest Eldridge (twenty-one-litre Fiat *Mephistopheles*) enjoyed a terrifying head-to-head contest along four and a half miles of dead-straight, tree-lined road at Arpajon, near Paris, in July 1924. Thomas won the first encounter on a technicality – the last time a Frenchman was to hold the title. Eldridge returned the following week. Stout fencing lined the route, to keep back the crowds. 'Eldridge's approach,' an onlooker recorded, 'was one of the most appalling sights which the writer has ever witnessed . . . The great red car approaching the starting line at nearly 150 mph, skidding continuously and violently and taking the entire width of the road to skid. At this horrifying spectacle the crowd left the rails as one man and took cover.' Eldridge claimed the record at 146 mph and pointedly put his Fiat ('The Fastest

Car in the World') on view in a Paris showroom opposite that displaying the one-week wonder that was the Delage.

The big difference between the pre-war and post-war machines lay in the engines. The Great War had brutally hurried up aero-engine design, with the result that at war's close there were suddenly lots of decommissioned, highly sophisticated, enormous, lightweight and very powerful aero engines lying around, stripped of purpose. In Britain the Aircraft Disposals Board had the job of selling off whatever ex-military engines it could, at remarkably low prices. Some adventurers claimed that a serviceable motor could be picked up for £25. For a would-be racer or record breaker the principle was straightforward. Acquire an engine cheaply, build a stupendous chassis to fit (or adapt some old pre-war frame), attach a couple of seats and a lightweight body – and that was it: far too much power for the tyres or chassis to cope with, but with the promise of much terrifying excitement. Brooklands, with its lavishly wide track and absence of tight turns, was about as well suited to the cult of the necessarily vast, unwieldy aero-engined racer as anywhere could be.

So, as well as Kenelm Lee Guinness's 350-hp Sunbeam and Ernest Eldridge's *Mephistopheles*, the twenties saw the appearance of Count Louis Zborowski's two *Chitty-Chitty-Bang-Bangs*, L.C.G.M le Champion's Isotta-Maybach, J.G. Parry Thomas's *Babs*, a Martin-Arab, Major 'Shuggar' Cooper's twenty-one-and-a-half-litre *Blitzen Benz*, a Cooper-Clerget, and Captain Alistair Miller's Wolseley-Moth. This last had a V8 Hispano-Suiza aero engine grafted on to an ancient chassis from a Napier shooting brake. Its bonnet looked like the prow of a torpedo boat and it was believed to be the most dangerous car of them all.

For much of the time these leviathans simply thrashed around the concrete in loose competition with whomever else was available. But the principle they embodied had already begun to make its way beyond the confines of the track. Deeply covetous of Eldridge's success at Arpajon, Brooklands fanatic Captain Malcolm Campbell bought Guinness's big aero Sunbeam from the Sunbeam Car Company, took it to Pendine Sands, in south-west Wales, and broke the LSR twice, in 1924 and 1925. Sunbeam retaliated by building themselves another, rather more temperamental racer – not around an old aero engine – and just managed to retake the record in 1926, the car being driven by Major Henry Segrave. After him J.G. Parry Thomas brought out his aero-engined *Babs* from the Brooklands sheds and took the record twice in 1926. And at the start of 1927 Malcolm Campbell arrived back at Pendine with his own, home-made Campbell-Napier aero-engined device and took back the record from Parry Thomas. A pattern had started to emerge.

3

The Hermit of Brooklands

For a year or so it looked as if John Godfrey Parry Thomas was going to be the key personality when it came to World Land Speed Records. Unlike many of the Brooklands crowd, Parry Thomas was no moneyed layabout. A vicar's son, he was born in April 1884 at Wrexham, just on the Welsh side of the England–Wales border, into a provincial, clerical household in which money was not abundant. But he was bright, inventive, and escaped to London's Central Technical College, where he trained as an engineer, before working for the electrical machinery company Siemens. A spell at Leyland Motors followed. So advanced was Parry Thomas in his thinking that he used the Continental metric system in preference to Imperial units; so captivated by his work that he would take a slide rule with him to the theatre, using it to work on problems during *longueurs* in the action on stage. At one point he planned a huge electrically powered airship.

But the key moment came when Leyland let him drive one of its super-advanced *Grand Luxe* Leyland Eight tourers at Brooklands. The sensation of the 1920 London Motor Show, the Eight was the most expensive car on sale in Britain (£3000 complete) and was called 'the Lion of Olympia'. Since it was actually Parry Thomas's own design, this was hardly an act of extreme liberality on Leyland's part. It was, however, enough to convert him utterly to motor racing. He left Leyland (who only ever made eighteen of the tourers) and went off to Brooklands for good.

Along with Major Ken Thomson – another engineer, whose family was from Rotorua, New Zealand – Parry Thomas started a business called the Thomas Inventions Development Co. Ltd, down at the aviation end. Thomson, shortish, egg-bald, acted as a socially neutral Rolls to Parry Thomas's Celtic Royce. And Parry Thomas was happy: he doted on Brooklands to the extent that he never moved out of the place, living next door to his works (from 1923 onwards) in a creeper-shrouded bunga-low called The Hermitage. He looked out on one of the flying-school hangars and shared his domestic life with Bess and Togo, two Alsatian dogs.

The notes of rusticity provided by the creepers, the cottagey front door to the bungalow and the determinedly back-woodsman's flagpole at one end were oddly contextualised by the light-industrial setting in which The Hermitage stood. Yet this was exactly what Parry Thomas wanted. His natural haunt was among the austerities of machine tools, fuel containers and drawing offices. No Bugattis or Bentleys for him. He was a desperately long way removed from the likes of Earl Howe and the Duke of Richmond and Gordon, and more or less the polar opposite of Woolf Barnato and Commander Glen Kidston. He was large, laceratingly sarcastic, wore gym shoes and a Fair Isle jumper and had little or nothing in common with the Brooklands smart set, for whom the place was Ascot without horses, and whose main function was to give him plenty of opportunities not to suffer fools gladly.

As for A.V. Roe, so for Parry Thomas: Brooklands was no pastime. He drove his own self-designed specials, winning thirty-eight races in five seasons, taking the Brooklands lap record in one of his cars, winning the *News of the World* Handicap in another, setting over a hundred class records. This never made him much money – a penchant for exotic Russian cigarettes being one of his few evident indulgences – but a high-minded forty-odd-year-old monomaniacal Welsh ascetic, living with a couple of dogs in a bungalow on an airfield, had little need of wealth.

On the other hand, he appreciated that money kept his business going and helped him to develop new products. He had had to give up a contract with Dunlop to test tyres to destruction on Brooklands' track: as Dunlop's rubber compounds improved, Parry Thomas realised that it was costing him more in petrol to wear out the treads than he was getting in reward money for each tyre destroyed. Having saddled himself with indefensible sponsorship deals like this, he came to see an attempt on the increasingly high-profile Land Speed Record as a more logical way to generate both publicity and income. It would take him away from his Brooklands fastness. But then all serious contenders faced this problem. You could keep Brooklands as the cradle of your ambitions and the place that first gave them shape, but you had to leave eventually.

This centrifugal force applied as much to Parry Thomas – in many ways 'Mr Brooklands' – as anyone else. He concluded that he would have to build, or acquire, a very big car and take it down to Pendine Sands, the only place in Britain where there was enough room to travel at over 150 mph. Already there were rumours that Sir Charles Cheers Wakefield, founder of the Castrol Oil Company, was planning a £1000 prize for whoever held the LSR, the prize renewing itself every year unless someone else took the record, in which case the honorarium went to the new holder. Sir Charles was generally known as a 'great sportsman'. This meant that he was happy to subsidise those competitors of whom he personally approved. Indeed, his generosity only shallowly concealed a strong and pervasive marketing impulse. In 1922 he was the first to use a light aircraft to signwrite the name of his company in the sky above London, and more or less everything since then had a similar motive behind it.

The Wakefield prize and some sponsorship money would be useful. Of course, building a very large record-breaking car from scratch would have been deplorably expensive. But there was an alternative. Parry Thomas was able to buy Count Zborowski's last project, the *Higham Special*, for £125, and render it usable. Zborowski had died in a crash at Monza in October 1924 and so had no need of a car which was essentially another *Chitty-Chitty-Bang-Bang*, merely graced with the name of his estate at Canterbury, Higham Park. This last *Chitty* was a primitive two-seater with a wobbly chassis and an American Liberty aero engine the size of a horse trough bolted on in front; in short, a dreadful white whale of a car. It was a sign of Parry Thomas's urgency that he even considered such a vehicle. Up until this point his cars had been thoughtful, principled designs, matured over time. Now, though, he was dealing with a real Brooklands machine – not merely because Brooklands was one of the few places in the world where it could be driven without immediately crashing, but because it was contingent, improvised, a hurried response to a pressing need, a Brooklands lash-up.

He spent another £800 doing his best to bring it up to scratch, toiling away in his workshop among the hangars, removing the second seat, improving the streamlining and making the engine even more powerful. He gave it the name *Babs*, possibly after one of his nieces, possibly after a woman named Barbara White, possibly after the nine-year-old daughter of sports car maker Archie Frazer-Nash; although decades later, elderly, unrelated women were still coming forward to claim this honour for themselves. He was so excited when he finished rebuilding the car one evening in April 1926 that he immediately took the monster out of its Brooklands workshop and drove ecstatically around the darkened Surrey lanes, without headlamps.

A few days later he was at Pendine, having transported *Babs* down on a Scammel six-wheeled lorry. Pendine Sands were, and still are, enormous by British standards. They have an unshrinking majesty about them – being some six miles long, golden-white in the sun, a shoddy grey in the more conventional rain, the River Taff debouching at the eastern end, the village of Pendine itself and a rocky bluff standing at the western end, their joint modesty counterpointing the vast flatness of the beach. To say nothing of the modesty of the Beach Hotel, where, in the 1920s, all speed kings put up, and where the proprietors, Mr and Mrs Ebsworth, filled the front bar with hams, hung from the ceiling to cure.

As well as Parry Thomas there was a team of fifty-three people in support. Among them were timing officials from the RAC, a doctor, representatives of the Shell-Mex oil company and a division of policemen wearing spiked helmets. The measured mile was indicated by masts stuck in oil drums which had been buried just below the surface of the sand. The endless rain and damp of the Carmarthen peninsula saw to it that *Babs* sank up to its axles in this same sand whenever it came to a halt. A gang of locals was deputed to push the car around until it could be wheeled on to duckboards. At one point Lieutenant Commander Mackenzie-Grieve, one of Parry Thomas's team, started to sink in his own Morris Oxford and had to be dug out. For this indiscretion he was later given a mock court-martial. Despite all this, on Tuesday 27 April, Parry Thomas, dressed in his trademark Fair Isle sweater, broke the 170-mph barrier on the wet, cold beach and took the LSR.

'With sheets of flame belching from its drain-like exhaust pipe and cascades of water in its wake, Mr J.G. Parry Thomas's giant 400 hp racing car to-day set up the world's fastest speed record on the sands at Pendine,' shrilled the *Daily Mail*, 'in spite of the fact that the driver was handicapped by having to steer with one hand.' In front of a crowd of several thousand Welshmen stretching along the dunes on the northern edge of the beach, Parry Thomas had set off to find that 'The petrol pressure was not sufficient – so I had to use the hand pump. This meant that I was steering all the time with one hand – rather a trying experience at such a speed.' No question that this was a tremendous achievement: single-handedly in almost every sense, he had added nearly 20 mph to the record, and *Babs* still had more to give, if only Pendine were longer; if only the rain would let up; if only the Beach Hotel had anything like proper engineering facilities, instead of a shed round the back of the bar.

Parry Thomas kept the title for almost a year. To prove *Babs*'s versatility as well as his own driving skills, he raced it around Brooklands, to the astonishment of the crowds; reaching, it is said, 160 mph on the Railway Straight. But competition for the LSR was increasing. Captain Malcolm Campbell's self-assembled Campbell-Napier was completed at the end of 1926 and in the new year he took it to Pendine. It, too, was a success, although not without much labour in the pouring Welsh rain. Campbell – soon to become one of the biggest names competing for the LSR – managed to take the record by a margin of 3 mph and went home in a state of mild conflict, quietly confident that his brand-new car had plenty of energy in it, but seething at Pendine's shortcomings.

Still, he had been pleasantly surprised not only by the newspaper attention garnered by his successful run ('Yesterday was suggestive of the Riviera in its mildness, the blueness of the sky and sea, and the gentleness of the wind . . .'), but also by the endorsement money he received from the likes of Claudel Hobson Carburettors ('World's Record'); BP ('For acceleration, speed and power, use "BP", the British Petrol'); and Castrol ('Captain Campbell's stupendous speed of 174 mph was made on WAKEFIELD CASTROL. The highest speed ever attained by a car!').

Parry Thomas fiddled more strenuously with *Babs* through the winter months. His heroism was being tested. Campbell was bad enough; but to add to that threat, the racer Henry Segrave was having a twin-engined car built for him by Sunbeam, who clearly would not give up their ambitions on the LSR. Moreover, the publicity which was essential to the project, and gratifying in its own way, imposed a burden of heightened expectations. 'New 450-H.P. Racing Car – Captain Campbell To Attempt New World Record,' read one headline. 'Most Pampered Car Never Moves Itself Except To Race,' said another. Journalists were turning up the heat, reaching for the language of war or grand opera: 'delirious speed', 'monster engine', 'muffled roar', 'monster unleashed', 'intense heat', 'goggles were sand-blasted', 'leviathan', 'hurled into the air'. Previously characterised as a 'well-known racing motorist' and an 'English driver', Parry Thomas was now also 'brave', 'daring', something other than a mere enthusiast. This, at least, was clear. The business of breaking the Land Speed Record was starting to acquire that most valuable thing, an aura.

At the most abstract level it was also a kind of non-violent colonialism. The nineteenth century's division of the geograph-ical world into a collage of protectorates, dominions, depend-encies and satrapies had long since run its course. By the 1920s the British Empire's territorial scope was at its greatest – comprising some twelve million square miles of land and maybe a quarter of the world's population – but it was a scope which heralded its own decline, as more and more nations within the Empire strove to loosen their ties with London. The aggres-sive land-grabs of a few generations back were now effectively ruled out by all civilised nations, as – supposedly – was open warfare, thanks to the cauterising effect of the Great War.

Nations could, on the other hand, bolster their prestige by engaging in a covert war to annex dots on the map or moments in technological history. The LSR already had a long and fractious story of national enthusiasms behind it. But it was far from being the only globally resonant endeavour.

While it was going on, Roald Amundsen was sailing through

the North-West Passage *and* reaching the South Pole; Mount McKinley was being climbed for the first time; Alcock and Brown were undertaking the first-ever transatlantic crossing by aeroplane; George Leigh Mallory and Andrew Irvine were dying in their fruitless assault on Mount Everest; the Schneider Trophy for seaplanes was inaugurated, immediately generating fierce rivalry between the French, British, Italians and Americans; Germany's *Bremen* was limbering up to seize the Blue Riband for fastest transatlantic crossing by ship from the British *Mauretania*; the Soviet Union, technologically backward as well as internationally opprobriated, sent a team of climbers up the highest mountain in the USSR and named it after Joseph Stalin; Charles Lindbergh was contemplating his historic first transatlantic solo flight; and in 1926 Alan Cobham landed his aeroplane on the Thames in front of the Houses of Parliament, having just completed an historic 28,000-mile flight from Australia, during which the aircraft was invaded by a colony of wasps.

If there was a hierarchy within these achievements, it was not always easy to make out. On the one hand, if you were first to fly non-stop across the Atlantic, then this became an imperishable fact, an appropriation of that page of the history books. Even now, people remember the names of Lindbergh and Alcock and Brown. On the other hand, such a deed often demanded an effective follow-up if it was not to become just a fabulous curiosity. As the pace of scientific change accelerated, so the ownership of an historical first – however bracing – quickly became redundant. Nevertheless, a newly established record for speed, or height, or distance, however impermanent, at least had the advantage of being contemporary, of demonstrating – for a year or so – that the country which set it was best able to exploit global technological advances. It was better advertising. So this particular kind of colonialism, this annexation of an abstract figure in the face of world competition, had a lot to be said for it.

It also dovetailed nicely with the problem of Britain's twentieth-century decline. Queen Victoria was barely dead before the *Contemporary Review* produced this threnody for a lost age: 'It is perhaps the grandest, and at the same time the saddest, spectacle in the world to watch the decay of a mighty empire. This spectacle is at present afforded by Great Britain with the whole world as spectators.' At most measurable points Britain was diminishing. Its share of the world's manufacturing output had decreased erratically over the decades; its overall share of global commerce was also shrinking. Invisible earnings from shipping, overseas investment, banking and insurance – which up until this time had richly filled the trade gap – were falling. Britain was moving from the status of creditor to debtor nation. Its armed forces had been cut back to a nominal core. It had just been able to absorb the financial costs of the Great War, thanks to the huge reserves it had built up in the preceding century. And compared with its European neighbours, it was still relatively strong. But, relative to its own recent past, it was plainly reduced. From Victorian powerhouse, in effect, to a land of gathering bathos – to Auden's English village, where 'Tudor cafés/Offer Bovril and buns on Breton ware'.

The extent to which the country seemed morally and psychologically exhausted was much remarked upon. The word 'decadent' began to be used about British society, and not as a synonym for 'hedonistic'. Women had won the right to vote, Bolshevism lurked on every street corner and in every drawing room in Fitzrovia, and the young had lost all sense of purpose. From Noël Coward ('The public are asking for filth,' said actor Sir Gerald du Maurier of Coward's *The Vortex*: 'The younger generation are knocking at the door of the dustbin') to lesbian authoress Radclyffe Hall; to Mrs Meyrick, the constantly arrested nightclub proprietress; to the first Labour Government of 1924; to the Balfour Report, gesturing in the end of Empire with its admission that the Dominions' 'tendency

towards equality of status was both right and inevitable' –
everything tended in one direction only.

Dr Arthur Shadwell, cholera expert, polemicist and author
of *Typhoeus or The Breakdown of Socialism*, wrote in *The
Times* in 1925, 'There really is something wrong with the
present generation: they neither work well nor play well. They
seem altogether lacking in energy and purpose.' Although
obsessed with sports and pastimes, the young of 1925 were
unable to translate their enthusiasm for play into competitive
will: 'They cannot hold their own against rivals who come
from countries which a few years ago were incapable of any
athletic prowess. Our representatives are beaten all round, more
often than not. We cannot find a boxer to stand up to a
Frenchman, let alone an American, and on the tennis-court the
modern athletic girl of whom we hear so much is no match
for her French rival.' His lament 'Are we really going down
the hill, as all our neighbours think and sometimes say?' would
have echoed in the minds of all right-minded readers.

Against this mournful background, success at the LSR – one
contest among many – had the potential to be talked up into
something stiffening, reinvigorating, just as any success on the
battlefield, chimerical or otherwise, leads to a rediscovery of
the national will. And there was another merit in chasing the
LSR. Although the sporting calendar was well enough stocked
with events, few had this kind of resonance, this international
reach. The Olympic Games, having restarted in 1896, were
only just beginning to resemble the crucible of national ambitions which they currently are. There were also international
tennis tournaments, cricketing round robins, a smattering of
Grand Prix motor races, boxing prizefights, golf matches and
sailing events. But their claim on the public consciousness was
limited to the extent that the national press was prepared to
give them space, radio at that time being only partially
interested, and television, the greatest sports impresario of all,
functionally non-existent.

Football was still a working man's bromide, biding its time before it became the biggest, richest, most international game. The first radio broadcast of a football match would not occur until January 1927. The first World Cup tournament would not take place until 1930; while the first UEFA European Cup had to wait until 1955. Domestic football drew big crowds, but was short of the correct aspirational qualities. *The Times* had described the 1914 FA Cup Final between Liverpool and Burnley as being 'Of comparatively little interest except to the Lancashire working classes', and little had changed in the intervening years. Britain had few world champions to point to, except in micro-events such as billiards or the 100-metre dash. There was a specific gap, demanding to be filled.

But being in the spotlight makes failure doubly unthinkable. Captain Campbell had written a letter to the *Motor*, just after Parry Thomas's successful 1926 run. It ended with a fine, hypocritical flourish: 'Whether these records stand or not matters little, as Mr Thomas will always have the satisfaction of having been the first man in recent years to have beaten the most coveted records by this huge margin.' Naturally, it mattered fundamentally whether or not the records stood: everything depended on your keeping the record. There was little more futile than being the last person to hold the LSR. Besides, what would any prospective challenger want, other than to beat the record by an even bigger margin? To reach the magic figure of 200 mph, perhaps?

By the start of March 1927 Parry Thomas was desperate to make progress and re-establish his place as the only worthy holder of the LSR title, the only true *auteur* – engineer, designer, fabricator, financier and driver. Campbell was rich and arrogant and Segrave had sporting pedigree; but Parry Thomas, the snaggle-toothed hermit of Brooklands, had *earned* the title. Now, though, he had influenza and the persistent sensation that he would get only one more effective run out of *Babs* before it was overwhelmed by other, newer, less homespun designs. Already it was starting to wear its amateurishness too openly. For all its fairings and bulges and swooping extensions around the rear wheels, and for all its attempts at low-budget streamlining, it was still a great white whale in which Parry Thomas sat up at the level of a delivery-van driver, the windscreen bolted in place in front of him on to a piece of wood, his seat resting on a set of timber-yard offcut floorboards and his back wheels being turned by a pair of enormous bicycle chains.

The chains, he was the first to admit, were an expedient: the cheapest and most practical way to get the power from the engine to the wheels. And, of course, chains, even very big, reinforced ones, will snap from time to time. Since they were sited on the outside of the car, a couple of feet from where Parry Thomas crouched at the steering wheel, they were, in effect, a pair of medieval flails, waiting to explode from their sprockets and fling themselves into the machinery, or round his head. This he was nonetheless prepared to live with, despite the danger and the degraded nature of the engineering.

So, reeling from his flu – he had to spend the entire preceding weekend in bed – and the smell of the aviation fuel poured into his car, he was on the Sands first thing on Thursday 3 March, wearing his Fair Isle sweater and leather driving helmet. He was nervous and lacked his usual concentration. The weather was unsurprisingly bad and the engine wouldn't run properly, pouring out black smoke. He made five, only marginally satisfactory, trial runs. Still, he turned to an onlooker and said, 'This is a winner for old *Babs*.' And after some grim adjustments to the plugs and carburettors, he set off for the sixth time, amid smoke and thunderous backfiring, to try to retake the record from his gathering foes.

Just past the measured mile, something shattered in the car. *Babs* went into a great, sheering skid, turned over, righted itself, caught fire and came to rest at the end of a last semicircular sweep at the edge of the sea. As the smoke cleared away, Parry Thomas was found, half out of the car, half incinerated, his shoes burnt away and the top of his head cut off from his forehead to the nape of his neck. He was so badly charred that the mechanic who tried to pull the corpse out of the car scorched his hands. Eventually they had to break his legs in order to extricate him. *Babs*'s bodywork was blackened all over and the rear offside wheel had been torn off and discarded farther down the beach. A crowd gathered, hats held down, coats flapping in the wind, to stare at the terrible battered wreck, framed in the semicircle it had gouged out of the sand.

It didn't take long for everyone to lay the blame on the offside drive chain; one of the two barely contained flails, which was presumed to have broken, sent the car out of control and scalped the driver. But the partial decapitation may equally have happened as the machine shot along the beach, upside down, with its driver trapped inside. The body was taken back to the Beach Hotel, where it lay awaiting the inquest on the following day. When this was over, Parry Thomas's team buried *Babs* in a sand dune, slit his leather driving coat and threw it in with the car, before erecting a stone cairn on top. His body was buried at Byfleet, next to Brooklands, his Avalon. The Thomas Inventions Development Co. became Thomson & Taylor, a bespoke motor engineering company for Brooklands habitués. Later on, Captain Alistair Miller moved into The Hermitage. *Babs* lay in the sand, rotting.

The pagan obsequies which surrounded Parry Thomas's death suited the landscape and the violence of his last moments. Elsewhere a more conventional panegyric note prevailed. He wasn't, after all, the first to die in pursuit of a record: in October 1913, for instance, poor Percy Lambert – the first man to do 100 miles in one hour – promised his fiancée that he would make one more record run and then quit. He went out at Brooklands, crashed his Talbot and was killed. His ghost, supposedly, still haunts the track. But Parry Thomas was, up to then, the most celebrated driver of his generation.

His death made the front pages – 'Parry Thomas Killed While Racing', '180 Miles An Hour To Death'. The *Daily Express*, despite capitalising on the shocking nature of the accident by reproducing large photographs of Parry Thomas and *Babs* on its back page, took a disapproving editorial line: 'Are these dizzy adventures in swiftness to be traced to a brave but foolish sensationalism, or do they really advance the causes of scientific developments and utility motoring?' Dr R.L. Thomas, who had presided over the inquest into Parry Thomas's death, saw things differently: 'I am not of the opinion of those people who are going to condemn record breaking. We all know that the history of England has been made up by pioneers, and these attempts by brave men only show that in 1927 the manhood of the British Empire is not dead.'

The Times went further, claiming that as a consequence of Parry Thomas's dying, the world 'is very much the better because there are still brave men who value achievement more than their lives', loudly saluting 'the spirit of idealism, the spirit which puts ease and safety and comfort and long life second to the achievement' – the spirit which, in the deepest analysis, 'has brought man from barbarism into civilization, and is daily bringing him out of error into truth.'

At the same time Parry Thomas retained something of a St John the Baptist figure about him. Partly, it was in the cruel beheading which killed him. Partly, it was in the way that the words 'dour', 'tough' and 'forbidding' attached themselves to his memory – the suggestion of a willed distance between himself and the rest of the world. And partly it was because his dying was like a prophecy. His relative prominence, heightened by his death, only served to emphasise how much more prominent his immediate successor would be. To put it another way, in his death he made plain the way for one to come after him, one mightier than him. Mightier than most, in fact: Major Henry Segrave.

4

Segrave at Daytona

《℃ ℈》

Henry O'Neal de Hane Segrave, simply 'de Hane' to his friends, was born in the United States on 22 September 1896. His father, Charles Segrave, was from a Wolverhampton branch of the Segrave family which had decamped to Ireland when his grandfather, Henry Segrave, succeeded to an estate in greater Dublin. The youngest of three sons, Charles then emigrated to Baltimore, Maryland, and made a fortune in real estate. There he married Mary Lucy Harwood, the daughter of a US naval officer, and H.O.D. Segrave was born in Baltimore. When Mary died after a sudden illness a couple of years later, the family returned to Wicklow, in Ireland. Here Segrave spent his early childhood. His father remarried – a Miss Jessica Stone – and presented Henry with a half-brother, Charles Rodney Segrave.

This multinational parentage caused problems in later years, when Segrave was famous. Was he English, British, Irish, American or, worst of all, an Irish-American hybrid? Jingoist Britons naturally wanted to claim him for their own, while Americans liked to taunt the British with Segrave's miscegenated background. On balance Segrave thought of himself as British. His father was Anglo-Irish, his schooling was English and

Ireland was still, thanks to the Act of Union of 1801, under the sway of the United Kingdom of Great Britain and Ireland, with representation in the House of Commons and a generation to wait until the recognition of the Irish Free State in 1921.

The 'de Hane' of which Segrave was so fond, came from his paternal grandmother, the daughter of Edward Francis de Hane, head of an old Huguenot family. The 'Segrave' part of his name harked back to distant Nordic ancestry: a Danish prince who had landed in England in the ninth century, seizing much of Leicestershire. This, with its associations of warrior tradition, blood and Valhalla, presented no problem to British supporters, who annexed it as a useful sign of aristocratic good breeding.

After a few years of bucolic enjoyment in Ireland, Segrave was subjected to a conventional English *haut bourgeois* upbringing, being sent to Bilton Grange prep school in Warwickshire and then to Eton College. Segrave arrived at L.S.R Byrne's house in 1910, stand-offish, gangly, not a good mixer. Aldous Huxley would have been a contemporary; also King Prajadhipok of Siam, Anthony Eden and Sacheverell Sitwell. At the start Segrave was dismissed as 'rather overgrown, rather muddle-headed'. In his four years at Eton he made no mark academically, but did have some success in rowing, one of the few team sports in which obsession and self-absorption can be harnessed towards a collective end. Tall oarsmen also tend to do better than short and Segrave's height could be turned to advantage by the geometry of rowing. He competed in a number of successful Fours and was considered for the school's first Eight. He was also socialised to the extent of being elected to 'Library', in effect becoming a house prefect.

His career at Eton ended just as the First World War began. Vigorously patriotic, like so many young men in 1914, he took advantage of the ongoing scandal of underage recruitment and, at the age of eighteen, talked his way into the Royal Warwickshire Regiment. This, from December onwards, gave him an accelerated induction into the madhouse of the battlefield. Among other things, he was caught in the disastrous offensive at Festubert in May 1915, where a bullet passed through his wrist. 'The Colonel wanted to have me returned as wounded,' he wrote to his father, 'but I didn't think it was bad enough, and when I had tied it up with strips from my shirt, could carry on.'

As it turned out, he was to be blessed by the blood of a Blighty wound a couple of days later when a bullet went 'through my left shoulder and passed out through the bottom of the shoulder blade'. He had to return to England to convalesce. This gave him the opportunity to rethink his military career, to look for something which was not only less crushingly immobile than trench warfare but which could satisfy his growing interest in things mechanical; which could offer movement, in other words.

The answer was flying. He took up a place at the Central Flying School in Upavon, Wiltshire, an institution formed in 1912, with the express object of training professional war pilots for the recently established Royal Flying Corps (RFC). In some ways this was merely a transfer from one kind of madness to another. The mild anarchy which characterised flying training in 1915, and the state of many of the aircraft sent to the front line, were a source of outrage to Segrave and his contemporaries from the moment they joined up. 'These machines,' he wrote home, 'are the most appalling death-traps I have ever come across.'

Despite its pre-eminence, Upavon offered instruction which was haphazard and without any kind of standardisation. Indeed, at that time more airmen were lost during training than in combat. Such pilots as survived were sent over to France after only a few rushed hours of dual and solo flying, in aircraft which, even when new, were barely finished, with their rigging imperfectly tuned and, on occasion, their controls so poorly set up as to render the planes lethal. The dope on the wings was improperly cured, the guns were sometimes misaligned and the engines were chronically unreliable.

Pusher biplanes, such as the FE2b and the FE8, were in vogue. By mounting the engine and propeller behind the pilot (and, in the case of the FE2b, the gunner, too) the aircrafts' designers avoided the then intractable problem of firing a machine-gun through a spinning propeller, at the same time as they gave the pilot a good view ahead. Drawbacks with this arrangement included the fact that any loose items in the cockpit could be sucked back into the propeller and spat out again like shrapnel; and that if the plane crash-landed, the engine was certain to break free of its mountings, plunge forward and crush the pilot and gunner in front. Segrave found himself on one occasion having to extract the remains of one of his closest friends from a pusher plane which had nosedived on to the airfield. The friend had been punched like a piece of sacking into the mud by his own engine.

Having outlived Upavon's under-resourced and periodically shambolic training, and after some fitful weighing of the odds, Segrave had his first successful air duel in April 1916. He noted – with a detachment that might almost be read as callousness – that the observer in the German aircraft was 'Killed stone dead' by a 'whole drum of ammunition', after which he 'saw him fall back in the body of the machine'. He then 'followed it right down and watched it crash close to a small village behind the German lines called, I think, Gheluveldt'.

Four more kills were to follow, before he was wounded again, this time more seriously. Accounts differ as to whether, in July 1916, a German anti-aircraft shell blew him out of the sky in his FE8; or whether his engine failed at 7000 feet and the plane fell to the ground on top of him like a heap of scaffolding. He was repatriated to the London Hospital in Whitechapel, where he was found to have head and stomach injuries and a shattered leg. Six bones had been broken and an amputation of his left foot looked likely. Luck again: the surgeons managed to insert a structure of silver plates into his foot and avoid the amputation. Segrave would walk with a limp for the rest of his life. But his limp was visually discreet, not so incapacitating as to stop him driving a car, and, best of all, a badge of courage.

When he returned to see his tutor at Eton ('A fearful clumping was heard, and in lurched Segrave, on crutches') he was transformed. 'He had escaped from hospital, hired a car, and here he was. But this was a different Segrave, brighter, quicker, more independent than he had seemed before.' The relationship between cause and effect was uncertain. 'Whether the comparatively uneventful life at Eton had laid the foundation for rapid development later will never be known,' swore the *Eton College Chronicle*, 'but that he was destined to distinction of some sort was obvious from this moment.'

Unfit for active service, Segrave found himself working at Flying Corps Headquarters at Adastral House, in central London, where the staff were, among other things, puzzling over the introduction of wireless radio to air warfare. Two years of fear, exhilaration, boredom and pain had turned Segrave's adolescent twitchiness into something more mature, more functional. He now had a fierce, directed energy and an ability to focus on the task at hand; both of which marked him out for preferment. In time he managed to work his way up to the position of Staff Captain, then Technical Secretary to the Air Council. Finally he was sent to the Special Aviation Mission to America, in Washington, DC, where he was attached to the British Embassy. He was also promoted to the rank of major. By the end of the war he had been decorated, mentioned in dispatches and got married (in October 1917 to Miss Doris Stocker, formerly a dancer at London's Gaiety Theatre).

From there he became, quite simply, Britain's most successful racing driver. Like the other demobbed Young Georgians then discovering motoring, he used speed as both a stimulant and a palliative, an excursion into fear which, unlike the traumas of the Western Front, could be progressively managed. Having bought himself a pre-war Opel in 1919, he won three races at Brooklands with it in 1920. Unlike many other post-Great War Brooklands motorists, however, Segrave was not rich. He had lost most of his inherited wealth immediately after the war when he started a motor business with the notorious Captain Alistair Miller. This venture collapsed within nine months, costing Segrave around £4000. The only thing keeping him and Doris from destitution was a job offered him by Kenelm Lee Guinness, now proprietor of the KLG ('Fit and Forget') Spark Plug factory in south-west London.

The racing Opel he kept going with his own small funds and his natural fixatedness. He called it 'the greatest thrill of my life' when he first went round Brooklands at 85 mph. 'That decided me to give up everything else and take to motor racing.'

Over time, though, the infatuation with speed intensified while the passion for Brooklands dwindled. It was not enough for Protean, ambitious Major Segrave to be just another motoring hack, his opportunities hobbled by the parochialisms of Weybridge and his own lack of cash. He needed a better car and more interesting places to drive it. So, in 1921, he used his limited Brooklands successes and his genius for self-advancement to talk his way into the prestigious Sunbeam-Talbot-Darracq racing team, convinced that he and the team could exploit each other to mutual benefit. Despite the French heritage evident in the firm's name, STD was a British outfit which had come into being in 1920, when Sunbeam of Wolverhampton formed a complex aggregate with the French Talbot and Anglo-French Darracq concerns, in order to build stylish, expensive tourers. The proprietor was French, too.

Louis Hervé Coatalen, the seigneurial, pragmatic Breton who ran the company, was convinced that competition success was the best publicity and (along with one-offs, such as the Sunbeam LSR car) was keen to go in for the new-look Grands Prix. Fiat were already making a name for themselves in Continental races and Coatalen intended to copy both their cars and their success. He offered Segrave a place in the team on condition that he fund all his own expenses and pay for any damage he caused to his car. Segrave finished seventh in the irksome 1921 French Grand Prix, during which the track more or less completely disintegrated. He also won the first 200-mile race organised by the Junior Car Club at Brooklands.

This was enough to persuade Coatalen to give Segrave a proper place in the STD team, which vote of confidence he repaid by winning four times at Brooklands the following year; and then by winning the French Grand Prix in July 1923, in a machine which was a racing Fiat in everything but name and colour. This victory in particular was freighted with special meaning. It was the first Grand Prix win by a British driver in a British car; and it was to remain the only Grand Prix win by a British driver in a British car until well after the Second World War. Winning the Voiturette Grand Prix at Boulogne, followed by the Spanish Grand Prix at San Sebastián a year later in 1924, confirmed Segrave's pre-eminence among British sporting motorists. He left his job at KLG in order to join the Sunbeam Car Company both as a works racing driver and as head of the London sales department at its showrooms in Hanover Square.

What was the secret of Segrave's success? Other than a clear natural ability to drive fast and a gift for finding his way to the centre of events? Much of it lay with the RFC. All racing cars posed a kind of barely quantifiable mechanical threat. Segrave's response to this problem was developed over time, but principally during his flying days, going back to the moment when he joined the Central Flying School at Upavon. Mechanical imperfection, human incompetence and arbitrary disaster were commonplace in the early days of the RFC. It was the atmosphere in which young pilots lived. Segrave's reaction was, like that of many people who work with danger, to combine two contradictory modes of being: he became a fatalist who nonetheless took endless pains to get things right.

When he turned from aviation to motor racing he won a

reputation for the fastidiousness with which he prepared both his cars and his tactics. As with the touch-and-go biplanes, he was merely the pilot, not the constructor. So he fought to regulate the behaviour of his machine the moment it was out on the track. In the case of the car with which he won the 1923 French Grand Prix, he was in it as soon as a prototype was available. When the team arrived at the fourteen-mile Grand Prix circuit just north of Tours, Segrave didn't even bother to unpack his bags at the local Hôtel de Bordeaux, but leapt into a tourer and started driving round the course.

Once the racing cars had been set up, he practised obsessively. He got his riding mechanic, Paul Dutoit, to time him through the corners. He rehearsed pit stops over and over again. He timed his rivals during their practice sessions. He saw to it that his own car was impeccably clean. He installed his brother, Charles Rodney, in the Sunbeam pits, as an assistant. As he had done in the 1921 French Grand Prix, he took his own physical fitness seriously, apart from his cigarette habit, which he found himself constitutionally unable to break. At the end of the Grand Prix, *God Save the King* was sung for the first time and someone tried to make Segrave drink a glass of champagne. Spartan by nature, he wanted cold water instead, but they had none.

Several years later he took to powerboat racing – in many ways even riskier than car racing. This wound him up so badly, as he tried to calculate the nice balance between obligatory risk and unquantifiable recklessness, that he became tense to the point of frenzy, yelling at colleagues and snapping at strangers. In fact, under pressure of any kind, he was notoriously petulant and irascible. A Brooklands diehard named Rodney Walkerley once found himself in the wrong place while Segrave was manoeuvring his car out of the paddock. 'He said, "Would you mind standing back please," in that somewhat high, Etonian voice and somewhat peremptory manner suitable to wartime Field Officers.' Stung, Walkerley thought him 'arrogant, aloof and superior', though he later amended his criticism to: 'He was very highly strung, but concealed it with his innate aloofness.'

Segrave was one of the first British racing drivers to wear a toughened crash helmet, as opposed to the more conventional cloth or leather flying helmet, whose purpose was mainly to keep the hair free of dirt and insects. The more self-consciously virile drivers mocked Segrave at first: the crash helmet betokened both neurotic professionalism and a prissy desire for self-preservation. And he kept with him a horror of being wished good luck, preferring instead to mull over the near-certainty of something failing radically, to calm his anxieties by familiarising himself with the prospect of disaster. At one LSR bid he spent his time beforehand chatting with a fellow speed king, an American named Tommy Milton, about famous track disasters in Europe and the United States. 'If my friends come round slapping me on the back and telling me I would surely win,' he explained, 'it might let me down. Milton's chatter will make me more careful. It has helped my morale.'

His last big British motor-racing appearance was at the first-ever British Grand Prix. This took place on 8 August 1926, inevitably at Brooklands, the only racetrack in the country. The first World Championship had been organised the previous year, taking in races in France, Italy, Belgium and the USA, with an offer to the RAC to host a race in Britain. After a year of havering the RAC suggested the Weybridge circuit. Hugh Locke King had died in January 1926, a white-haired figure wearing lank cardigans and padding around his back garden, who had nonetheless outlived all predictions of an early end. How proud he would have been to see the nine cars on the starting line (a good turnout for the year), apparently a vindication of the bet he had made with history twenty years earlier. Three of the starters were Talbots, one driven by Segrave. Sunbeam had given up Grand Prix racing as too expensive and handed competition work – and their premier driver – over to the other half of the STD combine, Talbot-Darracq in France.

Tickets cost 5/- a head. Sandbank chicanes were built on the Finishing Straight to mitigate the obviousness of the course. Silencers were worn, as ever, and a rickety footbridge was built over the Finishing Straight. It bore an advertising hoarding for J. Smith & Co., a Delage dealership. Yet the crowd turnout was less than impressive. According to one sorrowing newspaper report, 'Last Sunday proved that the English public will not take that keen interest in motor-car racing our friends do across the Channel. Only between 10,000 and 12,000 spectators paid to see the first international motor event run in this country at Brooklands, compared with the hundreds of thousands who flock to the grands prix motor races held on the Continent. Yet excellent arrangements for seeing every portion of the British Grand Prix race had been made by the RAC, no matter in what part of the Brooklands course spectators gathered.'

As it transpired, a French Delage won the race after the Talbots broke down, one after another. Thrills there were: for a brief period Segrave led the race and set the fastest lap time; Delage drivers were baked by their own exhaust pipes and had to douse their feet in buckets of water whenever they came into the pits – 'One could actually hear their boots hissing as they went into the water,' claimed Segrave later; Captain Malcolm Campbell led for a spell in his Bugatti. But the star of the event, Britain's original authentic motor-racing ace, never managed to finish. Having been in the lead, Segrave dropped back to second and then out altogether.

During this time he discovered first that his front wheels were about to fall off; then that his car was on fire; finally, that his supercharger was disintegrating. He left his car – so painstakingly prepared, so gallingly unreliable – in the pits, and began plotting his next move. Positively his last motor race would be a strictly contractual appearance for Sunbeam in May 1927, at a small-time meeting in which he had to drive a tourer round Brooklands with the hood down. Bored and disgusted, he parked his underperforming car on the far side of the track and quit motor racing for good.

Was this abrupt decline in fortune the reason why Segrave went over so whole-heartedly to the Land Speed Record? Partly. For a start, the LSR was already familiar ground. In March 1926 he had taken it on in a smallish, supercharged Sunbeam, specifically built for the purpose. The venue was the indifferent beach at Southport, Lancashire, over which Segrave had coaxed the neat but unsatisfactory racer to a speed of 152 mph across the flying kilometre rather than the mile. Enough, nonetheless, for the LSR. He held the record for all of a month, before Parry Thomas convincingly took it off him in *Babs*.

But could he think of nothing better than chasing the Land Speed Record? Surely a Grand Prix drive was worth more in every sense? Sunbeam's difficulties aside, much of the trouble with Grand Prix racing was that it was still in the process of inventing itself, with the result that too much of it was too contingent for someone as strategically focused as Segrave. One year, for instance, the French and Belgian Grands Prix simply disappeared from the calendar; another year it was the Belgian and the German races that were missing. When the AIACR changed the permitted specifications for Grand Prix cars at the end of 1925, half the top manufacturers dropped out, unable to sanction the cost of building new cars. At the Belgian Grand Prix of 1925 the Alfa Romeo team was so embarrassingly far ahead of the rest of the field that the drivers stopped for a meal during the race while their cars were washed and polished. The French Grand Prix of 1926 was so ill organised that only three cars made it to the starting line; two finished. It was not, all things considered, an entirely coherent option.

On top of this there was still no clear opening for a British contender. Twenty years had gone by since the inception of Brooklands, but all the big players were resolutely Continental (Bugatti, Delage, Alfa Romeo) or American (Miller, Duesenberg) and with Continental drivers (Benoist, Senechal, Chiron,

Campari, Divo, Wagner). Sunbeam had given up and small-time companies such as Alvis and Aston Martin made only occasional, futile efforts at filling the gap.

What, then, about the Bentley team and the Le Mans 24 Hour race? Fine, in its way – except that it, too, was riddled with drawbacks. For a start, you inevitably had to share your victory with both a co-driver and the famous Bentley name. Worse, the proprietor, W.O. Bentley, was frighteningly autocratic, expecting his drivers to follow team instructions scrupulously, obliging them to occupy second or even third place if it suited him; and anyway they had failed to win in 1925 or 1926, and so were not a bankable certainty. Besides, W.O. was busy acquiring a squad of loud, rich, hedonistic, Brooklands-minded sportsmen to drive his cars: 'Benjy' Benjafield, the extraordinary Woolf Barnato, Glen Kidston, Jack Dunfee, Sammy Davis, Sir Henry 'Tim' Birkin – the 'Bentley Boys'.

As an Old Etonian and honourably wounded major, Segrave could have held his own with such people. But as a compulsive obsessive who wanted to bestride the world and who preferred tap water to champagne, Segrave would have fitted in with the Bentley team about as well as a German spy. So, his yearning for speed, his *amour propre*, his desire for Britain to win and the shortage of other, available outlets impelled him towards the one thing which he could do better than anyone else: take the LSR. And Sunbeam, fed up with Grand Prix racing, but scenting a marketing opportunity in the record, were prepared to go along with him.

In this particular Segrave had a clear advantage over Parry Thomas. He didn't have to design, build or pay for his own record car. There was no question of *auteurism*, of having to demonstrate one's prowess in all divisions of the contest. On top of that – and crucial to his later success – Segrave was lucky enough to have the physical and personal qualities that constituted a hero in 1927. He was young, but not bristlingly immature: thirty years old – a bit younger than, say, debonair actor and singer Jack Buchanan; somewhat older than daring young Lord de Clifford, who had lied about his age in order to try to marry one of Mrs Meyrick's daughters.

He was also good-looking by the standards of the times. Admittedly, his gingery hair had thinned to the point of baldness and his large equine teeth betrayed his unquenchable dependency on smoking. But he was tall, trim, broad-shouldered (fans would remark admiringly how the width of his shoulders made it difficult sometimes for him to fit into a narrow racing car) and had deep-set, piercingly blue eyes. It was a twenties look – cautiously virile, a hint of active intellect in the high-domed head, nothing overstated. Parry Thomas, by way of contrast, was craggy, aggressively shaped like the Missing Link, in his forties, and had even worse dentition than Segrave.

Nor did Parry Thomas have any class to speak of – Welsh; Central Technical College – whereas Segrave had plenty. Things had not yet gone so far that one had to make excuses for being an Etonian and a major. Celebrity – as opposed to mere notoriety – was one of the functions of the titled and the socially smart, who were interesting merely because of who they were. Lady Diana Cooper, Lord Furness, the Hon. Colin Tennant, Lady Cathcart, Old Etonian financier and swindler Gerard Bevan, wrongly convicted pervert Sir Almeric FitzRoy, all paid tribute to a national predilection for social standing. Famous exceptions, such as Charles Chaplin, Jack Hobbs or Noël Coward, nonetheless did their best to fit in with the prevailing trend. George Bernard Shaw and Augustus John, artists and Celts, enjoyed a dispensation. Frankly eccentric aristocratic bohemians like Edith Sitwell and Lord Berners had it both ways.

Segrave's calling card was his Old Etonian background, an automatic leg-up into the public's critical indulgence. Once his good looks and his ability behind the wheel were added, he had an irresistible combination – one which Parry Thomas could only have dreamed of, back in his Hermitage.

But now Segrave was thinking along much bigger lines than Parry Thomas: exorbitantly big. For a start, the venue for his new LSR attempt was to be in the United States, at Daytona, Florida. And the car itself was to be one of mythically huge proportions.

At Segrave's urging, a suitably enormous, twin-engined beast had been specially built for him by the Sunbeam Motor Car Co. at the end of 1926. Designed by the dashing, moustachioed engineer Captain J.S. Irving, it was powered by two Sunbeam aero engines (by now third-hand, having been salvaged from a 1920 powerboat called *Maple Leaf VII*), both of which had been bolted on to a chassis big enough for a truck. Under the instruction of Louis Coatalen they had been named Matabele aero engines in order to evoke the fearsome martial spirit of the warrior tribesmen of Rhodesia. The Matabeles were fitted into the chassis back to back, and drove the rear wheels of the machine, *Babs*-style, through a pair of gigantic bicycle chains. The chassis, engines, wheels and the little space for the driver in between had then been covered over with a smooth aluminium skin, painted red and shaped like a poorly set jelly. The Vickers Aircraft Company and the National Physical Laboratory at Teddington both helped to develop the most efficient streamlining for this exterior. But, as the boys at the Sunbeam factory rightly observed, it looked like a slug.

When Segrave first set eyes on the naked chassis in early 1927, roaring and shaking away on its sooty test bed in the works at Wolverhampton, it struck him as a 'monster', 'gigantic'. Stripped of its red body shell, it looked like the insides of a tank: a dreadful mass of steel and iron and wiring held in a tubular steel cage, with a dismal little gap between the two brutish engines for the driver to crouch in. Tubes and hoses fed the engines air, water and doped fuel at a rate of 2.6 miles to the gallon. A quartet of forty-foot-long water-cooled exhaust pipes carried the flames and fumes out through a window into the winter air of the West Midlands. Segrave was forced to admit that it was 'the only time I can honestly say . . . I have stood in front of a car and doubted human ability to control it'.

At the Dunlop tyre factory in nearby Birmingham they were testing special high-speed tyres for the record attempt, on a purpose-built rig in a great shed. Observers had to watch the tests through peepholes in a reinforced partition as the tyres were apt to explode at high speeds. Two months before Segrave's record bid they ran a racing tyre up to 120 mph; just over half what he hoped to do at Daytona. Segrave was assured by Dunlop's technicians that the tyres for the LSR attempt would stay in one piece for a maximum of three and a half minutes. After a minute or so the tyre on the test rig duly exploded with a noise like a gun going off and hurled its tread, red-hot, through the open door of the shed and into the adjoining ground.

All that could be seen of Segrave when he sat in the machine was the little white pea of his crash-helmeted head poking out of the central section. The length of a suburban sitting room, 'the Slug' stretched so far fore and aft that the nearest patch of ground that he could see, when seated at the controls, lay a hundred feet away. A primitive metal hump in front of him deflected some of the oncoming wind turbulence while a padded headrest behind, loosely faired into the tail, allowed him to bang his head around whenever he hit a bump. He sat in a leather chair the size of a small saloon armchair, but without any seat belts. Before him were a gear lever, brake, clutch and accelerator; a steering wheel the diameter of a dustbin lid; plus a ship's engine-room array of instruments: twenty-eight of the things, including three radiator thermometers, six oil pressure gauges, eight magneto switches, one enormous master ignition switch and four rev counters. The whole vehicle weighed around four tons.

The engineers at Sunbeam had done their best to make the Slug safer by putting metal safety guards over the dangerous and archaic chains; by building an undershield beneath the car of six-millimetre steel plate, ostensibly so that if all the wheels fell off, the machine could skid along on its belly at 150 mph; and by integrating what was described as a 'stout steel hoop' for when the chains broke and the car rolled over and tried to crush Segrave under its own weight.

The news of Parry Thomas's decapitation reached Segrave while he was still in mid-Atlantic sailing across to the test ground. He made it his priority to have the chains on the Slug checked and rechecked on arrival in the States, acutely conscious of what had happened at Pendine and that in early tests back at the Sunbeam works it had taken less than a minute for the whirling drive chains to turn red-hot and fling sparks in all directions.

At the same time he understood the paradoxical element in all this. The record attempt depended on the risk of death to make it worth doing. If there hadn't been a good chance of the chains breaking and the car destroying the driver and itself, safety features or no, then the whole enterprise would have been diminished. Everyone else knew this, too. They all recognised that something sacrificial was being attempted. Major Segrave was, quite possibly, giving up his life for a cause.

And then there was the venue for the LSR attempt: Daytona Beach. The difference between Pendine Sands and Daytona Beach was as marked as the difference between, say, Osbert Sitwell and Douglas Fairbanks. Pendine was a hamlet surrounded by outlying cottages and reached by a couple of devious country lanes. Tourism brought in a seasonal income, attracted principally by the handsome six-mile beach. Farming in the hills reaching up towards Cardigan accounted for the rest. The population was measured in scores, rather than hundreds. There was one hotel but hours of rain. The nearest place of any size was Carmarthen, some fifteen miles away, and that was a small settlement dating back to the eleventh century. It was unquestionably a very British locale.

Daytona Beach, however, was the biggest tourist resort in

Florida – indeed, the whole of the south-eastern United States – and had been growing voraciously ever since the arrival of both the railway and the indefatigable capitalist venturer Henry Flagler, in the 1880s. Lying some ninety miles south of Jacksonville, it consisted of a rapidly expanding concatenation of towns lying on the edge of the mainland and facing a body of water, the Halifax River, which was in turn protected from the Atlantic by an enormous, straight, sandy beach. The Ponce de Leon Inlet terminated the southern end of this strand while a great rampart of sand dunes stretched back northwards. As at Pendine, the huge beach was the principal tourist draw. It was, however, not six miles long, but over twenty: a phenomenon of nature, both a gigantic bulwark against the ocean and a hedonist's delight, with its sunshine, its balmy temperatures in the seventies Fahrenheit, its superabundant space – five hundred feet wide at low water; hard and smooth as a table when the wind was in the right direction.

Mathias Day (after whom Daytona was named) had developed the original town in the 1870s; Henry Flagler drove the Florida East Coast railway down south, through Daytona and beyond; while Charles Grover Burgoyne extended and glamorised the downtown Beach Street area in the early twentieth century, galvanising the place into commercial prominence. The Florida land boom of the mid-twenties – the reckless speculation, the insatiability, the Mizner architecture – to some extent passed it by, being concentrated farther south in the area around Palm Beach.

But growth continued. In 1926 the settlements of Daytona, Daytona Beach and Seabreeze consolidated themselves into Daytona Beach. And by the start of 1927 the place boasted a pier, a two-storey casino (also used as a dance hall), an ocean-front promenade, the Burgoyne Gazebo (used as a bandstand), a boardwalk, an enormous saltwater public swimming pool with a great triple-arched tower to dive from and enough hotels to provide one for every resident of Pendine. The Esplanade

Burgoyne was lined with specially designed street lights, each one bearing five electric globes, to create a dramatic 'White Way'. On the door of the casino hung a poem composed by Burgoyne himself:

> Our latch string's always hangin' out
> For true friends old and new
> Come on inside, our hearth is wide
> We've saved a place for you.

Black cars lined up on the beach in the warm weather and disgorged a crowd of bathers directly into the water; who then mingled with the fully dressed beach walkers, picking their way over the sand, holding parasols against the Florida sunshine. In the winter months Saracina's Royal Italian Band came down from New York to give daily recitals from the conical-roofed gazebo. Palm trees grew in monotonous abundance, and, as testimony to Daytona's charm, up at the northern end, Ormond Beach, there were the great winter residences of field marshals of capitalism such as Henry Ford, Harvey Firestone and Thomas Edison – elderly men warming the blood in order that they might enjoy their money for one more day.

Thus, Daytona Beach offered the gamut of tourist experiences, from the gerontocratic ostentation of Ormond in the north to the meat-and-potatoes amusements of Esplanade Burgoyne farther south. It was calling itself 'The Most Famous Beach in the World' and with some justification: Miami Beach, two hundred and fifty miles south, had only recently been dredged out of the sludge of Biscayne Bay.

And this was where Henry Segrave had elected to attack the World Land Speed Record. He was going to do it on an immense American beach, five thousand miles from London and entailing – not the assistance of Lieutenant Commander Mackenzie-Grieve, some timekeepers from the RAC and six policemen wearing spiked helmets – but an army of helpers and backup people, including Kenelm Lee Guinness as acting team manager; William F. Sturm, his American agent; Steve McDonald, the tyre specialist sent over by Dunlop; Mr J.C. Calhoun, Chief of Police; the seven factory mechanics who had travelled out with the car; Mr Val Haresnape, Secretary of the Contest Board of the American Automobile Association (Head of the Board being Eddie Rickenbacker, the First World War fighter ace); Odis Porter, the official timekeeper; Walter A. Richards (of the Citizens' Committee and City Manager of Daytona); Frank G. Pearson, Secretary of the Chamber of Commerce. And then there were the squads of police needed for crowd control; the transportation specialists who had packed up the record attempt car; the team which had shipped the car down from New York to Jacksonville; the crew of the Cunard liner *Berengaria* on which Segrave had crossed the Atlantic, and so on.

Segrave's unstintingly narrow-minded backers had at first been so set against the idea of a transatlantic record bid that they actually refused to meet the expenses of shipping the car overseas and organising the speed trials. They wanted an entirely British success, down to the last grain of sand, rather than let it be compromised by any foreign involvement. Indeed, they left it to Segrave to fund the trip, smugly offering to repay him if he took the record. He knew, however, that Pendine was significantly too short for the sorts of speeds he envisaged and that Daytona Beach, as far as anyone knew, was the only place in the world where there was sufficient space.

The pier was the only snag. It emerged about halfway down the beach, effectively cutting it in two for Segrave's purposes and reducing the *piste* to ten miles. Still, this was four miles better than Pendine and there was less chance of rain, even in March. Consequently he had to scrape together some $25,000 himself (financial support eventually coming from Dunlop, BP, KLG Plugs and, unsurprisingly, Sir Charles Wakefield), arrange the transport and deal with the authorities in Daytona.

In addition, and even more impressively, he was instrumental in getting the Association Internationale des Automobile-Clubs Reconnus and the American Automobile Association to come together to recognise a single, unified World Land Speed Record. Until a few weeks before the Daytona attempt the two bodies had been living in parallel and mutually exclusive worlds. Not only had the AIACR refused to acknowledge the achievements of American record breakers such as Ralph de Palma, Tommy Milton and Sig Haugdahl (who had been using Daytona Beach as a track for a decade, and cheerfully attested to its suitability), but they had spurned earlier efforts by American luminaries such as Barney Oldfield, Bob Burman and 'Terrible' Teddy Tetzlaff. Yet, somehow, Segrave managed that most complex and implausible of tasks: he got the Americans and the French to agree on something. The day Parry Thomas died in Wales, the AAA and the AIACR were signing their concordat in Paris.

The justification for all this – Segrave's emotional double-thinks, the Slug's belligerent ugliness, the politics, the small army of assistants and hangers-on – was so that Segrave might travel at 200 mph in a dead straight line, for a mile; and then repeat the journey down the same mile at 200 mph in the opposite direction. In 1927 200 mph represented the *ne plus ultra* of man's legitimate ambitions. With great difficulty Malcolm Campbell had reached 174 mph. Parry Thomas had died trying to beat that figure. The luminous simplicity of the number suggested to some that it might conceal a dark secret. There was a body of opinion which held that neither motor cars nor the human anatomy were built to cope with travelling at 200 mph at ground level; that you would explode under the stress, or collapse internally or somehow just break into fragments. No fighter plane then in service could get above 200 mph, thousands of feet up in the thin air: 200 mph on the ground was like the sound barrier, a physical wall separating two distinct universes.

This partly accounted for the fascinated acclaim which met Segrave the moment he reached New York after his crossing from England in March 1927. In a full-scale rehearsal of the mania that would overwhelm him after his record, he was greeted at the quayside by a fleet of Cadillacs, all bearing Union Jacks. A police escort then turned on its sirens to clear the streets as he was driven to his hotel. A couple of hours later he found himself at the City Hall, the cynosure of a public reception laid on by Mayor Jimmy Walker, and broadcasting a speech to the American public.

When the time came for him to leave the city a few days later, he was obliged to take the liner *Mohawk*, rather than travel more conventionally by train, in order to escape the mob of press correspondents who were dogging his progress around town. Docking at Jacksonville, the boat was invaded by the Mayor and Corporation of Jacksonville, the Citizens' Committee of Daytona Beach – headed by the Mayor of Daytona Beach – the Committee of the Chamber of Commerce and more press men. On their arrival at Daytona a wholly different crowd was waiting for Segrave and his party, who by now found it hard to move around without another police escort.

At this point he found that he was unable to keep up with events. There were so many people begging for his attention that, as he wrote later, 'I have to this day no idea as to who they all were or what bodies they represented.' His notoriety did, however, mean that he didn't need special registration plates for the Sunbeam sports car he had shipped over; nor a special driver's permit. He was the guest of the State of Florida, and Florida was going to make sure that it fulfilled its obligations. But the state authorities had not anticipated the enormous numbers of spectators who turned up for the first test run on 21 March 1927. This drew a crowd of ten thousand sensation seekers, many of them hoping for an impressively sanguinary accident.

In the event, they had to watch Segrave hit not much more

than 100 mph. 'At this speed the car scarcely appeared to be moving,' he complained. 'Nothing much was learned from this test beyond the fact that the car was difficult to steer.' Added to this, there was nothing to prevent sand, engine oil and sea mist from blowing right up into his cockpit and blacking out his goggles. They rapidly improvised a way of stopping the muck from blasting in from the underside of the car. But the goggles themselves were being torn from his face by the wind, and had to be wedged under the edge of his crash helmet, which in turn was being wrenched from Segrave's head as he drove. By the time he finished his first test run he found that the air pressure had torn the strap through three of its fastening holes and that – even though the car was making no speed to speak of – his helmet was now wobbling around like a poorly fitting lampshade.

As a final complication, no sooner had Segrave got the Sunbeam moving down the course than a group of bystanders started their own cars and set off after him. These were joined by more regular US motorists, whose numbers were swelled by still more until at last he was being given chase along the beach by around three thousand private cars packed with rubber-neckers, in a motorised rout.

When Segrave had broken the LSR a year earlier, at Southport Sands, Lancashire, it had been in the British manner, in the wet, in front of a few hundred diehards smothered in hats and waterproofs. How could anyone British account for this enthusiasm: the fleet of Cadillacs in New York; the police escorts; the huge crowds watching his practice run? Well, Americans were the most car-minded nation in the world, with over twenty-three million vehicles registered by 1927, for a total population of around 119 million, with almost one person in five owning a car. This compared with rather less than a million cars for forty-seven million inhabitants in the UK, where around one person in fifty was a car owner.

The United States was mad for cars, for speed tests, for

motor racing, and speedways were springing up all over: from Fresno, California, to Kansas City, to Indianapolis. Local heroes like de Palma, Milton and Jimmy Murphy blithely broke land speed records in a manner largely unrecognised internationally, but to great acclaim back at home. Haugdahl claimed to be able to do 180 mph with relative ease at Daytona ('The car ran great'), provided his wheels were balanced properly. There was a culture hungry for motoring feats of daring and endurance, which Segrave's arrival to pitch at the magic 200 had tapped into. And, just to give things an extra push, there was America's abiding fondness for making a tremendous public spectacle out of almost anything.

Nevertheless, the Daytona authorities were appalled by the anarchy which accompanied the first test run, and set the second test, three days later, at 6.30 in the morning in order to pre-empt the zealots. And yet thousands of fans camped out all night on the dunes, so as not to miss a second of Segrave's increasingly molested practice time. After running the car from the northern end of the course, due south, just after dawn, he felt that this time he had put up a pretty encouraging performance. He then discovered that several of the more fanatical spectators had wandered on to the track, crossing and re-crossing the electric timing wires to give a series of completely false, and artificially low, readings. Seizing on this, the US dailies cried, 'Another English Failure' and, 'The Car That Would Not'.

There was nothing for it but to make an official attempt. By eight o'clock on the morning of Tuesday 29 March the beach had been cleared by the police and the officials had started to foregather. Mr Val Haresnape was present, as was Mr Odis Porter. The sand was in good condition – if the wind was from the wrong direction, the effects of wind and tide combined to turn the hard table of the beach into a mass of corrugations – and there was a stiff quartering breeze coming from the north-east. The sun was out. A judges' stand had

been erected at the edge of the course for the AAA representatives and other dignitaries. Some thirty thousand fans were
strung out along the dunes of the Ormond-Daytona Beach, in
a black pointillist mass. But where was Mrs Segrave? Where
was the hero's loyal helpmeet? Doris had stayed at home in
London, with their bulldog, Laddie, waiting for some curtains
to arrive. Even absent, though, she made an apt foil for Segrave's
simmering heroism.

By now Louis Coatalen had had '1,000 H.P. CAR BUILT
BY THE SUNBEAM MOTOR CO. WOLVERHAMPTON
ENGLAND' painted in large white letters on both sides of the
machine, to make sure that no one missed the essential point
that, as well as giving Segrave the chance to make history, this
was all business for Sunbeam. Building the fastest car in the
world, capable of doing 200 mph, would be something unique
to put in the advertising, provided the bid succeeded, and should
help to sell a few more of Sunbeam's fairly expensive consumer
motor cars back home. What's more, according to Mr James
Todd, Chairman of STD, the Slug had cost only about £1000
to build, given that the engines were already lying around the
factory, effectively free. It was costly as promotional tools
went, but not inordinately so. The US newspapers had, of
course, never heard of Sunbeam cars or Wolverhampton and
christened it 'the Mystery S', which sounded more showbiz.

The car was brought down to the start line, checked over by
Segrave and the mechanics. Segrave then clambered over the bodywork and dropped into the leather pilot's chair, where he sat,
staring at the dials and switches, pensively depressing the clutch
pedal. The mechanics used compressed air pumped in from
armoured steel bottles to start up the heavily doped rear engine.
Once this was going, Segrave used the rear engine to turn over
the front engine by working an inter-engine clutch, released by
a hand lever. The needles on the dials trembled into life. As the
clouds of smoke cleared from the exhausts, the mechanics scooped
up their equipment and moved away, leaving him alone.

Nothing in the world is as loud as the noise made by human contrivances, and the Slug was shatteringly loud. Its two immense twelve-cylinder piston aero engines were firing away without any silencers, and delivered a thunderous, chesty blaring which settled in Segrave's midriff, overlaid with countless metallic thrashings and clatterings. The whole was topped off with random battlefield detonations and crashes, as the fuel mixture exploded in the wrong parts of the engine. It was an inescapable physical presence, along with the stink of burning fuel, smoking engine oil, rubber and the tang of hot metals.

Segrave sat staring at the ribbon of yellow-white sand ahead, so wide when strolled across at low water, now apparently about as narrow as the tie round his neck, while the Slug rumbled and stank and rattled and flexed around him. He shoved the gear lever into first, eased up the clutch (it had a three-speed gearbox and a foot clutch, just like any car) and started off on the four-mile run-up to the measured mile. The machine was as big as a bus, but it was incapable of moving slowly, accelerating away with frightening alacrity in a cloud of black smoke, shaking and crashing over every indentation in the sand, barking explosively as Segrave changed gear.

For most of those up on the dunes, nothing seemed to be happening, until, after ten or fifteen seconds, they became aware of a droning sound moving towards them. Then the car itself appeared, curiously small and alone on the beach, hundreds of feet away. But the noise was impressive all right – a sound like a heavy bomber making a low fly-past, an authentic thunder that guaranteed the danger of the moment. A cloud of sand, water and exhaust smoke boiled up in the wake of the Mystery S and two stripes spooled out on the sand in the tracks of the tyres. The cameras clicked away and hastily wound on for a shot of the car's vanishing rear. The car was so menacingly ugly, while slim Segrave looked so small and vulnerable at the wheel. What if it blew a tyre (each tyre was experiencing a destructive centrifugal force of four tons at 200 mph)? What if it disintegrated (the air pressure on the front of the car was nearly a thousand pounds)? What if it crashed into the judges' stand?

Inside the Slug, Segrave was in fact trying hard not to crash into the judges' stand. The steering, which felt so light when the car was wheeled around at low speeds, was as heavy as a sack of coal once it had gone into top gear at around 130 mph. And when a gust of north-easterly breeze pushed the car to one side of the track, Segrave felt like the captain on the bridge of a ship, laboriously readjusting his course, rather than the pilot of a high-speed racing machine. A bit later, 'The steering wheel turned round nearly a full half-turn, without apparently causing the faintest difference to the direction.'

With his eyesight hopelessly blurred by the hurricane blowing past him and the vibrations of the roaring Slug, and the runway of the sand unravelling under him, Segrave could nonetheless just make out the black and red marker boards posted up to announce the start of the measured mile. Here he crossed the electric timing wires laid across the sand by the AAA and charged through the one mile out of nine which counted for the record. Having done this, he was caught by the wind and swerved again, mowing down a series of marker flags. He wanted to do only one thing: slow the car down.

So he applied the brakes, only to find that he had made a grave error. He had assumed that the wind resistance would slow the car down to about 75 mph without his so much as touching the brake pedal. Unfortunately, this was not the case. The wind resistance had little effect, and he was still travelling at high speed when he reached the end of the course. He had no choice but to stand on the brakes as hard as he could. But the car was so huge, and going so fast, that in seconds the aluminium brake shoes turned red hot, before reaching a temperature of more than 600°C. At this point they melted entirely, leaving Segrave still barrelling onwards in a four-ton car, with sand dunes to one side, the Atlantic on the other, and no way of stopping. To run into the dunes would wreck the car and kill quite a few spectators. To keep on in a straight line would drive him straight into the pier.

He opted for the sea and ploughed at 60 mph into the first inch-deep sheets of Atlantic water. Plumes of spray and steam gushed up around the wheels and through the bodywork, there was a terrible smell of incinerated brakes, the steering wheel tried to snap itself out of Segrave's hands as the Atlantic sucked at the front tyres, he braced himself in the rattling leather seat. But, amazingly, he and the Slug were unharmed. It churned out of the water like an amphibious craft and rumbled back towards the specially erected telephone box at the end of the course, where Segrave's goggle-eyed team was waiting for him.

Everyone calmed down and set to work. The Slug had its overstressed tyres changed and a whole set of new brakes put in, plus fresh fuel and water. Then it turned round and boomed back down the course with the wind behind it. Over the measured mile Segrave hit a staggering 207 mph, before bringing the car to a halt – this time without destroying anything. The drive chains, mercifully, did not snap. The timekeepers did their calculations.

Segrave had shattered the record. His average speed over the flying mile – the determining component of the LSR – was 203.7 mph, an increase of nearly 30 mph over the previous record. It was a startling result, better than almost anyone could have hoped. Nor had he been torn limb from limb by the experience, despite his encounter with the marker flags, crashing into the sea and reaching 200 mph. In fact, apart from some windburn on his face and a slight stiffness in the wrists, he was as fresh as a daisy. The whole thing had taken about half an hour from start to finish. The crowd had witnessed history – a command performance in fact – and loved it. He was the first man on earth to drive at over 200 mph and, grinning broadly, was chaired out of his car by cheering supporters.

Immediately souvenir hunters descended on the Slug. Two men stole the lenses from Segrave's goggles. A motorcycle cop took his belt, while William F. Sturm made off with his driving helmet, gloves and jumper. One man ran off down the beach clutching one of the Sunbeam's steel wheel covers, but the police caught him before he had gone more than a hundred yards.

Back in St John's Wood, Doris Segrave was unsuccessfully attempting a detached calm. Her husband had been quick to send a telegram: 'World's Record. Over 200. All is well, de Hane.' But the curtains had let her down. 'I just waited,' she told reporters. 'There was nothing else to do. For distractions I had my dog and the arrival of some curtains – which after all turned out unsatisfactory – for my drawing room. But it was the waiting!' Segrave's father took a beefier tone: 'At any rate, the boy's got grit,' announced Mr Charles Segrave. 'He's got courage. He's shown it. Why, when he stepped from the motor car at the end of the run there wasn't a tremble to his hands when he lit his cigarette.'

The London *Evening News* made its own small piece of history by holding a five-minute telephone conversation with Segrave on the new submarine transatlantic link, finishing at 4.30 p.m., London time. By 5.15 they had rushed out a special edition and got it on to the streets while headline writers on all the other papers were still mulling over some likely clichés. The advertising departments of Sunbeam, Wakefield Castrol, BP, Ransome & Marles Bearings and the rest sprang into life. BTH Magnetos declared themselves 'Unfailing in exacting tests and trouble-proof in normal duty'. Dunlop reprinted Segrave's cable to them: 'Hearty congratulations on wonderful behaviour of tyres during my record run. They are perfect. Segrave.'

Brooklands, too, cashed in with an adventitious reminder of its existence: 'High Speeds and Exciting Racing are Always to be Seen at Brooklands.' The Mayor of Southampton began drafting a speech of welcome for when Segrave's liner brought him home. But neither Segrave nor anyone else yet realised that an entirely new kind of fame had come into being.

5

A New Kind of Hero

((((⊙))

The front-page headlines fought to outdo one another. The British press announced, *inter alia*, a 'British Motoring Triumph', proclaiming Segrave 'The Fastest Thing On Wheels' while emphasising that it was an 'All-British Triumph Of Major Segrave', with key implications: 'What It Means To The Motorist'. 'On the burning sands of the famous Daytona Beach,' said the *Daily Telegraph*, 'Major Segrave, the premier of European racing drivers, sent his mystery car at the astounding pace of 207.015 miles per hour down the course, after beating up the track into a quartering head-wind that threw his huge racer into skids threatening instant death.'

The *Evening News*, having got its scoop the day before, capitalised on it with a follow-up interview with Doris Segrave. In this she tenderly averred that Segrave 'is still only a boy really – he won't be 31 until next birthday, and we have been married ten years, think of it . . .' She then tattled about his injured foot, revealing that: 'Up to three years ago the doctors persisted in advising him to have it amputated. But he would not let them amputate it and now it is much better and does not give him nearly as much trouble as it used to. But, of course, the foot is very misshapen.'

A couple of pages on, the paper's motoring correspondent was in a state of erotomania over the new hero. Starting with Segrave's 'steely-blue' eyes and moving on to 'a set of teeth almost too fine a dazzlingly white to be true', he sang of how 'When he is interested his eyes are wonderful. When he is as near to being excited as people playing his game allow themselves to get, his teeth glisten, radiate, and you realise that every minute of his waking life is lived very intensely indeed.' Concluding, the *News* offered this insight: 'Look at his face in repose and you see features almost girlishly handsome. Sit alongside him, on Brooklands, and as soon as his foot goes down his jaw squares up. His face changes. The whole man is transfigured. The laughing blue eyes become projectiles of . . . of Heaven only knows what, except that it looks like something that would *scorch* away obstructions!'

The American press, meanwhile, muffled the ambivalence with which it usually greeted any non-American triumph and took a typically prolix line: 'Human Bullet Flashes Over Sands In Blur – Hits 207 M.P.H. Clip In One Run – British "Hush-Hush" Car Faster Than Thought – USA Feels Pretty Slow'; 'British Speed King Hurtles Over Sands At 200 Miles An Hour – Dives Into Sea And Misses Death By A Hairsbreadth'; 'Major Segrave's Giant Auto Dashes Along Beach To Set Record'; '70,000 Americans (and John D. Rockefeller) Thrilled By Britisher In British Car.'

The significance of the last headline would not have been missed by its readers. Eighty-eight-year-old John D. Rockefeller, founder of Standard Oil and at that time widely believed to be the richest man in the world, was living in semi-retirement at Ormond Beach, alongside the other multimillionaires. No sooner had Segrave broken the 200-mph barrier than Rockefeller had himself chauffeured down from his home, The Casements, to the Sunbeam camp. There he praised Segrave's achievement, quizzed him on matters of car production in Europe and, at the end, produced four new silver dimes. This was one of Rockefeller's little gratifications, a way of conferring a Baptist's benediction on sporting figures and golf caddies. It was a tiny act of patronage, binding the recipient to him. He had the US Mint strike enough of these little coins every year to keep him permanently supplied. 'One,' he said, pressing it into Segrave's hand, 'is for your wife. You have one, yes? One is for your mother, one is for your father and the other for yourself.'

This was no small deed. It was confirmation that all America, metonymised in the form of J.D. Rockefeller – the human essence of American economic liberalism – had recognised Segrave's feat for what it was. Rockefeller also made sure to quiz Segrave, during their fifteen-minute chat, about the differences between European and American motor cars. Segrave, keen not to offend his American hosts, nor his British backers, reckoned that Europe was in the lead when it came to theoretical designs, while America was far ahead in mass production. This was carefully reproduced in a *New York Times* editorial two days later. Other generally approving quotes from Segrave himself were similarly preserved: 'Honestly, these Americans are wonderful,' was a typical example; and, 'I have never heard of finer sportsmen.'

Touchiness remained, of course. America couldn't afford not to be vigilant. Much was made of Segrave's American mother: 'Major Segrave is an American by birth.' Then, a couple of days after the LSR triumph, the *Washington Post* hurried out a quibbling essay on the decline of the British sportsman, to reassure any readers concerned that the Old World might have been reasserting itself over the New. 'Oxford University', the piece ran, 'are blaming the American Rhodes scholars for the failure of the British university to win sporting events. This is not because the Americans lack prowess, but, on the contrary, because they are so good that they discourage the English undergraduates from trying to make the teams . . . What is the matter with the English boy?' It was not always easy to see where formalised irony ended and earnest hostility began.

Nevertheless, following Rockefeller's blessing, there was a gala dinner hosted by three hundred of Florida's most prominent citizens, followed by an offer of $5000 a week to leave the Slug on display in the United States (rejected), followed by a triumphant return home on the *Berengaria* (on which Thomas Bowden, the chief pastry steward, unveiled a model of the Slug made of sugar and pastry). This was followed by a civic reception at Southampton, where Segrave's wife, father, stepmother, the Mayor of Southampton and representatives of the RAC and the Sunbeam Car Company greeted him. A large crowd pressed forward to see the car as it was craned out of the boat, but it was enclosed in a wooden crate and they had to be disappointed.

From there it was back to London, with a luncheon at the RAC in Pall Mall and a banquet on the same day at the Piccadilly Hotel. General Sir Ian Hamilton presided; Sir George Beharrell, the head of Dunlop, proposed the toast and praised 'the ascendancy of British design in motor car building', to which Segrave replied by describing the manner in which the Americans had greeted his result. Mrs Segrave was presented with a floral representation of the Slug. However much Segrave wanted to get back home to St John's Wood, he had to suffer these attentions, plus a broadcast for the BBC, the rush presentation of an exclusive Pathé newsreel at the Plaza Cinema (in which not the least interesting part was the way his car outran the pursuit plane, flying at over 130 mph), a public luncheon at Wolverhampton Town Hall, dinner at the Green Park Hotel (organised by his old comrades in the RFC) and lunch with the Overseas Club at the Criterion Restaurant. The Slug was put on display at Selfridges.

It was the full panoply of official hero worship, far more than Segrave was really comfortable with and as unnerving in its way as the hysteria manifested in the United States. It only ended with a celebratory demonstration run of the Slug at Brooklands at 4.10 p.m. on 6 June, in which Segrave nearly crashed the car in the rain.

But was Segrave's 200 mph a sporting event, an engineering feat, a post-Imperial colonisation of the record books, or a straightforward promotional stunt, selling the concept of British excellence? Segrave made no secret of the fact that, despite his buffeting by the wind and the strain in his wrists, he was not unduly tested by his record run. Although it took nerve and alert reflexes, it was over too quickly to need much stamina. There was less sheer athleticism involved than in contesting a Grand Prix or, for that matter, in a six-hour slog round Brooklands in pursuit of a clutch of Class F records.

Naturally Sunbeam (makers of 'The Supreme Car') and their suppliers felt that they were responsible for building a ground-breaking piece of machinery. But most of the radical thinking had gone into the tyres and the streamlining. The engines, splendid though they were, were fortuitous by-products of Sunbeam's aeroplane engine line (along with the Cossack, Manitou, Bedouin and Nubian aero engines) having been designed back in 1917 for an altogether different purpose. The relationship between car and aeroplane, companionable enough at Brooklands, was here reduced to simple parasitism, in which the car depended for its life force on an essentially separate branch of engineering. The chassis, suspension, steering and trans-mission (those terrible chains – cheap, simple and unavoidable since it was too difficult to make a solid driveshaft which could cope with the Matabeles' power) had no finesse, only strength.

LSR cars, their apologists argued, taught motor engineers much about the outer limits of engineering performance; this knowledge then percolated back down to the turgid Morrises and Austins on the high street. 'Practically every outstanding development in the motor car today,' insisted the *Daily Mail* shortly after Segrave's run, 'is the outcome of racing and record-breaking experience.' To which the *New York Times* countered, 'If Major Segrave's achievement of a speed of 211 miles an hour in his "Mystery S" car at Daytona is a triumph of British engineering, it is much more a triumph for his pluck and endurance.'

What was incontrovertible was that Segrave's success came at exactly the right moment to act as a tonic to Britain's sense of national beleaguerment, causing one fevered conservative later to write of Segrave himself, that 'The old principle of "blood will tell" is still true and that not all our ancient greatness of aristocracy has fallen into that decadence from whose effects we are assured that only democracy can save us.' Modernists could admire his youth, his good looks, his driving prowess and his un-British work ethic. Reactionaries could dwell on his Eton upbringing, his war record and his honest patriotism; they would also have approved of stories that Segrave had been seconded to Scotland Yard during the General Strike of 1926 in order to infiltrate and destroy Bolshevik cells in London.

So Segrave had either contrived his great success or had been lucky enough to take advantage of the mood of the time. He was the right person for the enterprise, with the right backing and the good fortune not to have to fend off simultaneous bids from either Malcolm Campbell or Parry Thomas. And there was one other key constituent part of his success in England: his exploitation of America to take the Land Speed Record.

If there was one country in the world which had manifestly stolen Britain's greatness, which had deprived it of its virility, it was the United States. Neighbours France and Germany posed constant challenges and offered the most barbaric affronts, but as nations they were at least intelligible in terms of their size and their ambitions. Mid-twenties America, on the other hand, was worryingly unbounded in its potentialities. The only major country (other than Japan) to have benefited from the First World War, it had stolen all the superlatives which Britain had spent the preceding 150 years accumulating for itself. It was now the greatest creditor nation in the world, the one with the greatest financial resources, the largest gold reserves. It was also the world's largest producer of both foodstuffs and manufactured goods. Its productive output in the 1920s was larger than that of the next six major powers combined. While Britain tried to lever a few last bits of economic value out of its increasingly fissile Empire, America simply went ahead and created the biggest domestic market in the world.

What's more, it was now possible to get some sense of what this meant in reality, as America's hold over the world cinema industry and its increasing colonisation of the popular imagination (by means of anything from Tom Mix to Gloria Swanson to the Paul Whiteman band) painted a picture, not of some freakish goliath, but of a modern, expansive other world, filled with motor cars, progressive architecture and copious sunshine, where the only significant vices seemed to be the excessive use of firearms, and Prohibition. The Wall Street Crash and the Depression were still years away. The realisation had dawned on the British that it was now quite impossible to condescend to the United States.

This presentiment had been in the air for a long time – since before the turn of the century. Indeed, as long ago as 1795 John Adams, about to become the second President of the United States, wrote to his wife: 'I wish that misfortune and adversity could soften the temper and humiliate the insolence of John Bull. But he is not yet sufficiently humble. If I mistake not, it is the destiny of America one day to beat down his pride.' By 1895 the United States was doing just that, leaning ruthlessly on Britain to resolve the Venezuela Dispute; at which Britain did indeed bend to the United States' will. At about the same time there were calls among more militant Americans to detach Canada from the British Empire and annex it wholesale as part of the United States.

A year or so later Fred A. McKenzie retaliated by writing

a satirically tinged essay deploring the hold American manufactures had over Edwardian England: 'The average man rises in the morning from his New England sheets, he shaves with Williams' soap and a Yankee safety razor, pulls on his Boston boots over his socks from North Carolina, fastens his Connecticut braces, slips his Waltham or Waterbury watch in his pocket, and sits down to breakfast.' From there the grim Yankee hegemony continues in the form of a New York electric tram to work, followed by an American elevator to take him up to his office, where 'He sits on a Nebraskan swivel chair, before a Michigan roll-top desk, writes his letters on a Syracuse typewriter, signing them with a New York fountain pen', and so on, until, at the end of the day, he unwinds at an American musical comedy before going to bed with a couple of 'little liver pills made in America'. The title of the piece was *The American Invaders: Their Plans, Tactics and Progress.*

By 1919 the British Admiralty was panicking over the fact that the US Navy had engaged in a shipbuilding programme which would give it numerical superiority over the British Navy. At the same time America was pitilessly insisting on the fullest repayment of Britain's war debts. By 1924 the Ford Motor Company had acquired a vast factory site at Dagenham, Essex, thus heralding its sinister intention to become the UK's biggest car manufacturer. And in 1925 General Motors bought up Vauxhall cars, with a similar end in mind.

As the 1920s progressed, the relationship between the two nations failed to improve, Neville Chamberlain noting at one stage that the Prime Minister, Stanley Baldwin, 'says he has got to loathe Americans so much that he hates meeting them.' The state of unease which existed between the ageing, declining superpower and the youthful, emergent one was by this time so well established that even the conciliatory *Times* could note that, 'As for American inventions, ideas and modes – they are simply thronging in upon us all the time. Voices from Pittsburgh are now heard across the sea by wireless,' while adding the minatory rider that 'It is not always easy to remember that the American is a foreigner.' And in the early thirties US commentator Raymond Gram Swing felt able to hammer another nail in the coffin which John Adams had started to build, by writing banefully in *Harper's Magazine* about 'the complete refusal of the British public to face the serious facts of their decline'.

Of course, when America did slump after the Great Crash, it fell further and faster than any of its international rivals. And, as was often remarked, its world political influence was markedly less than its raw economic influence. But in 1927 US supremacy looked permanent, and the British found themselves staring into a future filled with subservience to an ex-colony, with their best hope lying in maintaining an air of lordly sagacity, against which the gauche Americans as yet had no defence. America was supposed to be our friend, our collective cousin across the water, our gift to the world. But in some lights it also looked uncannily like our enemy.

What Segrave did next was at the time both radical and incomprehensible. Major Henry Segrave, the national figure and celebrated sporting motorist, turned his back on the Sunbeam Car Company and took a position as chief cement salesman with the Portland Cement Selling and Distributing Co., the makers of Red Triangle cement. It was as if Lester Piggott had given up horse racing at the height of his powers to become a hairdresser, and it quite wrong-footed his public. It appeared to be an absurdly self-effacing retirement for the fastest man in the world; an affront to the public's ambitions.

But Segrave was both heroic and prosaic. Off the track he was a quietly dressed, middle-class figure, married and living in a respectable suburb of London. As much as he engaged in highly demanding, high-risk activities, the obverse of his personality demanded safety: in this case, a respectable job in a respectable business with a reliable salary (his pay from Portland Cement combining with various emoluments he continued to receive from the world of motoring to give him an income estimated at around £8000 a year) in a field which was likely to offer steady growth. Better by far than the motor business he had involved himself in just after the war – that almost instantaneous failure, that £4000 crash. Better, also, than the Sunbeam Car Company, which had not only got rid of its competition department, but appeared to be quite exhausted by its LSR efforts, however successful.

In the same way his well-structured professional egotism was counterpointed by a piquant English modesty, an aversion to self-indulgence and an enjoyment of self-denial. Although one of his mechanics, Walter Fermer, later claimed that part of his job entailed driving a drunken Segrave and team back home after every successful motor race in the back of a Rolls-Royce hearse, Segrave saw drink as 'the refuge and sometimes downfall of far too many people': 'Finish the job before you start on the bottle is my motto.' Neither did he have any interest in food. His idea of a good meal was soup, mashed potato, poached eggs, maybe lemonade as a beverage. When he was stationed in Washington, DC during the First World War, his lunch was often no more than a double portion of waffles and maple syrup.

Small, English rituals also gave him pleasure. He had a suburbanite's love of tidiness, for instance, which compelled him, a few days after his return from Daytona, to muck out his wife's garage. The musical comedy personality Binnie Hale, star of *No, No, Nanette* and *Mr Cinders*, lived opposite the Segraves' appropriately unfussy house in Elm Tree Road. Emerging from her home one Sunday morning, she discovered the new national idol whistling and singing blithely as he scooped up old newspapers and domestic debris, lost in trivial gratifications.

England's greatest living sportsman also had a model railway layout on which he lavished great care and attention. Surprisingly, he wasn't the first Brooklands alumnus to take an interest in model trains. Just after the war Count Louis Zborowski had laid out a miniature narrow gauge railway in the grounds of Higham House. But this, like everything Zborowski built, was on the grand scale, eventually escaping the grounds altogether and becoming the kernel of the Romney, Hythe and Dymchurch Narrow Gauge Miniature Railway. Zborowski and his railway-mad friend Captain J.E.P Howey sent their back-garden locomotive round at such speed that it regularly came off the track.

Segrave would rather have died than abuse his train set in this way. Instead, he was happier to settle back wholesomely against his transformers and – on at least one occasion – address the British Movietone Newsreel cameras in his mellifluous baritone, saying that 'By the use of electricity in controlling your models you can make them nearly talk'; and, 'You can make the locomotive obey every single thing from a switchboard.'

It was his hobby – a word which he pronounced 'hubby', thus lending it an additional bourgeois grace note – and its little, predictable world gave him solace. He built his finest layout in a wooden shed in the garden of his house in Kingston, on the edge of south-west London, to which the Segraves had moved in 1928. Part of the track did exit into the open air, Zborowski-style, but the real business was all indoors. By May 1929 he had even created a cross-Channel rail link in one corner of the shed: 'I've gone ahead into the future and imagined, just for the sake of amusement, that the Channel Tunnel is complete.' He had a fully realised model of the platform at Dover Station, waiting for the last workmen's train to emerge from the Tunnel. A flick of a switch and out came the train, three overalled figurines standing in a flat wagon, followed by a crane and a Southern Region van.

'Now the first train from France is due to arrive – pulled by an electric locomotive of the type they will probably have to use in the Channel Tunnel when it's completed.' A light appeared, reflecting off the heavily rusticated Tunnel entrance. Then a tiny French train came into view, a train whose 'coaches are also the standard French coach used on the *Chemin de Fer du Nord*'. It pulled to a halt at the miniature Dover platform: the future in little in a shed in Kingston.

Back at the office, his enthusiasm for the cement and concrete business was so sincere that it even made its way into his ghosted autobiography, *The Lure of Speed*. As its title suggests, this is mostly a résumé of Segrave's sporting interests on land and water, the words being articulated by a well-known hack writer named James Wentworth Day, while Segrave himself provides the editorial thrust. As such, it comes up with odd philosophical analects: 'There is also such a thing as being slow and dangerous as well as fast and dangerous, and of the two I prefer the fast and dangerous driver, because provided he goes fast enough, he will scare people out of the way'; as well as meditations on the meaning of speed: 'In the future the speed which will matter will not be physical speed at all, but merely the translation of action.'

It also contains the authentic voice of Segrave the railway devotee: 'There can hardly be any doubt that a halt will have to be called in the national expenditure on roads. Great Britain absolutely cannot afford to discard the finest railway system in the world and build roads to take its place.' And it candidly plugs his current line of work: 'There is only one proper way to build a road for high-speed traffic conditions, and this has, I fancy, been abundantly proved in America. The highway should consist of two practically flat tracks of concrete.'

As things were to turn out, Segrave's move to the Portland Cement Selling and Distributing Co. was no wrong turn, but would fit snugly with everything else he did. And, as ever, he had big plans. By the end of 1927 he was ready to co-opt his new employers into his next – and even greater – project.

6

'Loyalty You Cannot Buy'

＜《 ୭》》

Segrave's ambitions were not good news for the forty-two-year-old motor racer, record breaker, insurance broker and company director Captain Malcolm Campbell. It meant that he would have to invest yet more cash in his life's work. Campbell was profoundly interested in money and always claimed that only the best in life was good enough, but his munificence extended exclusively to himself and to those projects which held his attention and remained interesting to him. He had inherited a fortune of around £250,000 from his diamond-broker father and had made another tidy sum on his own account in the Lloyd's insurance market. But he was no Woolf Barnato, no Glen Kidston. The rest of the world experienced his wealth capriciously and not often.

As is often the case with the rich, he could be mean in obscurely inventive ways. While overseeing the building of his first Land Speed Record car – the first of the great *Blue Birds* – he insisted on keeping his teams of mechanics happy by handing out tins of fifty Three Castles cigarettes, all of which were so old that they dated from before the First War. He haggled so often and so remorselessly with the local shopkeepers in Reigate that they resorted to quoting a specially inflated

'Campbell price' whenever he came in. And if anyone on the payroll used his money for tipping, he became incandescent at the idea of being exploited. 'If you want to impress taxi-drivers with your generosity,' he snapped, 'do it with your own money.'

But if anyone ever doubted how wealthy Campbell was, they only had to look at the chestfuls of cash he was pouring into his record cars. Having taken the LSR in 1924 and 1925 in his second-hand Sunbeam – the one Kenelm Lee Guinness had used at Brooklands – he had decided to go all out for the title and build himself a stupendous, state-of-the-art record-breaking machine – with which he took the title in February 1927 at over 174 mph. But this had cost him a troubling £10,000, with thousands of pounds more demanding to be spent if he was to catch up with Segrave's 203 mph. Parry Thomas had spent perhaps £1000 in total on *Babs*; Segrave had spent nothing at all, save the energy required to browbeat the Sunbeam Car Company and raise the funds to take his Sunbeam to America.

Personal wealth, of course, was not the only thing separating Campbell and Segrave. Segrave was a figure on to whom the public could project their own desires. His apparent coolness, his professionalism, his clear sense of purpose, his lukewarm personal habits and his quiet good looks embodied a particular English archetype whose depths were hard to fathom and whose surface suggested a kind of commanding inscrutability. Paradigmatically efficient, he even went as far as occasionally boring his own team. As David McDonald (other wise known as 'Dunlop Mac', the tyre company's racing expert) put it, 'Segrave's runs were all over so quickly and easily that they were almost disappointing.'

Campbell, by contrast, spent his life in a farrago of near-misses, of protracted flirtations with disaster from which he only just managed to extract victory. He not only had a Scottish name, with all Scotland's warlike and belligerent associations, but lived a life almost entirely devoted to contentiousness. He was small, slightly built. If Segrave was sometimes too broad-shouldered to fit comfortably into a racing car, it was a strange and daunting thing to see the squinting, relatively diminutive form of Campbell disappearing behind the windscreen of one of his LSR cars – which got larger and larger and more and more powerful over time – and flexing his little hands round the steering wheel, like a child with a toy too grown-up for him.

But, like the warrior chief he clearly imagined himself to be, Campbell had a hawkish nose, pronounced chin, eyes forever crinkled in fierce appraisal, and deep cicatrices in his cheeks: the lean, cruel facial characteristics of someone used to coercion. His smile was crisp and dazzling, an instrument of subjugation which he would turn on people, or behind which he would retreat in moments of uncertainty. As he got older and his vitality declined, he more and more resembled an implacable Mr Punch.

Campbell was also older than Segrave. He was born on 11 March 1885 in Chislehurst, Kent. His father, William Campbell, was a Victorian martinet who, at the age of forty-two, had married a 'beautiful' young woman named Ada. Beautiful she may have been; but she was also, according to Malcolm Campbell's granddaughter, Gina, 'insular, narrow-minded and selfish', and only seventeen years old. Having delivered herself of two children, Malcolm and Freda, Ada then established a trend of fierce marital disharmony with her husband, which carried over seamlessly into the next two generations of Campbells. And while William Campbell prospered at Andrew Campbell & Company, the family diamond merchants' business in Cheapside, in the City of London, Malcolm was sent, not to glamorous Eton, but to Uppingham, near Leicester.

Uppingham was founded in 1548 and had kept its head down for two and a half centuries before being swept up in the great Victorian public school boom and prospering accordingly. By the close of the nineteenth century it was a big, averagely thuggish boys' boarding school, filled with Victorian Gothic architecture and stuck in the mud and isolation of Rutland.

Campbell spent much of his early career at Uppingham failing the 'Fags' Exam' and being thrashed with the back of a hair-brush. Having got over that ('The series of vigorous hidings had made me so hardened that I took them as a matter of course'), he spent the rest of his time there learning little except the art of riding rams. This was the big thing on Sunday afternoons in the middle of nowhere, with time to kill and youthful testosterone to burn: to choose a ram in a field of sheep, run it down, climb on and ride it across the field, clinging to its horns and covering one's school uniform with rank lanolin. 'This rough work took its toll of Sunday garments.' Campbell had even less interest in academic matters than Segrave, but prided himself on his ram-riding and left the school with that as his principal accomplishment.

Malcolm's academic failure at school was taken for granted by his overbearing father. At the end of one term, faced with yet another report itemising Malcolm's lumpen performance, Campbell senior complained that his son had never won a single prize for any of the subjects he was meant to be studying. So Malcolm determined to prove the old man wrong. He spent the next term toiling at his studies, won an end-of-term prize, took it home in triumph, only for his father to look at it and announce, 'I suppose all the other boys must have been bad.' This was about the time that young Malcolm began to wage a long-term campaign against his father: as he saw it, the high-spirited insurrectionist youth toiling against the oppressive older regime. Names were called, beatings administered, parental commands audaciously disobeyed. The whole saga culminated one night in a terrific row, in the course of which Malcolm managed to pull a gas chandelier down from the ceiling of the family home. After that he vowed to leave for good.

He spent a couple of years in France and Germany, ostensibly studying. On his return he spurned the family diamond business; but, smothering his usual contrariness, allowed himself to be shepherded into Lloyd's of London, being apprenticed to a firm of insurance brokers, Tyser & Co. From there he moved

on to Pitman & Deane in Gracechurch Street. There he stumbled
on a pure money-maker when he developed a new kind of libel
insurance for newspapers. A spate of libel litigation had broken
out in the early 1900s (with one successful claimant winning
£1750 in damages) and Campbell spotted a market.

It took him six months to work out the best way to pack-
age his insurance scheme, and to persuade the Lloyd's under-
writers to back him. Fortunately, Lloyd's was going through
one of its more adventurous phases in non-marine insurance
and took him on. He then spent 'a great deal of time in climbing stairs in Fleet Street, urging papers to take up my new
insurance'. Finally Odhams, Southward and Company took
out a policy, and 'After that,' according to Campbell, 'success
was only a question of time.' His monopoly on the business
allowed him to make a good living without much effort. He
turned his attention to motorbikes, cars and Brooklands; and
in July 1913 contracted a lightning marriage to the wealthy
Miss Marjorie Dagmar Knott. Then, like Segrave, he joined
up in 1914.

When the war began Campbell was a second lieutenant in
the Royal West Kent Regiment, where he took over the transport
section and devoted his energies to getting his men to ride
horses and wear tremendously smart uniforms. For a while he
was a motorcycle dispatch rider, seeing action at the battle of
Mons in 1915. Again, like Segrave, he tired of Army life and
joined the RFC in 1916, passing out from the Special Flying
School at Gosport, Hampshire.

The 'Special Qualifications' in his service record made
mention of the time he spent before the war in France and
Germany, the fact that he had built a home-made monoplane
which flew for a hundred yards; and his racing at Brooklands.
'Knowledge of French & German,' it read. 'Built own machine
in 1909. Experience in high speed petrol engines from amateur
motor car racing.' It sounded impressive. But while Segrave
was pulling the corpse of his boon companion out of the mud,

or was being blown out of the sky in an FE8, Campbell was enjoying the relative drudgery of being a ferry pilot – that is, one whose job it was to fly fresh aircraft across the Channel to northern France and return beaten-up aeroplanes to England for repairs. The risk, evidently, was all in the flying: getting caught in fog or having to bring back an especially decrepit aircraft. Later on, he hunted Zeppelins and was promoted to captain; he was careful to keep the rank after the Armistice.

Events in Campbell's personal life ultimately had more impact on him than events in the war. While he was away on active service, ferrying planes back and forth across the Channel, the first Mrs Campbell was enthusiastically pursuing an affair with one of his business associates back home. The man's name was Reginald France, and the grounds for Mr and Mrs Campbell's subsequent divorce lay specifically in a long night of passion France and Marjorie spent at the Charing Cross Hotel at the end of May 1916. Campbell was traduced, in other words, and his already disputatious, fractious personality was given a further push towards discordancy.

The income he had derived from his insurance business (which he left soon after 1918), plus his inheritance, meant that by the start of the twenties he was extremely comfortably off. And in 1920 he met and married pretty, doll-like, impassive Dorothy Whittall, daughter of Major William Whittall. She had first set eyes on him at Brooklands in 1912. She happened to be spectating; he was competing. Rather, he was crashing his car spectacularly, right in front of where she stood. His sang-froid as he stepped from the shattered wreckage deeply affected her. 'His only expressions of regret,' she said later, 'were that he had endangered the life of his mechanic and that the car was in all probability damaged beyond practicable repair. I had the impression forced upon me that here was a man quite out of the ordinary.'

When they met again, eight years later, she was still in thrall to him. Only now, circumstances were different: he was damaged goods, permanently marked by the effects of his divorce. At the time the memory of Marjorie Campbell was swept aside in the fresh romance between Malcolm and Dorothy. It was only decades later, when things had gone terribly wrong, that Dorothy exhumed the memory of the first Mrs Campbell, recasting her, not as a love cheat, but as 'a very charming woman', who had 'a considerable fortune in her own right'. Campbell apparently owed to her 'a great deal of his success in his racing career during the year between his marriage and the outbreak of war. It was she who financed his purchase of racing cars' – Campbell had five – 'which he could not have bought but for her help.' And, 'It was she who gave him the first motor boat he ever owned – a luxury river launch, the *White Heather.*' This affection and generosity, we are invited to believe in Dorothy's memoirs, Campbell repaid by heartlessly absorbing her funds before tossing her aside like a spent chequebook.

But all this ugly revisionism was still to come. Derided by his father and comprehensively two-timed by his first wife, Campbell went ahead and married Dorothy, embarking on a new, post-war existence in which he was mistrustful of others and frequently prone to unmanageable inner conflicts. He was thus less of a catch than he first seemed.

From his new wife's point of view, these shortcomings came out most spectacularly during social engagements and family crises. Shortly after their registry-office wedding the Campbells elected to celebrate in a small way by having twenty or so friends over to the house in Kingston where they were then living. With the first guests about to arrive, Campbell decided that he had to go out and ride his horse in Richmond Park. Dorothy remonstrated. He lost his temper and stormed out of the house. An hour after all the guests had assembled and were toying inhibitedly with their cocktails in the drawing room, Campbell came back, sweaty and dusty in his boots and hacking jacket. He barked, 'Shan't be long' and disappeared upstairs.

Ten minutes later he had changed, literally and figuratively, and was complaisantly acting the part of host.

He did the same again when Dorothy was expecting their first child, in 1921. The birth was scheduled to take place at home. Campbell was at work. Dorothy telephoned him with the news that she had gone into labour, and would he come back to assist? He did so, but, overwhelmed by the exigencies of human need, he immediately disappeared to help a friend build a dog kennel. Finally Dorothy's parents arrived and, with the midwife, arranged Donald Campbell's arrival into the world.

Several years later Campbell had a launch party for the car showrooms in St James's Street that he had decided to take on. Come the day, the guests – motor traders, old clients, prospective new clients, money-men – turned up, and the drinks were poured. It then turned out that Campbell had spontaneously absented himself to go and take part in a hill-climb competition in France.

It was a recurring pattern: when they were about to move into a bigger, smarter house, Headley Grove, near Dorking, in 1936, as the packing crates and removal men turned up, Campbell took himself off for a cruise around North Africa, only returning months after the move was completed.

Campbell's inability to commit himself to any serious prior obligation included marriage. He felt free to chase after other women. 'We had not been married very long,' Dorothy wrote, 'before I was forced to the realization that there was another woman in his life.' A confrontation followed. He swore that the affair was over. It was. But then he started on another affair, and another, with the result that Dorothy 'came across letters from women, of such a character as to leave no doubt as to the relationship existing between writer and addressee'. Campbell didn't care about the distress he caused his wife. Out of indifference – or the need to sharpen the experience by spicing it with danger – one day he had sex with a woman on the tennis court at the family home at Povey Cross. Nine-year-old Donald found them *in flagrante*. Campbell also boasted of his couplings with tea-shop waitresses and took Donald, when he was old enough, on a tour of London's brothels.

By the start of the Second World War the Campbells were living apart. In 1940 they dissolved their marriage in a divorce of such spectacular messiness and acrimony that even the German invasion of Norway struggled to make headway against it in the national press. The messiness and acrimony arose not least because Dorothy Campbell, just like the first Mrs Campbell, was by this time a practised philanderer, whose infidelities had begun at the end of the twenties and carried on from there, although never reaching Malcolm's level of shiftless promiscuity. 'Loyalty you cannot buy,' was one of Campbell's steely apophthegms.

In the middle of this were Donald and his sister Jean, three years his junior. The story of Donald Campbell's relationship with his father is nowadays usually framed as a Sophoclean tragedy, ending in the half-willed suicide of the son in his jet-boat crash on Coniston Water in 1967. Campbell the father is generally represented as being imprisoned within an exceptionally narrow band of human capabilities, emerging as either a charismatic tyrant or as a mere sadist, unfit for parenthood at any level. Without a doubt he seems to have followed Larkin's edict that 'Man hands on misery to man', by imposing his own father's regime of beatings, denunciations and disparagements on his son. Even Jean, who ultimately became a loyal apologist, said after the event, 'He was very strict – poor old Don was always getting a walloping'. Poor old Don also had to get used to being called a 'clod' by his father and to being told that 'You'll never be as good as me. We aren't built the same way. You haven't got the guts that I have.'

Nevertheless, as soon as he was old enough to appear in public and pose for a photographer, Donald was used as a prop in Campbell's own publicity set-ups. He was pictured at

Brooklands, aged seven, in shorts, sandals and floppy hair. He
was allowed to christen one of his father's Water Speed Record
boats at Coniston, at the age of eighteen, besuited and mature.
He was taken out to the Bonneville Salt Flats in Utah, and he
was paraded at Brooklands in 1931 with the new version of
Blue Bird, peering sadly at the controls of the car while his
father turned away, frowning.

Donald's mother and sister were similarly co-opted into photo
opportunities, to consolidate the idea that Malcolm Campbell
was both fertile and fully rounded. In most pictures they look
anxious and unhappy, responding to the tension that Campbell
generated around him. One spectacularly ill-judged publicity
photo shows Campbell seated in a wing chair, glaring furiously
at the camera and clutching a live parrot, while little Jean
buries her face in her arms, Donald tries not to cry and Dorothy
stares tragically at the floor. But while the women were
frequently dispensable, Donald was a necessary foil for
Malcolm, the young prince adding lustre to the ageing king.
And yet why? Why did Malcolm Campbell allow the world
to see him repeatedly in the company of a 'clod'?

Because in this, as in so much else, Campbell was incapable
of applying any kind of editorial rigour to his emotions. Plainly,
Donald irritated Malcolm enormously. But then Donald was
quite an irritating child. He tipped oil around the excruciat-
ingly tidy garage at Povey Cross. He interfered with racing
cars in the pits at Brooklands – both his father's and those of
other competitors. He dismantled his toys and failed to reassem-
ble them. When his father was being interviewed by the *New
York Times* in a Manhattan hotel room, young Donald interrupted
'time and again' by bursting in, clutching a 'gigantic revolver
aimed at imaginary enemies lurking behind valises and trunks'.

At St Peter's Prep School in Seaford, Sussex, the boy was
broadly disliked for boasting about his father's exploits and
for selling forgeries of his signature to credulous friends. Sent
on to Uppingham, he was there given repeated drenchings in

water on account of his boastfulness; this, it has been claimed, led to the rheumatic fever which invalided him out of full-time education in 1937 and later out of the RAF.

And yet he saw his father as a truly great man and yearned chronically for his acceptance and his love. To this, Malcolm Campbell, in between the long moments of Victorian severity which marked so much of his parenting, sometimes responded. Donald drove him mad, but he *was* his son.

Consider the moment when Campbell arrives home at Southampton Docks on the *Aquitania* in 1933. He has just succeeded in his latest LSR bid in the States. A mob of people cheers his arrival, among them his wife and his eleven-year-old son, the boy now wearing a raincoat and a ludicrous bowler hat. Donald races up the gangplank to greet his father on deck. 'Congratulations, Dad,' he says, stretching out his right hand to shake his father's.

But Dad has got his wires crossed. Already perfectly rigid with tension on account of the presence of the newsreel cameras – conflicted again, feverish in his love of publicity, but fundamentally uneasy when it comes to public speaking – he has his hat clutched in his right hand and is too galvanised with nerves to switch it over to his left hand. Donald's right hand hangs in the air for a second, while it becomes clear to him that Dad is not going to shake it. Then it drops to Donald's side, an instinctive, mortified gesture of recoil. It looks as if Dad has delivered a brutish rebuff. Only this is not so. Finally Campbell senior untangles himself from the logistical crisis involving his hands, reaches down and squeezes his son's right hand in his left hand with what appears to be unpremeditated affection, saying, 'Thanks, old boy,' a note of candid relief in his voice. Donald smiles a pleased, bashful smile as Dad launches into his address to the cameras. It is a moment pregnant with indecisiveness and potential humiliation. Yet, on this occasion, Campbell comes out of it with his humanity just about intact.

*   *   *

If there was anyone whom Campbell regarded with more or less constant affection, it was the men who made up his Land Speed Record team. Dorothy remarked, enviously, that Campbell's *équipe* 'were men and brothers to be treated as such . . . They were admitted to a degree of familiarity not always usual between employer and employed. In fact, there was always an air of comradeship between Malcolm and his mechanics.'

And of all Campbell's team, the central figure ('He put the first nut on the first bolt') was Leo Villa. Villa made things possible, at the same time that Campbell was doing his best to make them impossible. Mechanically gifted, hard-working, prodigiously loyal, the twenty-three-year-old Villa joined 'the Skipper' in 1922, stayed with him until his death and then carried on as mentor and uncle-figure for Donald Campbell. Another photo, given by Malcolm Campbell to Villa in 1933: Villa and six other team members bear Campbell aloft after a successful run. In Campbell's hand, across the picture, is written: 'To Leo Villa my old friend of many campaigns In appreciation for all he has done, and to whom I owe so much of *Blue Bird*'s success. With thanks and best wishes from Malcolm Campbell.'

Campbell loved Villa about as much as he could love anyone. Theirs was a long and fractious marriage which never reached the law courts. But it is also true that, as he was with any kind of emotion, Campbell was contradictory about the love that he did feel. Such contradiction tended to come out in the form of the face-slapping which he inflicted on Villa for many years. This was his way of expressing closeness while at the same time maintaining an attitude of masculine distance. According to Villa, whenever Campbell and his team had broken a record, 'He came up to me and slapped me, quite hard, much too hard for comfort, really, across the cheek, and said, "Good old Leo." It was his way of letting off steam, I think.' It was a kind of brutalised affection, used at moments of high emotion.

Years after the great LSR adventures, Campbell was on his

deathbed. It was Christmas. Donald and Leo were gathered round in gloomy anticipation. 'With great difficulty he made us understand that he wanted to drink a toast for Christmas. Donald was dispatched for a bottle of champagne and the Skipper himself had a small glass of medicine in his hand, which he had great difficulty in holding. He was very ill and could hardly speak. Then suddenly he leaned forward, just as he had done so many times in the past, and slapped me across the jaw. With great effort, and very slowly, he said, "Good old Leo." They were the last words he spoke to me.' A few days later Campbell was dead, having yielded up this final token of kinship. Barely able to hold a glass of medicine, he had nonetheless levered himself up in his bed, slapped his 'old friend of many campaigns' as hard as he could and ground out his declaration like a Lear.

Villa was, therefore, the stoical lieutenant, intimate and unquestioning. But there were other, essential team members. One of the main figures in any record attempt was the engineer Harry Leech, among the handful of people who had actually survived the R101 disaster of 1930, in which the last great British airship had crashed in flames on a French hillside. Forever characterised in newspaper reports as 'the R101 Survivor', the toothy, bespectacled Leech had subsequently been attached to the engineering department of Southampton University, submissively taking his holidays to coincide with Campbell's land speed bids. Then there was Joe Coe, the engineer from Napiers, and the Dunlop brothers – Steve McDonald and David McDonald, respectively known as Big Mac and Dunlop Mac – who fussed over the tyres.

As a rule, whenever Campbell posed for the camera, he communicated nothing but unease. The exception was when he was with the team – Villa, Leech, Coe, Dunlop Mac – 'this gallant little band of very loyal supporters'; Campbell the warrior chief at the head of his pocket battalion. Then the smile was unforced, the posture natural. The frontispiece of his ghosted autobiography *My Thirty Years of Speed* doesn't show Campbell and his wife, or Campbell and his son, or Campbell and one of his cars. In fact, at no point does *My Thirty Years of Speed* even refer to the existence of Campbell's family. No: the frontispiece shows Campbell with his arms round 'his two mechanics and friends', Harry Leech and Leo Villa, Campbell wreathed in smiles, cigarette on the go, Leech and Villa beaming like the boon companions they were.

This kind of thing made Campbell happy, as did commanding the transport section of the Royal West Kent Regiment; inspecting Sir Malcolm Campbell's Own Sea Scouts; organising the first training school for the Metropolitan Police Flying Squad; and, at Daytona Beach, where these things were possible, hanging about with the boys of his LSR team and making sure they were entertained with local shows, parties, plenty of swimming and regular exercise. He was fulfilled in these moments, existing in a formalised setting, his position as tribal leader unchallenged and his status confirmed by the existence of his loyal second in command.

His financial blind spot was the Land Speed Record car *Blue Bird*, or rather, the succession of *Blue Birds* he built throughout the twenties and thirties for his LSR adventures. More than a blind spot: *Blue Bird* was an Aleutian Trench which absorbed oceans of money, psychic energy, physical strength. Rich, tight Captain Campbell felt nonetheless free to spend quite obsessionally from 1925 on, when the *Blue Bird* idea really started.

This was not long after he had moved Dorothy and his young son, Donald, into a fairly shambolic aggregation of farm-worker's cottages called Povey Cross, just south of Reigate (now hard by the perimeter fence of Gatwick Airport). The previous owner, an official of the London Fire Brigade, had used it as a weekend retreat, and done the bare minimum to bring this partly sixteenth-century building into the modern world. Nevertheless, an accelerated programme of building works made it habitable, as well as seeing to it that Campbell had some smart garages built for his constantly changing collection of cars.

But no sooner had the dust settled, and Mrs Campbell had begun planning her renovation of the 'sticky morass' which was the surrounding land, than the despotic Campbell had the chassis of his new record breaker moved in, in order to oversee its completion in time for the start of 1927. The Robin Hood Works, the engineering business run by Kenelm Lee Guinness near Kingston, had done the complex internal work. Now it remained for a streamlined body to be built up over what was essentially a huge single-seater racing car, with a Napier Lion aero engine (not a wartime cast-off this time, but direct from the makers) in front, and the driver seated behind the engine in the conventional position.

At once *Blue Bird* became a queen termite, fussed over by a team of eleven technicians led by Leo Villa. Everything about it was of laboriously superior quality. 'Don't believe in trash,' said Campbell. Vickers Laboratories stress-tested each component before it was bolted on, and the car had a hyper-complicated three-speed gearbox specially designed for it by an engineer named Joseph Maina. A squad of panel beaters worked through the night in order to keep to their schedule. The young family in the main house lay awake in their beds, listening to the thuds and clangs coming from the workshop; as did the Airedales and Alsatians Campbell had recently decided to breed. At any given point there were as many as thirty or forty of these creatures cooped up in the grounds at Povey Cross. They howled, hour after hour, as the hammering went on. Mrs Campbell, having been kept up all night by the panel beaters and the dogs, would come down to find pieces of machinery being worked on in her kitchen; and that the mechanics needed feeding, if not immediately, then at irregular intervals throughout the day.

Campbell's main endeavour in all this was to ignore his wife and children utterly, to lash his team on to greater efforts, and occasionally to yield to episodes of ineffectual spontaneity. One day he burst into the workshops clutching a bundle of neck-ties. He forced everyone to put on a tie before they continued working. Then, even as they were adjusting the knots, Campbell ran back in, yelling that the old granary – which the mechanics had been using as refectory and boarding house – was burning down. They struggled to put out the fire, but their failure to do so led to endless complications about finding lodgings for the team in the neighbourhood and working out new dining arrangements.

On another occasion Campbell simply dropped everything in order to take off for the island of Cocos, south of Costa Rica. He was in search of the treasure that many believed lay there. Five hundred expeditions have been mounted in search of this treasure; none has found it. Campbell left on Kenelm Lee Guinness's steam yacht *Adventuress* and came home a couple of months later, empty-handed, calling the venture 'futile'. From time to time he would unearth a fresh cache of twelve-year-old cigarette tins and hand them out like campaign medals. And so it went on.

A final push saw *Blue Bird* finished in time for Christmas 1926. New Year's Day 1927 found the team down at Pendine Sands, where things were hardly promising, given the weather and the predisposition of *Blue Bird* – and indeed, any stationary motor car – to sink into the soaking wet beach. Parry Thomas was also there, spying on them with a pair of binoculars, and helping to pull the car out when it started to go under. *Blue Bird* had to be parked on a couple of old metal advertising placards laid on the sand to spread the load. Then the gearbox failed and they took the car back to Povey Cross for adjustments.

They returned to south-west Wales in the middle of the month. The *Daily Mail* recounted this with a finely judged note of viciousness:

The short history of the new car has so far been full of disappointment. It took a year to build and cost its owner about £5000. Its log so far is as follows:

FRIDAY – It was carried to Pendine, a distance of 230 miles by motor lorry.

SATURDAY – Mechanics spent the day tuning the engine and generally getting the monster fit.

SUNDAY – The car was taken down to the sands. It plunged headlong down the slipway, causing some anxiety to its driver. It was started up, stopped with a jerk, and was then nearly swallowed up in the quicksand.

All through the night the eight mechanics worked to repair the gear trouble, and to-day the car did have a brief run. When it was started up a great sheet of blue flame from its open exhaust pipes singed a spectator's trousers.

It was still wet and impossible when they came back. Occasionally, bored, a long way from civilisation and by now starting to disconnect from reality, people in Campbell's squad would be inducted to the 'Pendine Club'. For this, one had to wear a lavatory seat around the neck while having beer tipped over one's head. Back in 1924 and 1925 Campbell had taken the record in the old 350-hp Sunbeam with relative ease, in the days when there was less riding on it, when Pendine seemed less hostile. Why did it have to be so arduous now? Everyone returned to Surrey yet again.

They came back to Wales at the end of the month. There was now hail and snow, gales and torrential rain. After one storm, on the night of 31 January, the beach was so covered in debris that it had to be hand-picked clean by the *Blue Bird* team and a group of local volunteers. Among other things, they recovered forty feet of wire hawser, two dead sheep and enough sharp shells to fill a medium-sized van. To get the beach to drain so that Campbell could drive across it at over 150 mph, they hit upon the idea of ploughing a drainage ditch in the sand. They found a plough and had it towed along by the van that had carted away all the shells. Leo Villa had a go at ploughing and twisted his thumb.

The costs piled up. The expensive, beautifully made Maina gearbox was already looking like a mistake, refusing to work properly and taking up so much room in the cockpit that Campbell could scarcely get in or out, and once in, didn't have enough elbow room to work the gear lever. 'Where the hell is Maina?' Campbell yelled. 'This is damn silly.'

One day he managed a really fast run, spoiled only by having to slow down in order to avoid the drainage plough, left at the edge of the course. He took comfort in posing rhetorical questions about his own car ('I spend all this damn money and what do I get for it?') and brooding on Parry Thomas's *Babs* ('That damned old chain-drive costs only half the money and it does the job.').

At last, on 4 February 1927, he got *Blue Bird* through the flying mile at an average speed of over 174 mph and took the LSR from Parry Thomas by a margin of some three miles per hour. There was water everywhere, lakes of rainwater and sea. Initially the car ground to a halt after travelling a hundred yards off its stands, but Campbell persuaded it back into gear and pressed on. His goggles were blown clean off his head at one point, leaving him blinded by spray and sand. But it was enough. His cloche-hatted wife came running across to him at the finish, waving a sheet of paper with the timer's results on it. Campbell was so excited that he kissed her ardently; she was so relieved that the nightmare was over that she let him. The *Blue Bird* team then carried him around the car on their shoulders and sang.

'I never want such an experience again,' he said to the press, his eyes still bloodshot from the blast of the gale. That night they threw an exhausted celebratory dinner at the Beach Hotel for all the people of Pendine.

Six weeks later Segrave shattered the record in Florida, became the centre of the world's attention and Campbell had to start all over again.

But then consider this. A couple of weeks before Parry Thomas took the LSR in 1926, Campbell was at Brooklands, demonstrating a Bugatti to a potential customer and personal friend, the Hon. Brian Lewis, later Lord Essenden. Lewis declared that the car couldn't manage 100 mph. Campbell leapt into the driver's seat, put Leo Villa in the passenger seat and shot off round the track, determined to prove Lewis wrong. As soon as he got up to speed, the Bugatti's bonnet flew open, was driven backwards by the force of the wind, hit Campbell on the head and knocked him out. Villa showed his customary presence of mind and managed to steer the car to safety at the edge of the track.

Campbell, however, recalled the accident as a providential encounter with Destiny, in which he somehow single-handedly and unconsciously drove the car back to the paddock, where he woke up with no recollection of what had just happened. 'By all the laws that we know,' he philosophised afterwards, 'my mechanic and I should have been killed that day.' He went on to explain that 'It is my belief that no man dies before his time, and I have never been able to explain these things.' According to Dorothy Campbell, another of his favourite expressions was 'It is all written in the book.'

The significance of this episode is not just that it hints at Campbell's well-attested fondness for mysticism, but that it suggests something of the way in which he mythologised himself, turning events into dramas, strophes in the epic poem that was his life. Villa always maintained that the flying bonnet (someone had forgotten to secure the safety strap which held it down) was an accident from which he and Campbell were both lucky to escape. He also maintained that it happened three years later than Campbell said it did.

According to Campbell, it *was* 1926 and it *was* an encounter with the Eternal, which happily demonstrated his ability to control a fast-moving car even when knocked out cold. It was an addition, in fact, to the Astonishing Story of Malcolm Campbell, the public figure. For, however much he may have been Segrave's inferior – older, less gifted, less handsome, the product of a smaller school, militarily lower-ranking, burdened by the imperfections of his LSR cars, an imitator rather than an originator – when it came to self-promotion he was unmatched. He understood completely that his exploits needed publicity to make them worth doing and that for the publicity to work he needed to offer an angle, a story, an image, a positive sense of how remarkable he really was.

Again, consider the name *Blue Bird*, which he gave his cars. Most famously, it applied to the LSR aero-engined monsters, as well as to his later Water Speed Record boats. It was then taken over by his son, Donald, and bestowed on his cars and boats, extending its usefulness well into the 1960s. But Campbell had been using it to christen his favourite racers from before the outbreak of the First World War. Up to 1912 he had, in fact, named his cars *Vanda* and *Flapper* – no worse than *Pooble*, *Toodles* or *Mud II*, which were also doing the rounds at Brooklands. He was on to a Darracq called *Flapper III* when someone observed that the name *Flapper* had brought him no luck whatsoever, and asked whether he had thought of changing it.

At that time the Belgian symbolist poet and dramatist Maurice Maeterlinck was enjoying international success with his play *The Blue Bird*. This was first performed in London at the end of 1909 and caused a minor sensation with its mixture of yearning fantasy and colourful proto-Jungianisms. Hard to credit nowadays, but this fairy tale for all ages about two children, Tyltyl and Mytyl, and their search for the meaning contained in the Blue Bird (aided by a Cat, a Dog, the physical manifestations of Death, The Perfumes of the Night, The Luxury of Drinking When You Are Not Thirsty, The Joy of Maternal Love, Fairy Berylune and many others) was deemed neither fey nor tiresomely unilluminating when it appeared on the London stage. Tyltyl's line, in the translation by Alexander Teixeira de Mattos, 'Why, that's the Blue Bird we were looking for! We went so far and he was here all the time!' more or less encapsulates the drama.

But there is a great deal of elaborate, indeed almost unstageable, visionary business between the start and the finish. This theatrical journey must have justified *The Times*'s critical reaction to the debut production at the Haymarket Theatre: 'An evening of unalloyed happiness. What an exquisite blend of fancy, wisdom, speculation, poetry, tenderness is this *Blue Bird*! It brings tears to the eyes and then chases them away with laughter.' This may make more sense when you consider that at the same time the Lyric Theatre was offering William Devereux's *Sir Walter Raleigh*, while the Palace Variety Theatre was doing *Special Cattle Show Attractions*. Maeterlinck's take on the world, dense with symbolism and radically benign, must have come as a delicious shock to the theatre-goers of the West End, glutted on post-Victorian materiality.

So, reasoned Captain Malcolm Campbell, why not appropriate 'Blue Bird' for the new name of his car? As an emblem of the desirable yet unattainable, it made sense for someone whose life was to be spent trying to snatch seconds out of the air. The other element of the equation – that what you seek is right in front of you, if only you know how to look for it – makes rather less sense for a man who spent so much time in such a tizzy of hyperactivity. But did Campbell ever see the play? Some said that he merely knew of it and recognised a good motif when he saw one. Others, that he had seen it, enjoyed it and succumbed to it – although, as he himself noted of the frugality which supposedly characterised his early life, 'Even when my business at Lloyd's prospered, I would not spend anything on theatres or similar pleasures.' Certainly there is nothing to suggest that he was a fan of the theatre.

He may, of course, have encountered Maeterlinck at Brooklands. He actually told Leo Villa that he and Maeterlinck were on conversational terms, and that a Maeterlinck with unusually Home Counties inflections had turned to him one day and said, 'Why not call your car the *Blue Bird*? It's a name that's brought me a lot of success.' Equally, he may have borrowed the name from Mrs Hilda Hewlett, Britain's first woman aviator, who, having learned to fly at the Mourmelon-le-Grand aerodrome in France, was not only on friendly terms with Maeterlinck, but returned to England in an aeroplane called *Blue Bird* and opened the Blue Bird Restaurant in 1910 at the Brooklands Flying Village. 'LUNCHEONS, TEAS, REFRESHMENTS AT POPULAR PRICES' announced the sign over the door, before the establishment burned down in 1917.

The idea of the 'blue bird' was anyway part of the general currency of thought. Campbell's cleverness was to appropriate it for his own use. And no matter how many times Louis Coatalen painted the words '1000 HORSE POWER SUNBEAM' and 'WOLVERHAMPTON' on the Slug (and on the wooden container in which it was shipped over to America), nothing had quite the resonant simplicity of *Blue Bird*, which eventually made its way – in the form of a little logo depicting the bird – on to cars, mechanics' overalls, tea services, motor yachts, greetings cards, a garage in Chelsea. So excited was Campbell by the *Blue Bird* idea that he decided to repaint his old Darracq *Flapper* in blue, the night before a race at Brooklands. All Surrey was asleep, but he managed to wake up an oil chandler and buy some paint from him. The next day he was on the starting line, his car bright blue, his racing overalls covered in patches of still-wet blue paint.

He couldn't have known where *Blue Bird* would take him, nor how useful it would become as a device in the promotion of his own career. Yet his talent for imagery and melodrama, plus a dauntless refusal to give up, meant that every setback was a potential springboard to future glory; every success a *tour de force.* He had fought his way to the LSR on Pendine Sands, only to have Segrave pluck it from his fingers like so much cheap coinage. Well, that was fine. It simply meant that he would have to pour more resources into the glamorous *Blue Bird*, take the LSR back off Segrave and, in the process, flesh out the creation that was Captain Malcolm Campbell.

7

Another Englishman in Florida

Henry Segrave had made Daytona the premier venue for record breaking. There was nothing for it but to follow his lead. Campbell's first trip to the United States set the tone for all the subsequent ones, containing as it did predictable elements of high drama, short-sightedness, glory and a passionate embracing of fame. He arrived at Daytona Beach early in 1928 and checked in at the Claridge Hotel. With him he had his wife, four mechanics, three cases of generic spare parts, a complete spare engine, two gas motors for starting the engine, ten cases of spare wheels and tyres, two cases of engine and gearbox spares, plus the car itself in its own vast packing crate. Then, on 15 February, he reached an average speed of nearly 207 mph and retook the record from Segrave.

In answer to the Slug, *Blue Bird* had been rebuilt into a Mk II version, in which the radiators were placed behind the rear wheels, in line with the body, to assist streamlining. R.K. Pierson, Chief Designer with Vickers Aviation Ltd of Brooklands, had developed the new shape in a series of wind-tunnel tests. Under the bonnet (now smoothly blanked off, an enormous Steely Dan) lay a new version of the Napier aero engine. So new was the

Napier Sprint Lion, as it was known, that it was still on the Air Ministry's secret list. Yet Campbell persuaded them to let him put the device in his car so that he might more successfully uphold British prestige – a clear demonstration of the new authority which the LSR commanded. The radiators alone cost over £400, were specially built by the Fairey Aviation Co. and were modelled on those used on First World War bombers.

Campbell's hopes had been lifted at the end of September 1927, when Flight Lieutenant S.N. Webster won the Schneider Trophy air race at Venice, flying an elegant Supermarine seaplane powered by one of the new Napier Lions. Even though the entire accumulated cost of Campbell's machine by now stood between £15,000 and £20,000, this news gave him courage after the toils of Pendine and the brusqueness with which Segrave had plundered the title for himself.

But what, in Campbell's eyes, really justified the terrible expense was not just the promise of beating Segrave, but the threat of genuine international competition. Tussling with Parry Thomas and Segrave was well enough, but for several years now stories had been circulating of an Egyptian prince's desire to capture the LSR with an extravagant hand-crafted vehicle whose whereabouts were being kept secret. Prince Djelaleddin was his name, and he had entrusted the design work of the record breaker to an engineer named Edmond Moglia. Suavely, they gave it the portmanteau appellation *Djelmo*.

The car first appeared in public in 1924, a vehicle whose smooth yet masculine lines prefigured those of Campbell's first *Blue Bird*. Years went by while it failed to perform satisfactorily in tests, until at the end of 1927 it was entrusted to Jules Foresti, a driver with whom Leo Villa had worked just after the war. The *Djelmo* team went down to Pendine Sands, in the inevitable rain, where Foresti got up to about 150 mph. At which point the car overturned in a terrible ball of spray, sand and steam. Foresti climbed out, to the amazement of on-lookers, and asked for a cigarette. And that was the end of

Djelmo: a failure, but in Campbell's eyes, a warning of what foreigners might accomplish, nonetheless.

In Germany, Fritz von Opel – of the famous car company – was working on a rocket car, an even more unquantifiable threat than *Djelmo*. In the end he took his single-seater *Raketenauto*, with its stub wings on either side, to the Avus track, near Berlin, in May 1928. There he electrically fired the sequence of twenty-four high-explosive rockets attached to the back of this bolide. The device reached about 140 mph. Women spectators screamed and fainted at the appalling noise. Von Opel, defiant in beer-bottle spectacles and flying scarf, pronounced himself satisfied and at once lost interest in the project.

The real action, though, was coming from contenders based in the United States. 'I feel confident that I shall be able to defend the British record against all comers in America,' Campbell said in February 1928, shortly before embarking on the *Berengaria* for New York. 'I believe that I shall be up against six competitors in the United States, representing all that American motor engineering brains can do. We shall probably go out on the Sands round about the same time as the Carnival Speed Week.' In fact, there were only two American challengers, but this was two more than Segrave had had to face. And each challenger epitomised both the best and the worst of contemporary American engineering practices.

The virtuous principle was represented by twenty-four-year-old boy wonder Frank Lockhart. Lockhart was a sparklingly gifted driver and engineer, whose career as a professional racer was barely more than a year old, but who had already won the Indianapolis 500 (in authentically filmic style, having taken over the car at the last minute) and had driven a small and relatively conventional racing car (enhanced, nonetheless, by his precocious engineering genius) at nearly 165 mph. Now he was at Daytona, sporting a clever, diminutive machine sponsored by the Stutz sports car company and called the *Black Hawk*, even though it was painted white.

In essence a sophisticated single-seater racing car, the *Black Hawk* was as neatly coherent in its design as Campbell's *Blue Bird* was awkwardly compromised. It had a comparatively small sixteen-cylinder engine built specially for its LSR task, as opposed to a huge aero engine coerced from a doubtful manufacturer via the British Government. It was slim, low and streamlined, as opposed to *Blue Bird*, which, on account of the bulk of the engine and the clumsy ironmongery of the transmission, had Campbell perched high up behind a bulbous fairing, like the lookout in an armoured car. The *Black Hawk* was all about the intelligent use of energy. It had integrity, purity of line and was driven by someone getting on for half Campbell's age – boyish, smiling, America's own Segrave, but with the extra credential of being able to manipulate a slide rule and use a spanner.

Playing the part of Beast to Lockhart's Beauty was a machine called the *White Triplex*, which, again, despite its name, was painted black. At least, it was painted black insofar as there was anything to paint. The *White Triplex* was a kind of automotive Golem, designed by J.M. White, a rich wire manufacturer from Philadelphia. White had the idea – the peculiarly American one, at that – of getting a car to travel at over 200 mph by the expedient of installing more very large engines in one car than anyone else. As it turned out, the most he could squeeze on to a rolling chassis was three Liberty aero engines, of the same type that Parry Thomas had used singly in *Babs*. This must have seemed unarguably right to White and the five mechanics who bolted the vehicle together: if one engine could get you to 170 mph, three should unlock the doors to a world of unimaginable speeds.

And there would be no need for streamlining or wind-tunnel testing or thoughtful suspension. Bestial energy was the key. A chassis like a giant's bed would serve as a platform, with a metal prow to cover only the first of the three engines, which were arranged in a rough wedge formation. This *reductio ad absurdum*, banteringly known as 'The Spirit of Elkdom', was to be driven by a necessarily muscle-bound journeyman racing driver named Ray Keech, whose tremendous forearms were like the hams which used to hang in the Beach Hotel at Pendine.

Hence the prospects for all three looked good in February 1928. Brains, brute force and that nebulous quality characterised as British know-how were to slug it out before tens of thousands of spectators for a prize whose worth was only now being guessed at. In the event, however, it turned out to be a no-contest. On the day of the race Lockhart got into a skid at around 190 mph and ended up crashing into the Atlantic, where he was almost drowned. Keech battled away in the *White Triplex* for a while, before a radiator hose burst, spraying his legs with scalding water. Both Keech and Lockhart landed up in Halifax County Hospital, thus reducing the fight to a solo round between Campbell and his own car.

Campbell had actually gone before either of them, apprehensive at the state of the beach and the tens of thousands of spectators waiting for him to make a mistake or get into a crash. Indeed, an error in practice damaged his shock absorbers and tore off part of the underside of the car. Then he nearly crashed the car again during the actual attempt, hitting a ridge in the sand at over 200 mph. The impact threw him upwards out of his seat, caused his goggles to be blown down from his eyes over his mouth and nearly hurled him from the moving car. Then the wheels momentarily locked and *Blue Bird* started to slide towards the sand dunes to his right. As much by luck as judgement, Campbell cured the slide by letting the two-and-a-half-ton car thrash around on the sand and steer itself towards the end of the course. After this he was too unnerved to stop and have his tyres changed at the end of the run or have a drink of water. Instead he stayed in the vehicle and shot straight back, his hands strangling the steering wheel. There was no bump on the return; but he was so exhausted by the first stage of the attempt that he could scarcely move the gear lever into top. At the end he had to be lifted out of the car and for a while was unable to stand.

And, despite the thousands of pounds he had invested in remodelling *Blue Bird*, and the months of panel-beating and tyre-testing that had gone into the machine, and the year that separated his attempt from Segrave's, all he had to show for it was the LSR by a margin of fractionally more than 3 mph. Just as when he had taken the record from Parry Thomas.

But Campbell's talent for self-mythologising got its first really big chance that day. Because, as anyone watching from the dunes overlooking the beach could see, he had *fought* his way to the record. The moment when *Blue Bird* hit the bump in the sand and started to swerve was a defining instant: 'I am no physical weakling,' he wrote later, 'and it required all my power to keep *Blue Bird* to an even course. The wheel had to be gripped. When I hit that bad patch, my muscles were being torn from me, and I had to wrestle with *Blue Bird* . . . When *Blue Bird* skidded and presented a broadside to the wind, well, I was Fate's plaything; and Fate decided to let me get back . . .'

Or, '*Blue Bird* was now all but out of control – caught by the side wind, and skidding in a huge cloud of sand at over 200 mph, while I was half-blinded because my goggles were jammed aslant across my face. If ever I imagined that my end had come, I believed it in the moments which followed, and it was instinctive action which saved my life . . .' Or again, 'I have read . . . somewhere, speculation to the effect that the human brain cannot function, cannot flash messages from mind to muscle when the body is travelling at the amazing pace of 800 feet a second. In all humility, I must contradict this speculation . . .'

The press connived in the process, arguing that 'Nerves of steel, a brain far more alert than the average, physical strength – all these are required for such an adventure as Captain Malcolm Campbell has just brought to a glorious conclusion'; and pointing out that 'Several multimillionaires who are backing

Mr Lockhart entertained Captain Campbell at dinner last night and commended him on his courage for driving yesterday at high speed during trials against expert advice.' Even Frank Lockhart was roped into glossing Campbell's near-disaster as a split-second triumph of nerve over happenstance, declaring that 'Campbell's performance gave me one of the greatest kicks of my life. It was a wonderful performance under terrible conditions.' The 'skid' became the governing image of the whole attempt – as depicted by contemporary motoring artists such as Bryan de Grineau – the 'skid' and Campbell's stark brilliance in saving the 'skid'. 'England's "speed wizard" or "speed king" as he is variously described, is the hero of the hour throughout the United States.'

From then on, to Campbell's intense satisfaction, everything else fell into place – making the struggle at Pendine a year earlier suddenly seem ridiculously small-time. In the States they marvelled at 'The greatest speed ever officially registered by an automobile', which had been renamed, incidentally, the '"Hush Shush 1"'. Campbell's past successes amazed them likewise: 'He has won almost two hundred trophies which have a melted-down value of ten thousand dollars.' At home, too, the press were keenly overexcited: 'Motor Speed "Record" Captain Campbell's Success'; 'Britain Beats Speed Record – Secret Engine'; 'England's Speed Wizard – Capt. Campbell Hero Of The US'; 'Capt. Campbell's Triumph – Americans Fail'.

And there was plenty of quality advertising to bolster the editorial, as Dunlop, Napier, Pratts Ethyl ('The fortified fuel that fortifies your engine'), KLG, Vickers Armstrong and Wakefield Castrol ('The efficiency that spells speed to the record breaker means economy to you') blurted out page after page of material. Among which was the following announcement: 'Buying your car NEW or SECONDHAND? Let Malcolm Campbell, the famous racing motorist, help you choose your next car. For £50 and upwards you can purchase by Part Exchange or Deferred Payments a guaranteed model tested in

Malcolm Campbell's own works.' And there was a photograph of Campbell, plus the St James's Street address of the car dealership he was involved in at the time: 'Consult Malcolm Campbell about your next car.'

Everything was coming together. Once Frank Lockhart and Ray Keech had been eliminated, Campbell was free to become the toast of America. At Daytona he was strenuously plied with Prohibition-breaking bathtub hooch, Leo Villa watching with dismay as some of this spilt on the boot of a Ford sedan and stripped the paint clean off. Better was the genuine Scotch which the Daytona police had wisely saved and which they served at a banquet given to commemorate Campbell's new record.

By the end of February Campbell and his wife were in New York, at the Hotel Pennsylvania. A few blocks from their front door were the studios of the WJZ radio station, from where Campbell ('still stiff in the shoulders') broadcast a characteristically wordy and inaccurate speech to the nation. 'My American friends,' he began, 'it seems to be a little presumptuous for an Englishman to be talking about speed to an audience in a nation that has a world-wide reputation for doing everything rapidly and especially for being addicted to extremely rapid transit . . . I should like to dispel any impression that I am a professional racing driver. I have always been an amateur . . . I have raced on practically all the speedways of Europe on motor bicycles and motor cars . . .'

Shortly after this he was hurried off upstate to Buffalo for a congratulatory dinner with the President of the Dunlop Tyre Company. From there he went on to Washington, DC, where he officially trumped Segrave at last. On 1 March he was presented with the Daytona Beach Trophy – a vast, two-handled silver cup – by Charles G. Dawes, the Nobel Prize-winning Vice-President of the United States, in the presence of Sir Esme Howard, British Ambassador in Washington. He returned home on board the *Berengaria*, the big *Blue Bird* crate covered in messages ('Good Luck'; 'Dunlop For Ever'; 'Come Again,

Daytona Beach Police Dept, Guy Hurd, Chief of Police') and gleaming with satisfaction.

After that his celebration lunch at the Connaught Rooms back in London might have veered towards anticlimax were it not for the combined presence of the United States Ambassador in London, Alanson B. Houghton; Sir Charles Wakefield (inescapably the host); Henry Segrave; Sir John Studd, the Lord Mayor of London; and, most unnerving of all, Sir William Joynson-Hicks, the breathtakingly right-wing Home Secretary.

The US Ambassador started off in a robust frame of mind, conscious of the indignity of having to defer to a British audience. 'When a man goes to the United States to win a speed contest, he has got to go quickly,' he said, to indulgent laughter. 'Captain Campbell has beaten the Americans fairly and definitely on their own soil. But it is no secret that Americans intend to *bring the trophy back*.' This garnered a healthy round of applause; as did Sir Charles Wakefield's presentation to Mrs Campbell of a diamond and sapphire brooch representing *Blue Bird*. She had spent most of Campbell's Daytona record run at the beach, paralysed with nerves and with her face buried in her hands. The brooch was a 'token of the unfailing support of her faith and courage, so wonderfully justified'.

But it was Sir William Joynson-Hicks who took the occasion by the scruff of the neck. Perfervid anti-Communist that he was, 'Jix' had not only helped to mastermind counter-measures against the General Strike and (bolstered by his association with the Public Morality Council) was about to launch into several months' persecution of Radclyffe Hall, but was prone to come out with such inflammatory statements as, 'We conquered India as the outlet for the goods of Great Britain. We conquered India by the sword and by the sword we should hold it!' He was known as 'the Policeman of the Lord'.

Clearly, 'Jix' was deeply inspired by Campbell's achievement. 'The event we are celebrating,' he began, 'is a disappointment only to those gloomy people who lament the fact that England is becoming *decadent*. Our guest is a lineal descendant of the great men of the past. The old Elizabethans would have welcomed him to take his place with Drake, Frobisher and Raleigh.' The Policeman of the Lord was already reading things into Campbell's record that Campbell himself might not have anticipated. 'While we have lost one or two other things,' he went on, 'we have won this splendid contest with the same engine that won the Schneider Trophy in the air' – a pause for this magical evocation to take effect – 'and we have won it by British character, British engines, British power, British pluck and British sportsmanship!' The response to his speech was loud and sustained cheering, in the middle of which Campbell sat, smiling his brilliant, defensive smile and bashfully wagging his head.

Campbell had arrived. He was now, abruptly, so celebrated that the popular press used him in jokes. The *Daily Mail* said of playwright Edgar Wallace, 'Mr Wallace writes plays about as fast as Captain Campbell drives a motor-car.' The *Daily Express* made a conceptualised Campbell a key player in one of its 'Little Man' cartoons. (The 'Little Man', soup-strainer moustache, bowler hat, short, anxious, the conscience of the *Express* readership, is tied to the front of *Blue Bird*. Winston Churchill, at the time an erratically spendthrift Chancellor of the Exchequer, sits in the cockpit, wearing overalls and a racing helmet, reading about Campbell's triumph. The tail of the car has '800 Million Pounds Per Year' written on it, while a banner flying above reads 'DEBTONA BEACH'. The 'Little Man', as 'Mascot', calls out, 'I say, don't you think you might slow down a bit this time?' To which 'Captain Churchill, Driver of the Blue Budget' replies, 'Slow down? Why, Captain Campbell says there is no limit to speed!' It should be added that whenever Campbell referred to Daytona, the natural semi-strangulation he applied to any diphthong – plus whatever unconscious anxiety he was experiencing about the expense – made it come out as 'Debtona'.)

All these gratifications rooted themselves deeply in Campbell's mind: the presence of the American Ambassador; the public acclaim; the relegation of Henry Segrave to mere hanger-on at Campbell's triumph; the adamantine rhetoric of Sir William Joynson-Hicks. No matter that it had cost a small fortune to get there: at last there was a clear relationship between Campbell's investment and the goods it delivered. No matter, either, that he had broken the record by only 3 mph and that, a few weeks later, Ray Keech, out of hospital and bursting with aggression, would steal it off him by just over half a mile an hour (and be mobbed by delirious American spectators). He was already in another, headier world, a world as far removed from poor, trudging Parry Thomas and the rain-lashed beach at Pendine as he could be. Girding himself with this new sense of impregnability, he went off and proved himself mistaken once again.

8

Under an African Sun

⟪ ⟫

Campbell believed he had identified a problem with the LSR set-up and was keen to fix it, turning the solution, he hoped, neatly to his own advantage. The mixture of thinking he applied, however, was an assemblage of the straightforward and the helplessly perverse.

First, there was Daytona Beach. Although clearly a step up from Pendine, it had its drawbacks: namely, its bumpiness (that 'skid'), its dependency on wind and tide, and the fact that there was nowhere to run to if things went wrong. The dunes on one side, the Atlantic on the other, made for a worryingly narrow track at over 200 mph. He didn't want to die in the attempt, nor did he want to kill anyone else. Then there was the fact that Segrave had got there first. Campbell felt compelled to use whatever resources were available to achieve glory, rather than mere fame. So he needed to stake out his own territory, discover an apt theatre of his own, rather than tag along after the younger man.

And then there was the problem of America. However excellent the facilities and however amiable they were when you got there, it was an awfully long way to go. Surely there was somewhere nearer, and, with Sir William Joynson-Hicks's words ringing in his ears ('Drake, Frobisher and Raleigh') perhaps within the British Empire? So that his LSR bids might be made, if not on British soil, at least on Empire soil, or sand, or desert? An All-Empire bid, with All-British Engineering and Materials: this would captivate the world and leave him unassailable.

The rest of 1928 was spent hunting down an acceptable alternative to Daytona Beach, Campbell adopting the same mental posture of simultaneous wilful denial and irrepressible credulity with which he had gone in search of hidden treasure on Cocos Island in 1926. The Empire precondition was plainly less important than simple proximity, for he investigated sites in Spain, Belgium, Portugal and the Syrian Desert, just west of Rutba, in western Iraq.

Then someone told him about a magical desert plateau in the western French Sahara, high above sea level, lonely, flat, hard and almost endless. The French authorities seemed baffled by the notion of a great solitary racetrack in the middle of the desert, but Campbell – in one of his displays of heroic obsessiveness – hired an aeroplane and flew himself over the desert to look for this spot. And he found it: south of Reganne, in Algeria, and some six hundred miles north of Timbuktu. As described, it was pancake-flat, smooth, durable, and also over four hundred miles from the nearest railway line, rendering itself effectively inaccessible and therefore unusable.

On the way back from this disappointment Campbell and his travelling companion, Squadron Leader D.S. Don, were flying along the north Moroccan coastline in the direction of Oran. Here their plane crashed on a beach in Riff territory, an ungovernable part of Spanish North Africa. Temporarily held against their will by, in Campbell's words, a 'bearded, dirty, evil-smelling crew' of Riff tribesmen in 'dingy skirts', Campbell and Don were released after several hours, only to fall into the hands of more Riff. Now they found themselves trapped in a two-storey hut, forced to eat 'rancid butter' and 'harsh sour bread' and drink 'water that was almost black'.

A night went by. The sleeping Riff 'were twitching and muttering, very like dogs in uneasy slumber'. When dawn came the two airmen made a run for it over the bodies of their captors, fled for the shore and started to struggle along the coastline, west towards the city of Tetouan. They clambered over headlands and beaches and swam round otherwise impassable points. Campbell swore that they travelled seventy miles along the North African littoral in this way, before being rescued at last by some nervous Spanish officials.

Campbell was back in Surrey when a Dr Marin wrote to the *Cape Times* of South Africa, announcing that he had heard of Captain Campbell's struggle to find a suitable place to let *Blue Bird* out and what about the dried-up lake bed four hundred and fifty miles north-east of Cape Town, called Verneuk Pan? Amazingly, the newspaper sent an assistant editor out to Verneuk Pan to see what was there. More amazingly, he confirmed what Dr Marin had claimed. There was indeed a vast, flat, dried-up lake bed on which it hadn't rained for years. He reported that it was so bare and so flat that he had driven along it for several miles at 70 mph without touching the steering wheel of his car. The principal drawback, of course, was that it, too, was hundreds of miles from anywhere, halfway between Cape Town and the Kalahari Desert. There was a railway line, but it stopped a hundred and twenty miles short. This, though, was still better than communications in the western Sahara, where there were no railway lines at all. And it was within the Empire.

It was an indication of Campbell's desperation that he seized upon Verneuk Pan as the answer to his prayers, heedless of the fact that 'Verneuk' is Afrikaans for 'to cheat'. Daytona Beach lay invitingly on the eastern seaboard of the United States, tried and true in its way, and as crammed with the appurtenances of modern living as Verneuk Pan was devoid of them. But Campbell had turned his back on it. By now, the end of 1928, he had remodelled *Blue Bird* for the second time and was urgent in his need to be seen to make progress. The aviation-standard £400 side-mounted radiators had been junked from the car as soon as the last Daytona attempt was over and were sold as scrap for a few pounds. The struggling car builders Arrol-Aster, of Dumfries, had been pleased to take on the job of reworking Campbell's record breaker, hopeful that some of its lustre would rub off on them. As it turned out, they went bankrupt a year later. In the meantime they put the radiator back in the nose of the car, trimmed the tail fin off the back and added some optimistic fairings around the wheels.

It was looking, if anything, even more substandard than before. In some senses it resembled a cannon with a tapered muzzle; at the same time it was ludicrously phallic, its genital profile confirmed by the bulking-up of the rear quarters and the protuberant seating arrangements. Despite Arrol-Aster's best endeavours in their rainswept works, it had an amateurish feel to it, less coherent even than in its first incarnation at Pendine. In fact, it looked like a muscle-bound version of some of the freaks and misfits which used to haunt Brooklands before the war – the streamlined Itala of R. Wildegose; the pencil-shaped Sunbeam *Nautilus*. It advertised its own lack of vision.

Nevertheless, at the start of 1929 Campbell and his team were ready to transport the car, fifty-six cases of spares, three dozen tyres, eight hundred gallons of fuel and five hundred spark plugs to seething Cape Town. Colonel Lindsay Lloyd, Clerk of the Course at Brooklands, was with him; Campbell reckoned to spend £1500 on fares alone. He arrived on the *Caernarvon Castle* in February and docked at the harbour off Mouille Point. From there he drove to the Queen's Hotel in Oudtshoorn, managing to lose his briefcase, filled with important papers, on the way. Yet neither this, nor the significance of the name Verneuk, nor the fact that Oudtshoorn was close to Cape Town, off which, in the seventeenth century, the Flying Dutchman was believed originally to have foundered, put him off.

What did Campbell think he was doing? Why had he spent so much time, money and effort in search of an alternative to Daytona Beach? Nearly a year had gone by in scouring the face of the earth for somewhere that – as it would turn out – was worse than Florida. It was symptomatic of the fact that much of what Campbell did was a willed digression, a flight from the matter in hand. From his first encounter with cars, his first engagement with the sorcery of rapid movement, he had used them as ways to evade demands being made on him, to neutralise the importunities of the present. Incredibly, despite all the other claims on his attention, Campbell was the most active participant Brooklands ever knew. The only driver to race there in the 1910s, '20s and '30s, he amassed well over three hundred entries in twenty-six different makes of car, including Bugatti, Alfa Romeo, Mercedes, Delage, Fiat, MG and Sunbeam. His nearest rival, Captain Alistair Miller, could only manage 179 entries; Woolf Barnato 172. In comparison, of the four thousand-plus drivers listed as entering events at Brooklands, a third only ever participated in one event; three-quarters participated in five events or fewer.

Campbell, on the other hand, not only enjoyed racing: he was unable not to race. When the Campbells were living in Kingston he would drive home from his work in the City, urging himself to get into a duel with any other speed enthusiast he might find on the same stretch of road. These races would often take him straight past his own front door and on to Esher or beyond, before he snapped back into the real world and came home for dinner, long after dark. And then, having churned through his evening meal, he would grab a different car from his garage and chase off into the night, while wife and children stared after his retreating tail lights.

But cars were not the only bromide with which he tried to still his frenzy. He experimented with several lifetimes' worth of hobbies and pastimes – all of which swirled around, coalescing and then collapsing over time – without ever settling on one that satisfied him. Collecting chinaware, silverware and old books all went through the mill of his temporary obsessions. The chinaware, accumulated almost at random, was eventually pronounced by an expert to be worthless. The filigree silverware didn't fare much better and had anyway to contend with the dazzling contents of Campbell's trophy cabinet ('The largest one-man collection of motoring prizes in the world'). The antiquarian books were bought one day on impulse as a job lot, which then provoked Campbell into commissioning a handsome set of library shelves on which to display them. He never read the books – barely opened them, in fact – but appreciated the tone they lent his home.

Indeed, the house at Povey Cross (nowadays a Grade II listed building) with its minstrels' gallery, its half-timbering, its sixteenth-century ambience, its surrounding tussocky fields, would have been very much of the fashion for the mid-1920s. The non-specific Tudorbethan look was the one to which many aspired – fresh and honest-seeming as it was after High Victorian – and Povey Cross was at bottom the real thing. So Campbell liked to litter it with books and apt period knick-knacks. A claymore hung in the hallway. Campbell claimed that an ancestor had used it at Culloden, but his biographer James Wentworth Day was convinced that he had bought it 'from an antique dealer in the Edgware Road who specialised in weapons'. The important thing was to maintain the appearance of cultured authenticity.

Freemasonry and the Scout Movement were given a look-over. A troop of Sea Scouts named themselves 'Sir Malcolm Campbell's Own' before he lost interest in them. Towards the end of the thirties he was nevertheless presented with the Scouts Gold Thanks Badge for his services to the Carshalton District. A picture-collecting craze went the same way as the book-collecting craze, as did a fleeting interest in oriental carved ivories, another in billiards and another in fishing. There was the dog-breeding, which peaked with around forty dogs, caged up around the grounds of Povey Cross, dwindled to around half that number, kept on long chains as a deterrent to burglars (enough to add 'a sinister touch', according to Wentworth Day), before finally falling to one or two.

Golf had a slightly firmer grip on Campbell's imagination: he had nine-hole courses laid out at Povey Cross and at Headley Grove. The advantage of having his own golf course was, principally, that he could cheat without excessive difficulty ('I'm not going to count that. I'm going to drive another ball'). Motor yachting also kept his interest, while a model railway fared less well. Inspired by Segrave's perfectionist's set, he had an unsurprisingly huge one built at Povey Cross, ostensibly for young Donald. When Donald crashed a train in front of a newsreel team, his father masterfully took over the layout as his own, before he got bored and allowed it to be removed and put on show at Selfridges department store.

In the latter part of the 1930s one of his final obsessions involved the design and construction of air-raid shelters. Readers of *The Times* were intrigued one day by the news that Campbell was 'building a bomb-proof dug-out 8 ft. below the surface of Headley Grove. "My motto is prepare for everything," he told a press representative who watched him at work yesterday.' The estate gardeners at Headley Grove had been joined by a team of hired labourers, who between them were building a shelter consisting of 'two compartments 6 ft. 6 in. high. The sides are 18 in. thick and the front 2 ft. thick. Wireless and a self-contained electric lighting set will be installed when the shelter is completed. The roof will include a sheet of armour plate and will have a total thickness of about 8 ft. The dug-out will accommodate 30 people. Seats will be provided and beneath the seats will be boxes for provisions.' Dorothy Campbell noted that the air-raid shelter 'became quite a show feature of the place', creating 'much interest, especially of a local nature'.

The locals plainly thought Campbell mad. But this did not stop him, a year or so later, from asserting at a Foyle's Luncheon that 'every possible measure for safeguarding the civilian population should be adopted'. His own prescient suggestion was 'the construction of gas and bomb-proof underground garages in London and provincial cities'. But soon the Second World War would be upon the country and Campbell would be off, hoping to join the Commandos.

These were the more ephemeral hobbies; but there were also persistent, immovable fixations, marking out Campbell's progress through life. Motoring was the main one. A chronic desire to find buried treasure was another. In fact, the search for buried treasure can be seen as a ready metaphor for almost everything else he did. Campbell was possessed by the conviction that he would one day find that secret hoard which lay somewhere on the face of the planet, darkly obtainable by the right man, and from that point on, make sense of his life and the world as a whole. He searched for treasure most conspicuously on Cocos Island. He also wrote forewords to a couple of books by the treasure-fixated writer Harold T. Wilkins: *Modern Buried Treasure Hunters* and *Treasure Hunting: The Treasure Hunter's Own Book of Land Caches and Bullion Wrecks*. And he was at it for many a weekend, at home in Surrey. But he was not merely hunting for treasure during these weekends. Rather, he was searching for either the perfect metal detector or the one authentic spiritualist who could sympathetically intuit the presence of metals beneath the earth.

How did he conduct these searches? He sealed up the family silverware, coin collections and jewellery in biscuit tins and buried these around the garden. Whichever hopeful prospector had turned up that day – mystic; diviner; or technician cheerlessly brandishing some hulking mass of valves and batteries – would have to find whatever Campbell had hidden in the grounds while the latter stood back, frowning. None of them ever succeeded and Campbell would then banish them, while at the same time itemising still more of his possessions to inter for the next visit.

To retrieve his buried possessions, he had, of course, to find them himself. So before their burial, he made sure to set out a clear list of instructions, detailing the location of each cache of valuables. But this was buried treasure he was looking for, not a gas main: it had its own conventions, its own aesthetic. The instructions he drew up were couched in the style of *Treasure Island* or *Chums* magazine. There were few specifics, but a great deal of pacing distances out in strides of indeterminate length, from starting points which were not always accurately pinpointed. The result was that some of his property never saw the light of day again.

Campbell liked to see himself as daring and piratical in his own right (the early chapters of his autobiography *My Thirty Years of Speed* are rich in stories of shooting incidents, pre-Great War German-baiting, underground explosions and mechanical thrill-seeking), but his search for hidden treasure comes across much like his search for the vanishing point of absolute speed. It bespeaks a profound unhappiness, an unhappiness that could only be calmed by the magical or the unattainable. As Maeterlinck put it, 'It seems likely that the Blue Bird does not exist or that he changes colour when he is caged . . .'

When war was declared in 1939 Campbell naturally got even busier, cramming gold and silverware into biscuit tins and soldering the lids shut, afraid that the Germans might invade his home. Thousands of pounds' worth of property disappeared into the ground. The immense trophy collection, housed in a glass-fronted cabinet that ran the length of a wall, was harder to hide. Campbell decided to build a false wall in front of the cabinet, so as to confuse German looters, with the trophies – as well as the family tableware and silverware – immured for the duration of the war.

In 1945 what items could be recovered from the ground were found to be irretrievably tarnished. Those in the walled-in cabinet were little better. Because Campbell had failed to allow for any ventilation in the secret space, the damp had got to the mahogany cutlery holders and the plinths for his trophies, and reduced them to mush. Ivory knife handles had likewise spoiled. It was, by any lights, a disaster.

The interdependent ideas of secret treasure and rigid containment threaded their ways through Campbell's life. Part of the time he buried things or boarded them up. At other times he simply obsessed over the question of orderliness, the necessity for efficient taxonomies. His workshops were kept in a state of permanent high discipline: it was a matter of totemic significance that his tools and equipment should be clean and in the right place at all times.

His personal appearance, too, was neurotically neat and glossy. In an age when most professional men strove for a decisive crease in the trousers and a disciplined parting in the hair, Campbell had a positively enamelled finish. Even after a Land Speed Record attempt, his overalls – the *Blue Bird* symbol neatly embroidered on the front – would look crisp; his tie jutting fastidiously from the folds, like a spare epiglottis. And one of the things that gave him greatest pleasure was painting and labelling tins and boxes to contain all the little precious bits and pieces which had accumulated in his garage – in which to bury small prizes among the dross of life.

The voyage to South Africa was, at heart, another expedition in search of buried treasure, the treasure being the perfect, undiscovered wasteland of Verneuk Pan, the record breaker's Land of Beulah. It didn't take long, though, for a progressive and irresistible sense of failure to start creeping over the attempt. When the *Blue Bird équipe* at last got to the Pan – the car was transported in a crate on a huge Thornycroft lorry – they pitched camp, with tents, water containers, tea, stews and tinned fruit, and a gramophone. Then they found that, although big enough – perhaps thirty miles long and fifteen wide – the Pan's dark surface was roughcast with pebbles, small bushes and worst of all, tiny, razor-like slivers of shale. The whole track would have to be cleared and levelled before *Blue Bird* could so much as turn a wheel. It was determined that they would need to hire some four hundred native workers. Since there was almost no one living locally, hundreds were sent up from Cape Town to the remorseless heat of Verneuk at the height of the South African summer.

Scorpions and puff adders lurked in the scrub. Temperatures in the shade were well over 100°F. Traders at Brandvlei (the nearest dorp, sixty miles away) looked forward to doing good business in petrol and whisky. Campbell himself arrived by aeroplane and immediately declared, 'Verneuk Pan is the most wonderful stretch of flat country I have ever seen.'

It quickly became clear, though, that the task was hopeless. The hired workers found the conditions intolerable and soon started to fall sick, while scores deserted. After days of toil they had cleared four hundred or so yards of track out of a projected total of sixteen miles. In the absolute parched wilderness, surreally flat and treeless, a kind of negative of Surrey, the little quarter-mile strip lay beneath the sun, pointing east–west, like the outline of a herbaceous border. 'It would have been much better,' intoned the *Autocar*, 'for Campbell to have gone to Florida rather than to Africa.'

So the Chief of the Provincial Roads Department at Cape Town loaned Campbell the services of an engineer named Nesbitt to solve the problem. Nesbitt decided that the best option would be to scrape the abrasive top layer off and lay a fifty-foot-wide road made of mud taken from the lake bed. The Town Council of Germiston, just south of Johannesburg, offered a steamroller and driver free of charge. This was transported as close to Verneuk Pan as road and rail would allow. The steamroller's operator then drove non-stop for over a hundred miles across the desert to get to Campbell's camp. In a display of breathtaking pertinacity, they managed to scrape the surface clean, smooth it and level it, very nearly to the point at which it was ready to use.

Meanwhile the handful of journalists who had been sent out to cover the record attempt found themselves going insane with boredom. One day they discovered a tortoise shambling across the track. Naming it *Blue Bird II*, they determined to enact Aesop's fable of the tortoise and the hare, with the tortoise playing itself and *Blue Bird* the sleeping hare. The tortoise covered a distance of twenty yards and seven and a half inches, before retreating into its shell and refusing to re-emerge. It was declared victor *in absentia*.

Then it rained. Up until this point the total rainfall for the preceding four years had been half an inch. Now it poured down, an almost tropical deluge lasting an entire night. Tents were blown down in the rainstorm; the workmen's shelters were demolished. Afterwards the track lay under six inches of water and every single motor vehicle was immobilised.

Worse things were happening to Campbell himself while this was going on. He had been using his aeroplane to get himself to and from civilisation in Cape Town. One flight turned tricky and the plane crashed in the middle of nowhere, with him alone at the controls. He suffered a cut mouth, a gashed nose, the loss of some teeth and a severe shaking. Another plane came out to rescue him, but this also crashed on landing at Cape Town, a gust of wind turning it over, and reopened all the cuts Campbell had just received in his first crash.

Trying to recover from two air crashes in a row, Campbell was obliged to watch his wife leave for England in the company of the Hon. Brian Lewis. Both had come out to lend support during the LSR bid. Lewis was a keen racing driver in his own right and, notwithstanding the accident with the Bugatti bonnet, was counted by Campbell as one of his closer friends. But Dorothy Campbell announced that she was unwell, that the strain of Verneuk Pan was too much for her, that she must return home. Campbell demanded that she stay. She refused.

Lewis – small, attractive, flirtatious, amusing – disappeared off with her, ostensibly to make sure she survived the long boat trip back. As it turned out, soon after the pair returned to England they took a flat in London and began an affair.

And on it went. No sooner had his wife gone off with Lewis than Campbell trudged back to Verneuk, just in time for the floods. The team was marooned for a week, forced to subsist on a diet of brackish water and tinned salmon. Campbell obliged himself to be forbearing. Soon the waters would clear away and the track would be rolled smooth again.

He would then have to deal with the fact that the relative thinness of the air – the Pan was over two thousand feet above sea level – would drain power from *Blue Bird*'s engine. He had to beat Ray Keech's 207-odd mph, but it would be as much as he could do to reach 215. On top of this, his eyes were starting to trouble him. In the awful emptiness of the Pan, one yard of baked brown earth looked like any other yard. When he finally got round to driving *Blue Bird* he couldn't tell where the middle of the track was or how near he was to disappearing into the scrub altogether. There were no dunes, no Atlantic Ocean to chaperone him. He ordered a broad white line to be painted the length of the course, straight down the middle. This would be his guide, the one thing to which he had to cling while everything else was failing about him.

He flew back to Cape Town while the track was receiving its final preparations. It was 11 March 1929, his birthday. He was forty-four years old. Morosely partying, he consoled himself with the thought that at least he could soon get on and attack the record, that destiny would be his to command once more. But in mid-drink, quelling the memory of the tinned salmon and the water that tasted of puddles, he was given a message by the local Reuters correspondent. Had he heard that the heroic Major Henry Segrave, who had been in Florida all this time with a brand-new car, had just shattered the World Land Speed Record, at 231 mph?

Campbell absorbed the news, took a deep breath and forced himself to send a congratulatory telegram of clenched abruptness: 'Damn Good Show – Campbell.' Then he grimly got on with his birthday.

9

Segrave's Golden Arrow

《① ②》

All the time that Segrave was working for Portland Cement he had been a slave to a double agenda. He had to sell cement for his employer and get a new car built for the LSR. Showing a real economy of energy, he got two senior directors of Portland to provide the initial finance. Once the company's Henry S. Horne and Oliver J.S. Piper had agreed sponsorship, Segrave, the ruthless energiser and administrator, got the rest of his backing from Dunlop, KLG Plugs, Napier, Vickers, Charles Cheers Wakefield – the standard retinue of supporters. To design the machine, he employed Captain J.S. Irving once again.

Like Segrave, Irving had had to quit Sunbeam and get another job. He was now working for the Sandberg specialist metals business; but, charged with this precious new commission, Irving took a sabbatical at Sandberg, engaged a team of seven engineering draughtsmen and took over a secret office at the top of a building in central London. 'The glamour of speed,' he wrote at the time, 'is one of the very oldest of human emotions and, like that of music, is truly universal in its appeal.' What was more, 'Extraordinarily fine qualities are bred in both men and women by this habitual overcoming of danger, and that nation is most virile which possesses these pioneers in greatest number.' He was really writing about Segrave, of course: about the nimbus of success which haloed him.

When Irving's design finally appeared in public at the start of 1929, it turned out to be wonderfully ambitious, an embodiment of progress, speed, mystery, a Futurist sculpture. And, as in a sculpture, its form, its scale and its materials were functionally indivisible, each essential to the whole piece. The engine was at the front, driving the rear wheels in the approved manner; but Irving had the brilliant idea of sending the power to the rear wheels down two driveshafts, running either side of the car, between which Segrave sat. Campbell's *Blue Bird* had but one driveshaft, on top of which Campbell was forced to perch. Segrave, on the other hand, was right down low, as was the entire car – a mere three and a half feet tall at its highest point. No clumsy frontal radiator either, but a trefoil shape, fitted snugly round a Napier Lion aero engine (as used in the 1927 Schneider Trophy winner, but a more up-to-date version) and tapering to a low, feral point. The radiators (made by the Gloster Aircraft Company) ran along the sides, two great slabs between the wheels.

At the back was a vestigial vertical fin, a kind of aeroplane tail with amputations, supposedly to steady the beast at high speeds. Wind-testing was done at the National Physical Laboratory. And – the quintessence of purposeful menace – there was a telescopic rifle sight on the bonnet, just in front of Segrave's seat, with an aiming device on the nose of the car, so that he could point it accurately at the measured mile on Daytona Beach. As the car designer Anatole Lapine would later observe of Porsche racing cars, it incarnated 'the winning look that weapons have'. It was twenty-seven and a half feet long and painted gold from nose to tail. Naturally, it was called the *Golden Arrow*.

The gilded body was made by coachbuilders Thrupp & Maberly, more used to constructing bodies for Bentleys and Rolls-Royces. Kenelm Lee Guinness's Robin Hood engineering works in Putney Vale, which had done the foundations for Campbell's *Blue Bird*, bolted the engineering parts together. The chassis, looking exceptionally trim and up-to-the-minute in comparison with that of the Slug, was propped up on old railway sleepers in a brick-lined corner. Segrave would burst in from time to time, in his usual terse frenzy: 'He'd come rushing in, darting here there and everywhere,' said a KLG worker, 'having a good cuss when he found the jobs he'd expected to be finished hadn't even been started.' Having cussed, he would take a breath, then lay his full charisma on the work-force. 'He'd go and talk to the lads for ten minutes or so, and just *charmed* the jobs out of them . . . they'd work hours and hours of overtime for him.'

The finished car was said to have cost £18,000. Before it left for America, it was put on display at the Rootes show-rooms in Piccadilly. There it was revered by, among others, HRH the Prince of Wales; Mr Stanley Baldwin, the Prime Minister; Sir William Joynson-Hicks; Sir Samuel Hoare, the Air Minister; and Sir Austen Chamberlain, the Foreign Secretary. Even today, residing in splendour at the Beaulieu Motor Museum, it looks more meaningful, more perfectly conceived, than its neighbours.

Segrave was, of course, in his inevitable state of prophy-lactic gloom, shortly before going out to Daytona to attack the record. Sitting at home in Kingston with Laddie, the latter now half-blind and so enfeebled with age that it had to be carried to bed, he said, 'Poor old fellow. He will not be here when I return.' Then, quickly correcting himself: '*If* I return. Do you know, I have awakened night after night in a cold sweat? In my nightmares I have dreamed that I have failed . . . The contemplation of possible failure sends a shiver down my back. I would not be able to face the public.'

On this occasion, however, he had good reason to agonise over potential disaster: death was now stalking Daytona Beach. A couple of days after Ray Keech had stolen the LSR from Campbell on 22 April 1928, young Frank Lockhart, America's own golden hero, had taken his rebuilt Stutz *Black Hawk* down to the beach for a fresh assault. He had crashed in February of that year, trying to beat Campbell's record; but it had only taken him a few weeks to straighten out the car's frame and get over his own cuts and bruises. Everything had been going well and tremendous speeds were predicted of the boy genius.

It was 25 April when, after a couple of warm-up runs, he put his foot down to attempt the record in earnest. He shot along the sand in his elegant little car, when a tyre burst at over 200 mph. The *Black Hawk* skidded, then leapt into the air in a succession of appalling somersaults, hurling him into the air before crashing to a halt upside down, a great gout of oil leaking from the engine, like a wound. Lockhart's unconscious body lay fifty feet away from the wreck. By the time they got him to Halifax County Hospital, he was dead. He had just turned twenty-five.

However dreadful this was as a national sporting tragedy (and however much it affected Stutz, who called a halt to their racing activities), it was a promotional gift to Segrave and the organisers at Daytona, a ratcheting-up of the tension which helped to ensure that a huge crowd of spectators turned up for his drive in March 1929. On arrival at Daytona, Segrave acknowledged Lockhart's fate in the note of doomed pessimism with which he viewed the attempt. When a reporter asked, 'Do you think you have an even chance for your life at anywhere near the speed you expect to attain?' he answered, 'Much less. About one chance in ten, I should say off-hand.' On another occasion: 'When I saw the course I said to myself that this beach was going to "Turn me over".'

Quite apart from the thrill of death now hanging over Daytona, the exoticism of the *Golden Arrow* and the presence of Major Segrave himself, there was yet another element in play. It came from the *White Triplex*: the three-engined beast owned by J.M. White which had hospitalised its driver, Ray

Keech, on its first appearance at the start of 1928, but which had gone on to set a record of 207 mph later that year. The record that Segrave was now attempting to beat.

It was this awful device that was once more being wheeled out, eleven months on. Keech had refused to drive it ever again. So had most of the other professionals White had approached, one of whom, Bill Muller, claimed, 'A dozen experienced drivers have refused to drive that haywire job. I am expecting news of the death of anyone who tries it.' Up-and-coming Wilbur Shaw (later to win the Indianapolis 500) was eventually fingered by White as the most likely pilot of the *Triplex*. He, however, was sitting out a ban imposed on him by the American Automobile Association for a rules infringement. White tried to buy off the AAA, but they wouldn't play. Given that everyone else had turned him down, he was eventually left with only one available driver desperate enough to want to occupy the *Triplex*'s distressed-leather seat.

Lee Bible was a forty-two-year-old auto mechanic who had spent the previous months looking after the *White Triplex*, tuning its three engines and fiddling hopelessly with its backyard suspension. Having tried his hand at being a railway fireman, a telephone linesman and a taxi driver, Bible – married, with two children – had recently bought himself a garage and settled upon cars as a career. He was also an 'outlaw' driver: unlicensed by the AAA but picking up drives at dirt-track races whenever he could. And he took the LSR seriously. It was an affront to his patriotism that the prize should be so easily taken by Britishers who never got their hands truly dirty in the cause; and who never got killed. Bible believed completely in the ethos of the *White Triplex* and in the American virtues of pioneering self-reliance, simplicity and strength which it embodied. He called it the 'opportunity of a lifetime' to be allowed to try to steer it. So it was arranged: Segrave would make his attempts first; Bible immediately afterwards.

*   *   *

It was remarkable, in the circumstances, that any record-breaking happened at all. The *Golden Arrow* team had to wait three weeks before the sand was level enough to make a practice run. Until it reached Daytona, the *Arrow* had hardly turned a wheel; no one knew quite what to expect. Eventually conditions improved enough for Segrave to go for a trial run; at which, to his delight and surprise, the car hit 170 mph without even straining. Another week went by, the weather taunting the two record breakers. Then, on the morning of 11 March 1929, the wind and tides were right once more. An astonishing 100,000 spectators turned up to watch. The *Golden Arrow* was wheeled out on to the course. Everything felt good; conditions were as right as they ever were on Daytona Beach, although plagued by a bright, diffuse mist. There was plenty of time for two runs before the tide turned and the sea started coming back up the beach. Segrave thought he might try for the record.

The measured mile was over four miles away from his start line and quite invisible in the sea mist. Segrave had arranged for a 500-candlepower red arc light to be hung fifty feet above the beach at the point at which the measured mile began, and another light at its far end. He squinted over his gun sight at the point where the dim red disc of the arc light would appear, and shot off the line, able to see not much more than three-quarters of a mile ahead, the beach alive with tiny gullies and standing pools of water, a side-wind beating against the car. There was drama: a pipe burst, spraying steam and hot water from the furious engine across the aero screen behind which Segrave crouched. But prescient Captain Irving had incorporated a fallback for just such an eventuality. By pulling a lever, Segrave could release chemically super-chilled ice from a built-in icebox to cool the water and calm the spray and steam.

At around 200 mph he did this, reached the end of the course just by the pier, stopped the car, had all the tyres changed, the hose reconnected and more ice tipped in, then howled back south towards the Halifax River inlet, 'a projectile screaming through the air'. In fact, the noise of the engine was heard by the crowd, rather than by Segrave, who was only conscious of 'the roar of the wind past my ears' and 'the flag posts rushing by', which 'looked just like one straight line drawn on a piece of typewriting paper'.

And that was that. He climbed out of the now begrimed *Golden Arrow* and discovered that, once again, he had comfortably demolished the record. Not by some paltry increment of a half or 3 mph, but by 24 mph, leaving the new LSR at just over 231 mph. Doris Segrave was present this time, sitting in a private box beneath the judges' stand, hiding her eyes and sniffing from a bottle of smelling salts. As soon as Segrave drew to a halt, she dropped the salts, ran to the car and threw her arms round his neck. Cheering broke out along the dunes as the result was announced. Segrave sat on the edge of the great golden car, chewing gum, grinning for the crowd, shaking hands with Daytona's Mayor E.H. Armstrong, occasionally petting Doris fondly.

Even the *New York Times* was impressed: 'The clocklike precision with which the English driver ran through his dazzling performance thrilled the spectators quite as much as the spectacle of his giant arrow-shaped car as it bellowed down the course and the announcement of the wide margin by which he had broken the former record.' It had taken under an hour from start to finish.

The whole spectacle was striking. If there was a drawback it was that, like any massively competent demonstration of skill, it diminished itself by the degree to which it made itself look unchallengeable, beyond normal human expectation – 'almost disappointing'. Segrave himself did nothing to heighten the imaginative drama of the moment. Even after his record run, he was still accentuating the negative, retroactively countering any misfortune that might somehow have got in between him and his success, insisting that 'I had a foreboding that things would not go right. Everything had gone so well before under the engineering of Captain Irving and the management of William Sturm . . .' And, abstinent as ever, he declared, 'In my party there are twenty-five English people. Oh yes, they're celebrating. They're drinking champagne now. But not me! I'm going to bed. The fact is I am very tired. Now that it is all over there is a sort of relaxation . . .' Of course, Lee Bible still had to go out and make his run. 'I shall watch it from the grandstand,' Segrave announced, boyishly. 'What a holiday!'

Bible was on fire to make his reply. As soon as Segrave had calmly reset the mark at 231 mph, Bible shot out on to the beach and flogged the *White Triplex* up to 127 mph before retreating to work on the engines. The weather became unsettled and rain fell heavily. Segrave encouraged Bible to wait for it to improve before taking the car out again. The American interpreted this as a piece of characteristic British false counsel.

The next day, 13 March, he was ready to go, despite the worsening conditions. The beach was full of corrugations and patches of standing water which were like an adhesive, erratically and unpredictably dragging at the wheels of his car. But Bible was determined, and managed to wrestle the *White Triplex* up to around 200 mph in a practice run. This was all the encouragement he needed. 'It looks like a good day for a record,' he announced. Starting at the southern end of the course, he decided to make the leap from also-ran to national hero, to smash Segrave's record just as Segrave had smashed Keech's. A cameraman for RKO Pathé Newsreel, Charles R. Traub, set up his equipment a hundred feet away from the electric timing tape at the end of the measured mile. 'If you want to see some real action,' he told an acquaintance, 'you'll get it right here when that fellow takes his foot off the gas crossing the finishing wire. At that speed, something is going to happen!'

Something did happen. The *White Triplex* thundered over the finishing line on its final run, Bible hunkered down at the wheel as if trying to protect himself from an avalanche, smoke and spray billowing out behind – and then, in an instant of

oklands racetrack: work in progress in 1906, right at the beginning of Hugh Locke
g's great scheme.

cking on the Members' Hill during a meeting in the mid 1920s. The approach to
readed Members' Banking can be seen in the upper right-hand corner.

John Parry Thomas takes the LSR at Pendine Sands in 1926. The car, *Babs*, stands in fro of the Shell banner. Parry Thomas stoops over a rear wheel.

A rear view of 'the Slug', guarded by a Brooklands policeman.

nry Segrave, in the *Golden Arrow*, has just set a new record of over 231 mph. languidly shakes hands for the cameras with the car's designer, Captain Irving.

Segrave at Windermere in 1930, surveying the lake. This is one of the last photographs taken of him.

Malcolm Campbell
frantically wipes the sand
and spray from *Blue Bird*'s
windscreen while driving
150 mph on Pendine Sand

Better: Campbell at
Daytona Beach.

Acclaim in the streets of
London: Campbell and
wife Dorothy are parade
on his triumphant return
home in 1931. A few we
later he was knighted.

final version of the *Blue Bird* LSR car, displayed for the newsreels in front of
mson & Taylor's, Brooklands, January 1935.

cessful run over and Campbell demonstrates both the steadiness of his hand and the
ess of his nerve.

George Eyston earning a living breaking records in a MG Midget ...

... and the awesome *Thunderbolt* under construction at the Bean works.

John Cobb emerges from his
tourer at Brooklands …

… and exits, airborne, from
the Members' Banking
in the *Napier Railton*.
Amateur photographers
illicitly snap him from the
edge of the concrete.

Cobb suffers Reid
Railton to offer up
the lid of the *Railton
Special* for the benefit of
the press.

The entire bodywork could also be lowered on to the chassis with Cobb at the wheel. Ken Taylor gesticulates.

Cobb at Bonneville, having just driven at 350 mph. Soot blackens the back of his car and the line painted on the white salt is just discernible as it heads towards the distant mountains.

extreme and terrifying kinetic violence, the car was exploding towards the sand dunes in a series of elephantine leaps, tearing the wheels and bodywork from the chassis, and plunging straight towards Traub and his camera. Traub threw himself to one side. The *White Triplex* twitched in its flight, swerved away from the camera – which unheedingly filmed the whole catastrophe – and ploughed into Traub, slicing him in two. Bible's body was flung on to the sand, his neck, arms and legs broken. Mrs Bible, who had been watching all this time, became hysterical. J.M. White collapsed with grief. As soon as order was restored, Mayor Armstrong closed the speed trials and declared two days' public mourning. He was then quick to remind the public that the beach would, all things being equal, reopen in a year's time for another speed meeting.

The Segrave party was less sanguine than the Mayor. Segrave's father, back in London, was beside himself at the thought that Henry might take the *Golden Arrow* out again, in order to raise the record further. 'For God's sake telephone my son at Daytona, and tell him not to go through with the test tomorrow. It is terrible! It is terrible!' he cried. Then he added, 'Please tell my son that it is my *express wish* that he should not take the test.' But Segrave was ahead of him. 'Please tell my father that I promise him I will not go in the car again. That to-morrow morning it will be safely packed in a crate ready for shipment to England.' And that was the end of Segrave's record bid.

In the shock of the moment the *Washington Post* discovered that it had a duty to opprobriate the whole principle of record breaking: 'This is an excellent time for the AAA to withdraw all connection with these foolhardy speed trials. The machines used are not automobiles, and the public is not benefited in any way by the clipping of seconds off the "world record". It is a senseless, suicidal sport that should be suppressed in the interest of the dependent wives and children of speed maniacs.' Shortly after this, Ernest N. Smith, General Manager of the AAA, launched a counter-attack, arguing that 'High speed is recognised as the laboratory for the testing of new designs and innovations in the automotive world, and on this ground such trials, conducted at Daytona, Fla., and other places, are likely to be continued.' This was in turn denounced by Colonel C.G. Vincent, head of Packard's engineering department, for whom 'the feat of Major Segrave in driving more than 231 miles an hour added nothing of value to the industry.'

The *New York Times* was in a similar mood, demanding of its readers, 'What is the good of such performances, since no motorist on the road would want to drive a machine like the *Golden Arrow*?' Moreover, 'We listen not incredulously to predictions that the German device of rockets will shoot planes across the Atlantic at the rate of 500 miles an hour . . . The speed mania grows by what it feeds on. Thirty years ago no one was crazy about speed.' A Mrs Hinda Burke, from the Washington, DC area, joined in, complaining to the press about 'the growing custom of comparing these stunt makers' – the LSR kings – 'to great figures of the past. Why, the heroes of the past went through more excitement and danger, where they had to think and act quickly, than is possible at this stage of existence. Only theirs was real, not worked up by propaganda and cheap sensation.'

The American Establishment was unmoved by these protests. The first time Segrave broke the record at Daytona Beach he had an audience with John D. Rockefeller. The second time he over-topped even that. On 27 March he was granted an audience with the President of the United States, Mr Herbert Hoover, in the White House. This was really impressive. Not only had he compelled the respect of America: he had now done it twice in a row, and at the highest level. The British habit of attributing any success to good fortune was a preventive against the sting of failure whenever the nation's representatives attempted the same thing again. There was a small underlying assumption that the British could only ever successfully manage something once. Twice was, by definition, rare and remarkable.

Sweeter yet for Segrave and Britain was the way that, after his audience with the President, he was taken along Constitution Avenue to the steps of the Capitol, where his double triumph was recognised by the presentation of the Daytona Cup by Vice-President Charles Curtis and Sir Esme Howard. Segrave then delivered an acutely judged speech of thanks, in which, as in his discussions with Rockefeller, he was both quick to remind doubters that he was English, not Irish-American, and eager to offset America's failure to gain the LSR against its superiority in all other things. 'When an Englishman is in the United States to compete in an event of international importance,' he said, 'the eyes of the people are centred on this nation; and the friendly treatment and co-operation accorded him are certain to have an everlasting and favourable effect.' More specifically, 'America should be proud of the Contest Board of the American Automobile Association, its governing body of racing. I can say frankly, you are miles beyond our own racing committee in organisation, in methods and in efficiency.'

In New York crowds were gathering to stare at the *Golden Arrow*, placed on display until the time came to crate it up for its return to England. And British American Tobacco filled the pages of the American press with ads for Lucky Strike cigarettes, showing Segrave in helmet and goggles, announcing to the reader, 'I reach for a *Lucky* instead of a sweet'; and, 'After the strain of my ride the toasted fragrance of *Luckies* was like a tonic . . .'

Back at home, far from registering boredom at Segrave's apparently facile success, the British public was extravagantly moved by it. Audiences cheered when the news of his record was announced from the stages of theatres and music halls. The national press cleared the front pages: 'Land Speed Record Smashed', it cried; also, 'Great British Victory' and 'All-British Triumph'.

By the time the White Star liner *Olympic* reached Southampton on Saturday 13 April, with Segrave on board, he was being deluged by uncritical acclaim. He had received well over a thousand telegrams of congratulation in the States. In the time between docking at Southampton and ending up at the May Fair Hotel in Berkeley Street, he received a further two thousand, among which was one from HRH the Prince of Wales expressing his pleasure that the record had been brought back to England. Even before the *Olympic* had tied up, a barge came out to deliver a message from the King. 'On your arrival home,' it read, 'I send you my hearty congratulations on your splendid achievement in winning for Great Britain the world's speed record for motor cars'; it was signed, 'George R.I.'.

No sooner had Segrave read this than he was waving at the cheering mob on the quayside before being taken off to the South Western Hotel, in Southampton, to broadcast to the rest of the nation. At 10.15 p.m. he was live on the BBC's 2LO transmitter, in a talk entitled *Breaking the World's Speed Record*. In the course of this he revealed that on the first run at Daytona he had been bothered by something sharp sticking through the cushion of the *Golden Arrow*'s seat. It turned out to be 'a metal paperweight in the shape of a turtle with a long pointed tail'.

The next morning he was up early, to catch the special train from Southampton to Waterloo. This had a twenty-five-foot-square placard on the front of the locomotive, reading 'WELCOME HOME SEGRAVE'. It pulled in at Waterloo Station beside an enormous bower of flowers and bunting, as for the arrival of royalty. Here the Lord Mayor of London, the Mayor of Westminster and Sir Charles Wakefield protected Segrave – bowler-hatted and wearing an overcoat and an Old Etonian tie – from the emotions of the waiting crowd and bundled him into a Rolls-Royce Sedanca de Ville which then set off at the head of a procession of sixty cars, each bearing the legend 'Welcome Home Segrave'. Schoolboys held up banners reading 'Good Old Segrave' and '231 mph – Crikey!' The cars made their way through wet London avenues, the trees still leafless, while crowds six deep pressed towards the leading vehicle, stopping the traffic. Cheers and applause rang out all along the route. Police on horseback trotted back and forth, trying to manage the press of humanity.

Into Old Palace Yard, in front of the Palace of Westminster, they swept, before making their way into the Victorian reproduction-Gothic majesty of St Stephen's Hall. Here Mr Douglas Hacking, Parliamentary Secretary to the Department of Overseas Trade, made an official speech of welcome. Then it was out into the rain again, down Great George Street, past Horse Guards Parade, along the Mall and St James's Street, past thousands more yelling enthusiasts, and finally to the May Fair Hotel. 'WELCOME SEGRAVE,' it said in flowers above the entrance. Someone fired off a maroon; another well-wisher dropped a few shreds of paper from an upstairs window in the semblance of a tickertape welcome.

From then on, Segrave and his party were in the hands of the Society of Motor Manufacturers and Traders, who had laid on a reception at which two little golden models of the *Golden Arrow* were presented: one to an increasingly dumbstruck Segrave; one to Captain J.S. Irving. Both were also presented with a five-foot-long floral model of the *Golden Arrow*, carried by two grinning bellboys.

Sunday was a day off, barring more telegrams, importunings and messages of support. Monday the 15th saw the real orgy of public approbation. The *Golden Arrow* had been placed on display at Selfridges, on the ground floor. By mid-morning a queue stretched round three sides of the building, filing past the car at the rate of fourteen hundred people an hour. A small boy peered at the machine: 'How on earth could Segrave fit into that tiny seat?' he asked. His friend replied, 'He could do anything, he could.'

Later that day the RAC threw a celebratory dinner at its

headquarters in Pall Mall, under the Chairmanship of Sir Arthur Stanley, and in the presence of the Prince of Wales. Decorations and white ties were worn. Sir Charles Cheers Wakefield was present, as was Mrs Doris Segrave in a low-cut, sleeveless dress and shingled hair. Having suffered on the sands of Daytona, she could now relax and enjoy the benefits, not the least of which was hearing the Prince of Wales laud her husband.

Evidently the Prince found something in Segrave with which he identified; or for which he longed. Both were of an age: the Prince thirty-four, Segrave thirty-two. Both shared a certain asexual smoothness of appearance, a retiring masculinity that was true to the times. Heroism was something which Segrave embodied, but which the Prince had been denied when constitutional imperatives forbade him from seeing active combat in the Great War. It was something which the troubled royal brooded on, and which – a few weeks earlier – had made its way into a speech he gave to members of the Institute of Transport, of which he was Honorary President: 'I would like to describe Segrave as a hero . . . I think, without exaggeration, that we can put his effort to regain the world speed record as one of the bravest, one of the most sporting efforts ever made . . . I am sure that all of us take our hats off to Major Segrave as a brave man and a very fine sportsman.'

It was hard to tell who was more intimidated. 'Major Segrave,' he began, to rapturous cheering from a predominantly male audience, 'has just proved to the world that a British motor-car with a British motorist is the fastest thing that travels on dry land.' Potted palms towered over the slight Prince; candles burned in sconces on the walls. Segrave sat a seat away to the Prince's left (Sir Arthur Stanley between them), inclining his head with a certain hunted modesty. A barker stood louring at the Prince's back.

There followed some observations about courage in the face of the unknown: 'He took the chance, and he did that which no human being had ever done before. Thanks to his nerve he has won through successfully.' Then there was something to bring a lump to every throat: 'When we had grace before dinner we thanked God for the good dinner we were about to receive, and I could not help saying to the Chairman, "Thank God Segrave has come back safe."' Louder, more prolonged cheers welled up at this candid articulation of emotion. And this from the Prince of Wales himself!

As if recognising a lapse, the Prince then swerved back to the less dangerous subject of 'this great British achievement': that 'The British motor-car, the *Golden Arrow*, which enabled Major Segrave to put up his world's record, was more than a motor-car. It was the British motor-car manufacturers' challenge to the world!' Cheering and table-banging at this; followed, two days later, by an opportunistic national newspaper advertisement, sponsored by the Society of Motor Manufacturers and Traders, boosting British cars and openly thieving the Prince of Wales's turn of phrase. 'The *Golden Arrow*,' it read, 'was more than a motor car: it was the British manufacturers' proud challenge to all nations.' And, in case one didn't fully get the point, 'British industry is a sturdy creature plentifully supplied with backbone.'

Segrave's reply was cooler than the Prince's opening speech, tempered by his usual unease in the face of ostentation, although one contemporary account described him as 'looking considerably better than he had done before'. Clearly stirred by the idea of a confederacy of speed kings, he paid tribute to 'a great friend', who 'was in Africa now attempting to do the same thing. And had he been successful before we sailed to America, we would not have gone. Because just so long as an Englishman holds the trophy, it does not matter who that Englishman is.' The 'great friend,' was, of course, Campbell, still sweating and cursing in South Africa, still failing to make progress. This thoughtful inclusion of Campbell in the celebrations 'struck the correct note, and sounded as though it came from the heart', but would only have helped to emphasise the gap – geographical and professional – which lay between them.

Just as important, however, was the homage he paid to his other rival: Lee Bible. Bible, with whom Segrave experienced 'a definite feeling of friendship and comradeship', had by now been doubly doomed. Not only had he given his life for the cause; but his death, by providing an essential reminder that the LSR was dangerous and its champions were courageous, made an even sharper setting for Segrave's success. It was the least he could do, to acknowledge the debt.

As soon as Segrave had finished speaking (to generous applause), Sir Charles Wakefield was on his feet, readying himself for the moment when he awarded him the new gold Wakefield Trophy, designed by the artist Phoebe Stabler, plus £1000 a year, until the record was broken again. Sir Charles thought that 'All would agree . . . Mrs Phoebe Stabler has caught the inspiration of "The Spirit of Speed" and thus perpetuated a tense moment in the history of international sport.' Loud cheering; and the chance to gaze on Mrs Stabler's design for the Trophy. Strongly Deco in its vocabulary, it was an androgynous female nude figure leaping forward at an angle of forty-five degrees, anchored to a plinth by her right toe and a sheaf of napery emerging from her loins; while both Mercurial wings and electric lightning bolts shot backwards from her shoulders. The whole manifestation was gilt, weighed nineteen pounds and was a couple of feet tall. In comparison with the pared-down masculinity of the *Golden Arrow* itself, it looked contrived, incoherent. It had no function other than to advertise itself. Segrave nevertheless accepted it with good grace.

He carried on experiencing his triumph. Following his dinner at the RAC, he endured a round of lunches and receptions (the Connaught Rooms, the British Racing Drivers' Club) and starred, with the *Golden Arrow*, for a week at the Regal Cinema, Marble Arch, in a film about the Daytona record run ('which not only includes many breath-taking scenes of the great race itself but also the preparation of the wonderful racing car, Segrave's departure from England, his arrival in

New York and in fact a history in little of the whole triumphal event'). The newspapers swelled with their usual promotional chorus (Castrol, BP, Ferodo, Vickers Steels, BTH Magnetos, Hoffman Bearings, Acetex Safety Glass). Segrave was booked to appear at the *Daily Mail* Schoolboys' Exhibition at the beginning of the following year. Madame Tussaud's put a model of him in the Sporting section.

In all his public appearances Segrave was scrupulous to pay homage to his mechanics, to the *Golden Arrow*'s manufacturers, to Captain Irving. But the fact remained that he was the centre of attention, the *locus* for the dreads and longings of the ordinary people of England; and of the Prince of Wales. He had outstripped his competitors and stood alone, lionised and inimitable.

By rights, however, Segrave wasn't entirely alone. In June 1929, just a few months after Segrave had stunned the world at Daytona, Sir Henry 'Tim' Birkin and Woolf Barnato had co-driven a Bentley Speed Six to a record-breaking first place, ahead of three more Bentleys, piloted by Glen Kidston, Jack Dunfee and 'Benjy' Benjafield. It should surely have meant everything to have been part of such a rampant victory, and indeed for the Bentley Boys it did. But for Segrave their achievement was simply not big enough. It made the papers all right (although with nothing like Segrave's Daytona *éclat)*; motoring enthusiasts knew all about Bentleys and the Bentley Boys; it even became a little piece of motoring history. But the Bentley Boys were generic, subsumed into the greater whole; rather than British victory, they were interested in team success.

Indeed, W.O. Bentley had issued especially stifling orders that year, in order to confuse the rival Mercedes team. He made his drivers win the race as slowly as they could, in order to give onlookers the consoling impression that the cars would have nothing left to give when they reappeared the following year (it worked: Mercedes overdid it in 1930, blew up and Bentley won again). Wild man Jack Dunfee was so furious at having to cruise round the track at touring speed that he demanded, 'Do you want me to get out and push the bloody thing?' And then, both before and after the whole heavily managed event, there was all the partying and drinking and womanising. Had he been a Bentley Boy, Segrave would have found himself awash with loathed champagne at some bacchanal in Berkeley Square, in whose south-eastern corner the Bentley Boys kept their flats, and which was known by London cabbies as 'Bentley Corner'. It was not, in any way, Segrave's idea of fulfilment.

In truth, Segrave had much more in common with the famous aviators of the day, whose occupation was also solitary, heroic, touched with a degree of romance – and inherently progressive. After all, the lineaments of the modern world were now clearly discernible in the forms of radio, the telephone, the supremacy of the United States, Modern Movement architecture, air travel, the motor car. Segrave was a part of this. Bentley's huge, atavistic machines (Ettore Bugatti called them 'lorries') and the frightening immensity of the Le Mans circuit all harked back to the early days of racing, to the great pre-war endurance tests. But Segrave's *Golden Arrow* expressed the possibilities of the future, like Charles Lindbergh's *Spirit of St Louis* or the *Graf Zeppelin*.

And like, say, Sir Alan Cobham, who (sponsored by Sir Charles Wakefield) had flown the first round trip from England to Australia and back in 1926, Segrave was both a barnstormer and a technocrat. Standing there in his breezy white overalls, he appeared as someone outside the boundaries of the old social order, his driver's outfit and his crash helmet rendering him socially neutral, the apostle of a deracinated and mobile world. Cobham was thick-set, bullish, wore a thick moustache and came from simple farming stock; Segrave was tall, slender and an Old Etonian. But under the new dispensation they had much in common. A year later attractive Amy Johnson would detach herself from her working-class Hull background by becoming the first woman to fly solo to Australia, subsequently rejigging her accent into something more like Standard Received Pronunciation and entering into an arranged marriage with her daredevil co-aviator Jim Mollison. She, too, would occupy the same kind of ideological public space as Segrave and Cobham. She, too, would be a modern hero.

And, beyond this, Segrave personified the aspirations of the new suburbanites, the suntrap estate dwellers and Stockbroker Tudor devotees, who were emerging, not around the old railway networks, but around the new, sweeping arterial roads which radiated out from the big cities. For them the car had begun to shape the city outskirts at the same time as the city outskirts were shaping the car, until there was an unassailable symbiosis between them. If not 'poetry and tragedy, love and heroism', the arrival of the commonplace suburban car was at least the means to a kind of democratic liberation. When BP rushed out their statutory advertising flannel after Segrave's Daytona success ('It pays to use BP – The Petrol that Packs a Punch'), these new motorists understood that this wasn't so much a claim of technical superiority as an appeal to their longing for escape.

Segrave was an enabling figure, a man who embodied both the exclusivity of the past and the technological egalitarianism of the future. He was upper-crust, but a suburbanite in Kingston; an Old Etonian who liked model trains; a daredevil pilot of modest personal habits; he was close to his father, married to Doris and broke world records. And in 1929 he could be read by millions – without undue difficulty – as a kind of Lindbergh of the trunk roads, a Prince of Wales of the bypass.

But there was still another milestone to pass. There was the knighthood. Aldwick Bay, near Worthing, has generously been called 'the Sussex Riviera', and it was here that King George V was convalescing after the bronchial illness which had kept the nation beside itself with apprehension over the winter months. Sir Arthur du Cros, a pioneer of the pneumatic tyre, had made his establishment on the front, Craigweil House, available to His Majesty. Large, with double bays on the south-facing side, done up in late-Victorian Modern a bit like the Savoy Hotel, Craigweil was appropriately dull, impressive and anonymous. Bognor was a mile to the east, not yet Bognor Regis.

In deference to the King's illness, the New Year's Honours List had been held back until the start of March. When it did appear the newly confirmed Knights Bachelor were drawn from conventional stock: judges, local politicians, governors of the Empire, an editor, some philanthropists. A.V. Roe was a mild exception, knighted 'For distinguished services to British Aviation'.

But Segrave, like Sir Alan Cobham before him, leap-frogged the entire process. Such was the pressure to give him his full due, to confirm his apotheosis, that he was allowed to skip the procedure of the Honours List and was rushed down to the south coast in a closed car, while the King was rousted out of bed in order to knight him. He had to be smuggled into Craigweil House by a side door so as to dodge the press corps outside. Thus, on 27 April, the King received Segrave in the library, overlooking the sea, and knighted his exceptional subject, Major Henry O'Neal de Hane Segrave, in a front room in Bognor, making chit-chat with him as the watery spring sunshine streamed in through the windows.

Campbell continued to flog away in South Africa, more or less unnoticed. As time passed, the weather became autumnal. In the early mornings listless spectators stood around in hats and overcoats, watching the shadows gradually shorten. The white line stretched east–west along the dark Pan, a memento of failure. On his return to England, Segrave had callously, but accurately, wished 'Captain Campbell all the best of luck at Verneuk Pan, but I do not expect, considering the difficulties he's up against, that he will be successful.'

Eventually Campbell took out his penile *Blue Bird*, more or less for the hell of it. On Sunday 21 April he got it up to 218.5

mph, destroying two sets of special Dunlop tyres in the process. It was evident that the car couldn't be made to go any faster. So, on his very last set of tyres, and against the advice of the Dunlop team, he decided to annex a pair of lesser records: the World Land Speed Record over five miles and five kilometres. These unresonant targets duly met, he packed up and headed for home. Shortly before leaving Cape Town he gave a radio broadcast, spiritedly and disingenuously reassuring his audience that the Verneuk Pan could be made into 'the speedway of the world'. To which he would return, a year later, 'in a monster car which I am going to call the *Springbok*'.

His stoicism was remarkable. The whole trip had cost him in the region of £7000. He had failed to take the LSR. His wife, he was certain, had gone off to start an affair with one of his closest friends. He had lost some teeth. His eyesight was starting to fail. Resignedly, he unpacked *Blue Bird*, settled it in its garage at Povey Cross and considered what to do next.

A reception dinner given for him a month later by the Society of Motor Manufacturers and Traders was starkly bathetic in comparison with the enthronement of Segrave. Yet he put on a brave face and went along to the RAC, where, only a few weeks earlier, Segrave had had the world at his feet. There he listened to a Mr R.H. Blake, on behalf of the Society of Motor Manufacturers and Traders, offer a tribute 'From Motor Builders, to one who, in spite of adverse circumstances, has shown what is possible for the British-made car'. Campbell was then handed a silver cup to go with the many other silver cups in his trophy cabinet.

In return he forced himself to render his failure in the best possible light, arguing that 'The disadvantageous circumstances had to be taken as the luck of the game, which must confront anyone carrying on pioneer work . . .' Segrave was there, too, applauding politely and looking suitably serious when Campbell came out with the phrase 'pioneer work'. It would rank as one of the lowest points in Campbell's life.

10

Death by Water

୧୧C ୭)⟩

Segrave was already plotting his next move. He left the Portland Cement Co. and became Technical Advisor to the Aircraft Development Corporation, where he began work on designing the Segrave Meteor fast touring aeroplane. He had now taken the Land Speed Record three times, each time more effortlessly than before. There was no sense of challenge left. 'It calls for determination, rather than genius,' he observed, 'for there is no dreaded rival to outstrip, no stimulus of competition and little room for the exercise of judgement.' In fact, 'According to my own experience, conditions are straightforward enough up to about 180 miles an hour.' It was only after that they were 'apt to be far more difficult, not to say exciting'.

   Hence ennui positively saturated his voice as he sat in the *Golden Arrow* at the very start of January 1930. He and the car were the star turn at the *Daily Mail* Schoolboys' Exhibition in the Horticultural Hall, Westminster. As well as the *Golden Arrow* there was the Schneider Trophy-winning Supermarine S6, victoriously flown around the Solent by Flying Officer Henry Waghorn in September of the preceding year. And there was Campbell's *Blue Bird* to complete the set. This last had been paraded through the streets of London a month earlier like a captive elephant, as part of the procession for the Lord Mayor's Show; Leo Villa at the wheel. 'Next most famous among speed cars,' the *Daily Mail* reminded its readers, cruelly.

A group of silent, staring British schoolboys stood ranged around the *Golden Arrow*, witnesses to a miracle. Segrave wore a trilby and spoke in a languid monotone, explaining how 'This is the car which went to America in February of this year to try and get back the World Speed Record then held by America at a speed of 207 miles per hour . . . And, as you know . . . we were lucky enough to get this record back . . . the maximum speed that this car did, being an average of 231 and a half miles per hour . . .'

Having put the event in context, alluded politely to the Americans and observed the convention of attributing any success to good fortune rather than cleverness or skill, Segrave faced the task of bringing the moments of the record attempt back to life for his audience. The most, however, that he could manage was a weary confession of how little time it all took: 'This car has actually only been driven . . . for about ten minutes of its total life . . . In that time' – he prodded a finger into his left eye to winkle out a particle of sleep – 'we were able . . . to do the record . . . and complete the job . . . and come back here.' There was a terrible sense of exhaustion hanging in the air.

The adulation of the crowds in London, the knighthood, the use of the word 'hero' by a star-struck Prince of Wales, even the invitation to design a special bodywork for the Hillman car company, were not enough. He had already attempted to retire after his success at Daytona in 1927 – 'I have raced for eight years and already exceeded my allotted span of luck. I shall tempt fate no longer' – but had come back. Immediately after Bible's crash in 1929, however, he was determined to give up cars, but was also more circumspect in his language: 'I am not prepared to say whether I shall definitely give up speed racing, both on the track and elsewhere. I am making no decision in the matter until I get back home.'

This sounded a little furtive; and it was. Although he had lost interest in motor racing of all kinds, he had fallen in love with speedboats; and shortly after his Daytona success he went off to take part in a race at Miami Beach against the American powerboat king Commodore Gar Wood. Following his first inspirational encounter with Wood in March 1927, Segrave ('tall, slim, handsome, clothed in white tropic knickers,' according to a contemporary American account) had had his own powerboat, *Miss England*, built in 1928 by the British Power Boat Company around the inevitable Napier Lion aero engine (roped into yet another unfamiliar application) and shipped it out along with the *Golden Arrow*, precisely with the intention of taking on Wood. 'Double Death Gamble,' a headline had said. To his tremendous excitement, he then managed to beat Wood in their *mano a mano* competition in Miami, not least because Wood's boat broke down before the end of the race.

The thrill of powerboating (as Malcolm Campbell had already noticed, travelling slowly on water was as rousing as travelling fast on land) confirmed his repudiation of cars. Yet Segrave wasn't promiscuous in his ambitions. Rather, he was a serial monogamist who had now fallen out of love with the Land Speed Record, was becoming passionate about speed on water and had an as-yet Platonic interest in the air. From now on, speedboats would fill his mind with the persistence of a waking dream.

There were good reasons why. For a start, speedboating involved real competition, in the form of Gar Wood. Wood was a multimillionaire inventor and industrialist (his fortune came from hydraulic lifts and hoists), boat racer and designer, twice holder of the World Water Speed Record, an incarnation of virile American potentialities.

Secondly, there was the International Harmsworth Trophy. Instituted in 1903 by Sir Alfred Harmsworth, proprietor of the

Daily Mail, this was awarded to whichever boat (not more than forty feet in length; any number of engines) won the annual International Harmsworth Trophy Race. Naturally, Harmsworth had invented this prize with a view to seeing the names of British winners liberally inscribed on it. But, after some skirmishing between the French and British at the start of the century, the Harmsworth fell neatly into Wood's hands in 1920 and for nine years he had held on to it.

Sportswoman Marian Carstairs had already spent several years and tens of thousands of pounds trying to win back the Trophy in her *Estelle* powerboats, but with no success. 'Joe' Carstairs – or 'Betty', as Marian was sometimes known – was a charismatic tattooed British lesbian oil millionairess and close acquaintance of Malcolm Campbell (with whom she was photographed in March 1930: 'Joe' in the passenger seat of a Bugatti, wearing a beret, long scarf, purposeful expression, cigarette nipped between her teeth, Campbell at the wheel, looking giddily pleased with himself). She was addicted to speed, although her truest love was very possibly a stuffed leather doll named Lord Tod Wadley. Despite her wealth and her passion, she had failed to lay a finger on the Harmsworth. Segrave, however, had his inviolable sense of mission; plus Charles Wakefield (now Baron Wakefield of Hythe) to bankroll him for a new boat, *Miss England II*. This combination of wealth and self-certainty would – they were both sure – not only bring back the Harmsworth Trophy, but also claim the outright Water Speed Record, and thus defeat the muscular Gar Wood on both counts.

There was an extra congruity in this, as Britain had twice won the Schneider Trophy for aircraft, and was set to win it a third time (and hence outright) as well as take the overall World Air Speed Record from the Italians, in 1931. Taking the Water Speed Record would not only be an achievement in itself, but would set things up nicely for the globally imposing three-hander of land, air and water speed records. It would also pose a mass of severe technical problems for Segrave to solve, which was, after all, what he really liked doing. The Prince of Wales called him a 'hero'; the national press called him a 'wonder driver'. But his heroism was a heroism that eschewed the big, mad gesture, the act whose daring is predicated on its lack of sensible forethought. His bravery only emerged after he had first borne down on specific problems, seeking to resolve them by the application of intelligence.

Powerboats were so full of difficulties, however, that even Segrave found them hard work. To get a boat to go really fast through the water, you had to use a hydroplane – that is, a boat whose hull is built in a stepped form, the step or steps acting to push the craft upwards so that it rides on top of the water, rather than ploughing through it. This had been standard practice for powerboats since before the war, but it was still a deeply puzzling science and one which relied mainly on empirical trials with different shapes and different types of wood. As a result, perfectly right-looking powerboats would often turn out to be unable to rise out of the water, or 'plane', while others thrashed up and down at speed – 'porpoising' – for no clear reason.

Gar Wood, fifty years old, white-haired and positively musty with boating lore, was prone to come out with precepts such as 'Your boat is too light. You should have more weight for your horsepower' (to 'Joe' Carstairs). Explaining to Segrave that he was wrong to put the engines at the back of the boat, he said, 'I want those engines ahead of me when we crack up. If your hull blows to pieces, what chance have you? Those engines are a wall of steel in front of you.' And, as a general maxim, 'There are too many unknown factors about speed on water. We've taken our boats out on the river many times and have blown quite a few scientific theories to pieces.'

It was not only hard to predict the performance of any boat which was placed in the water; it was hard also to predict the behaviour of the water itself. The beach at Daytona could be wet, dry, smooth, lumpy, covered in shells or abrading itself in a gale. But at least it was to that extent consistent. Water, however, is capricious and contradictory. It is a fluid medium which becomes enormously hard when approached at any speed. It can appear as smooth as glass, but exert a terrible drag on any object moving through it. It can be flat calm, but in three minutes and with a rising breeze, covered in the kind of small ripples that make a rapidly moving powerboat leap up and down in a destructive frenzy. In these conditions, a boat – which has no suspension of any kind – simply crashes into any wave it meets, or slams down on to the surface of the water, like a filing cabinet landing on a concrete floor.

Added to this is the question of getting whatever power you have, to drive you forward. By 1930 there was plenty of brute force in an average aero engine; but, cribbed by the technology of the day, it necessarily ended up turning a two-bladed metal propeller about a foot across and dissipating its energy in a ball of spray. Everything was problematical.

It was, in some ways, like a return to Segrave's early days with the Royal Flying Corps, in which nothing could be predicted with much certainty and almost every flight was a metaphorical, and actual, leap into the unknown. Worse, it was forcing him to occupy the terrain that men like Frank Lockhart and Parry Thomas had found themselves inhabiting – stern theoreticians who had nonetheless been obliged to leave the plans behind and trust to luck. Quite quickly, Segrave reached that stage of extreme preoccupation in which he would come down to breakfast in his new, unostentatious, squarely bank-manager-Tudor home in Coombe Warren, Kingston, and say to Lady Doris, 'I'm sorry, D, I can't speak today. I've got to think.'

In June 1930 *Miss England II* was taken from its workshops in Cowes, on the Isle of Wight, and transported up to Lake Windermere. There were two of the latest Rolls-Royce V-12 aero engines installed at the back of the boat; as used in the

Schneider Trophy Supermarine S6. The craft itself was thirty-two feet long and weighed over five tons. One of Segrave's big ideas was to make the front step – the one that did most of the work, getting the boat to plane – movable, held in place by enormous bolts, so that he could experiment with different settings. Engineer Fred Cooper had designed a new kind of high-speed propeller, which promised a lot but which came with no guarantee.

Windermere itself, about a mile wide and almost twelve miles long, is the biggest body of water in England, and was just about long and straight enough for Segrave's purposes. The team put up at the Old England Hotel, Bowness-on-Windermere, right on the water's edge. The sun, uncharacteristically, poured out of the sky as Lord Wakefield, wearing a frock coat and barely tall enough to come up to Segrave's waist, made an address: 'If *Miss England* attains her double object – if she succeeds in passing the one hundred miles per hour mark for the first time on water – she will not only bring back one of the world's most coveted prizes to this country, but will have engraved Britain's name on yet another milestone of progress.' Segrave stood at Wakefield's right hand and frowned. His knighthood seemed to have rendered him even taller and slimmer than before; his overalls appeared an even more unearthly dazzling white against the utilitarian grime of the boat sheds. The day before, he had surveyed the course. On his return he told a bystander that it was 'the most dangerous game I have tried'.

He was now working to a different imperative – the national, rather than the personal. Up to the point at which he had taken the LSR in the *Golden Arrow*, Segrave was still – just – a sporting gentleman motorist; a semi-professional pursuing a specific end partly for his own satisfaction, partly for the prestige these things brought back to England. Although tens of thousands of spectators had seen him in Florida, and although he had been granted an audience with the President himself, his actions were, to that extent, unembarrassed by larger concerns. In the intervening year, however, he had become national property, an iconic personage. 'When Segrave was knighted,' yelped J. Wentworth Day, 'the whole flower of knighthood bloomed again.'

In practical terms this made it possible for Segrave to get access to two brand-new Rolls-Royce engines – still the pets of the British Air Ministry – as well as to the bank account of Lord Wakefield. In psychological terms it stripped him of any protection he might have claimed for himself as a sports-man. Now he was an official legate for Britishness. Without a doubt his ego was up to the job: it was ego, talent and self-belief which had got him this far. But everything else had moved on to a higher level of expectation. And, for the first time since his underachieving involvement in the British Grand Prix of 1926, he was performing as the star turn in front of a British crowd, with all the burden of anticipation that this entailed.

The trials began. On 10 June the £25,000 boat, white and slim like Segrave himself, slid away from its mooring, while Segrave and his two mechanics fired up the engines. Scores of day boats floated in *Miss England II*'s path, like the impor-tuning spectators at Daytona Beach. Lady Doris Segrave watched from the shore with Lord Wakefield. Segrave and his assistants, Michael Willcocks and A.V. Halliwell – the latter on loan from the Rolls-Royce company – disappeared off down the lake, trailing smoke and an intimidating rumble.

The trials were tantalising and frustrating. The Water Speed Record, set by Gar Wood in March 1929, was just over 93 mph. On their first run Segrave and his two mechanics hit 94 mph before the high-speed propeller split in two, gouging a deep groove in the hull and nearly wrecking the boat. The propeller was replaced and the next day Segrave made a succes-sion of test runs along the measured mile at just over 100 mph. Being tests, of course, they didn't count for the record. The next day, 12 June, they went out and the propeller snapped again. Segrave's infallibility was being tried. Powerboating, the great unquantifiable, was yielding; but uncertainly. It was reported in the papers that 'A special representative from Detroit – where *Miss England II* will meet the American boats in an attempt to win back the British International trophy in August – is cabling daily reports of *Miss England*'s tests.'

Clearly, the record was very nearly his, as long as the weather held and the propeller stayed in one piece. And as long as the timekeepers were there – a prosaic difficulty which held no easy solution, as Segrave noted on 12 June: 'I am not going to take any more risks,' he said, 'but I've got to have a shot for the record to-morrow, because the timekeepers must leave for the Isle of Man TT races on Saturday.'

'Tomorrow' was Friday 13 June. If this disturbed him, he didn't show it. Displaying a mettlesome rationality, he ignored all superstitions – despite one of the timekeepers cheerfully remarking that 'In view of the date, I'd better have your auto-graph now' – and prepared the boat for its first record run.

That day he was grimly confident. The weather was still fine. A big crowd was out, day boats and steamers lining the course. Bathing beauties posed on the marker buoys. If there was a cloud on the horizon it was that there weren't enough new, specially made steel-reinforced lifejackets to go round. Only one had so far made it up to Windermere. Segrave disdained conven-tional lifejackets as 'useless', unable to offer any real protection if the boat crashed at speed. Reinforced ones might possibly be worth wearing. But if there was just one steel jacket available, then he would wear no jacket at all, rather than take the one on offer and put his life above those of his two mechanics. So, jacketless, Segrave, Halliwell and Willcocks fired up *Miss England II* and growled out on to the shining, liquid course. There Segrave made two runs, one in each direction, reaching over 101 mph on one run and duly breaking the Water Speed Record, the average coming out at nearly 99 mph.

This was surely enough. British prestige had been manifestly upheld. Had this been Daytona, had it been the Slug or the *Golden Arrow*, one suspects that Segrave would have left it there for the day and gone away to plan his next move. But this time he was seized by a terrible impatience, a need to reach an even higher speed, a 100-mph average, before the time-keepers packed up; or by a kind of rapture of the deep; or by a novel hysteria, a by-product of being the iconic Sir Henry Segrave who no longer yielded to nice calculations of risk, but faced them down.

Instead of returning to base, he remained in the boat with Willcocks and Halliwell, turned it round and shot back down the lake for a third go. Soon after it hit planing speed and was thundering down the course in a cloud of spray and smoke, *Miss England II* gave a jink to one side and leapt into the air, its engines roaring. Segrave, Willcocks and Halliwell were flung into the water. *Miss England II* crashed beneath the surface of the lake with the force of a bomb going off. A few seconds went by. The stern of the boat bobbed up, a hole torn in the hull, the bows filling with water.

Willcocks was pulled out, alive. To the horror of his wife and four-year-old son, Halliwell had disappeared completely. A Mr P.F. King of Troutbeck, spectating from a day boat, jumped fully clothed into the lake and pulled Segrave from the water. He was taken unconscious to the Old England Hotel, where doctors attended him. Despite suffering a broken arm, broken ribs and a fractured thigh, he revived enough to speak his epitaph: 'How are the lads?' he asked Lady Segrave. And then, 'Did we do it?' She assured him that they had got the record. Shortly after that he died of multiple lung haemor-rhages. Halliwell's body was later found, still clutching the pencil and notepad with which he had been jotting down instrument readings.

No one had a definitive explanation for the disaster. The boat may have hit a half-submerged log or bottle at 100 mph.

Or perhaps the movable front planing section – the one held on by bolts – had been torn off by a rogue wave crossing the lake's surface. After the 1929 LSR, Segrave had written that as one 'gathers speed, one slowly feels the whole thing gradually getting little by little above human control'. As it turned out, this, with its nervous gradualism, its sense of dislocation and its undercurrent of fear, was a fair summation – not just of that fatal day, but of the ten years which had preceded it.

The Establishment which had helped to create Segrave duly abandoned itself to grief. The King sent a message to Lady Segrave, in which he recalled 'with pleasure the occasion at Bognor Regis when he conferred a knighthood on Sir Henry, and his Majesty mourns the death of one whose intrepid adventures on land and water were the admiration of all the world'. The Prime Minister, Ramsay MacDonald, declared that 'Segrave's death is a sad sacrifice. He will always hold a conspic-uous place among the speed pioneers, and the achievement which cost him his life will be a lasting record.' Lord Wakefield lamented: 'To say he was the most courageous man I ever met is only a small part of my conception of him . . . Although always bearing the greatest burden, he supported and encour-aged his colleagues by his rocklike strength and endurance.'

And *The Times*, with a pinch of equivocation, wrote: 'The spirit that urged Segrave to speed is a great and noble thing. It is the spirit of adventure, of courage, of honourable emulation, which, however useless its objects may be, is in itself a higher thing than that which would suffer human life to drag listlessly on in grooves of habit and indifference.'

Segrave's importance in life was measured by the scope and scale of the elegies on his death. They were international in reach: from the *Miami Daily News* ('Major H.O.D. Segrave, British annihilator of space on land and sea, won not only the international race for speed boats at Miami, but he captured the heart of America'); to the *Liverpool Echo* ('In these dolorous days, with weak-kneed depressionists all too numerous, let us, who have faith and hope, say that there is nothing wrong with England as long as she has pioneers like Segrave'); to Commodore Gar Wood ('His loss, I know, will be mourned by every sportsman. He was a great gentleman'); to the Paris-based *Echo des Sports* ('Sir Henry will leave an imperishable mark in the memory of those who knew him. His death calls forth not only the regrets of his own country, but the regrets of the entire world'); to the *Dublin Evening News* ('Stilled is the bravest heart that ever beat/Quiet the soul that never knew defeat/Smiling and cool you faced the eyes of Death/For England's honour gave your latest breath').

Conventionally, what one mourns is the loss to oneself – clearly so in the case of the *Daily Telegraph*, which lamented the passing away of an epic, irreplaceable figure, a character from Baroness Orczy or John Buchan, a Sandy Arbuthnot with a sense of propriety: 'Tall, slenderly built, erect, with piercing deep-set eyes and a hawk-like face, he was all that imagination called for in a speed king. He had nerves, but they were nerves of steel, a vivid imagination, controlled by a cool brain . . .' The *Telegraph* was bemoaning the loss of its chance to believe. The poet, adventurer and political Scaramouche Gabriele D'Annunzio was so shocked by Segrave's death that he wrote a poem and sent it to Lady Doris. She was so moved by D'Annunzio's poem that in return she sent him the steering wheel from Segrave's wrecked boat. He mounted the black, mangled wheel as the centrepiece of a shrine in the Stanza delle Reliquie at his residence on Lake Garda.

Segrave's funeral was on 17 June, at the Golders Green Crematorium. A large crowd turned up to try to get in, but was held back by a police cordon. Inside, there were four mourners: Lady Doris, Segrave's father, his stepmother and Lord Wakefield. Wreaths, sent from all over the world, filled three cars. They were driven away afterwards and laid on the cenotaph in Whitehall. At the same time a memorial service took place in St Margaret's Church, Westminster. This drew representatives of the Prince of Wales, the Prime Minister, the Rolls-Royce Company; also Mr Gordon Selfridge, Captain Malcolm Campbell and two French dignitaries who placed a wreath of red and white roses on the altar. The church was filled to overflowing and two hundred members of the public had to stay on the pavement outside.

This separation of duties – the public and the private displays of mourning – pointed up something fundamental about Segrave's life. To the extent that he was public property, he brought forth expressions of grief from any number of quarters; the world seemed to have known him and found something profound in him. His success was so complete, it drew into it everyone else's aspirations and ambitions. People saw in him, in his unblemished achievements, what they wanted to see in themselves. But at the crematorium at Golders Green, the private Segrave – who distanced himself from the world by always remaining in motion – disappeared into the flames. Despite the presence of Lord Wakefield and the second Mrs Segrave, it's hard not to believe that only Doris and his father were truly close to him. And later in the year Segrave's father went up in a Segrave *Meteor* aeroplane, carrying his son's ashes. It was a moment of private theatre: at Lady Doris's request, he scattered them over the playing fields of Eton.

11

Knighthood and Politics

《◖ ◗》

The decade had started on a note of lugubrious symbolism with the death of Sir Henry Segrave. This was promptly followed by the crash of the R101, the state-of-the-art British airship which was meant to open up valuable new international air routes and act as a floating embodiment of national prestige. The R101 exploded spectacularly when it hit a hillside near Beauvais in northern France on 5 October 1930. Forty-eight of the fifty-four people on board were killed, including Air Vice Marshal Sir William Sefton Brancker and Lord Thomson, the Air Minister. The British airship programme was stopped immediately.

By the second half of 1930 unemployment in Great Britain had risen to well over two million. Glorious autonomy and the national destiny so manifest in the nineteenth century – as of a great liner sweeping towards its home port – were gone. The United States' introduction of the protectionist Smoot-Hawley Tariff helped to accelerate the collapse of industrial production all over Europe. Britain's trade surplus of over £100 million in 1928 would, by 1931, have been transformed into a deficit of £114 million. In the same year His Majesty

the King took a voluntary pay cut of £50,000. Pretty soon
Germany would default on its post-war reparations payments,
the Bank of England would be losing gold at the rate of £2.5
million a day, the exchange system would fall apart and the
American banking system would start to collapse. Another few
years after that, Fascism would have established its dank
cellarage in the centre of Continental Europe, and all that would
be left would be the dizzying prospect of a world spiralling
down into war again.

Captain Malcolm Campbell's response to the raw disquiet of
the time was to build himself a new *Blue Bird*. Ever since it
had come back from South Africa, ungarlanded and with the
miasma of failure clinging to it, he had been brooding on its
deficiencies. 'That damn car,' he would say. 'Heaven knows
what it cost me, and what's the use of it?' But at the start of
1930 he found his way down to Brooklands, where Ken
Thomson and his erstwhile chief mechanic, Ken Taylor, were
running the engineering business they had built out of the
remains of Parry Thomas's Inventions Development Co.

The star of Thomson & Taylor was now thirty-five-year-old
Chief Designer Reid Railton – a kind of caricature scientist: tall,
pencil-thin, bespectacled, ill articulated inside his suit. His face
was lean, Jesuitical. In later life he wore a dental plate. When
it developed a hairline crack, rather than take it to a dentist, he
adopted the engineer's solution to micro-fractures by drilling a
tiny hole at the end of the crack in order to safely distribute the
stress. He also suffered from migraines, which he would cure
by burning blisters on his forehead, on the basis that the pain
of burning (intended and therefore manageable) overwhelmed
the pain of migraine (unintended and therefore oppressive). Rest
cures in the Alps failed to make much difference.

Walter Hassan, a well-known Bentley modifier who subsequently became a key figure with the Jaguar Car Company,
worked with Railton. He found him 'very gifted, with a terrific

ego, and was very sure of himself. He never discussed anything with anyone, he was so sure that his ideas were right.' Searching for an encapsulation of the man, Hassan ended up with 'rather snooty'.

An arrogant oddball like this was just what Campbell needed. 'Is there any way of getting some more speed out of this old car,' he begged, 'to save a lot of time and expense?' Fixating on Segrave, Campbell assumed that his absorption into the world of speedboats was temporary; that in a year or so Sir Henry would be back at Daytona to kick more sand in his face. Railton reckoned *Blue Bird* in its Verneuk Pan form 'appalling', but Campbell was rich, the project was, for all its shortcomings, glamorous and intriguing, and there was only so much work going around for small, intensely specialised businesses like Thomson & Taylor.

What's more, Campbell had managed to lay his hands on two new supercharged Napier aero engines, despite the initial resistance of the Air Ministry. He was materially assisted in this by none other than 'Joe' Carstairs, who gave him £10,000 – money which she would once have spent on her own racing projects, but which she now handed over to the irresistible Campbell. 'The greatest sportsman I know,' was how he subsequently described her. Bitterly, she complained that 'Usually he drives like an old woman.' Reid Railton chafed at the machinery he was now committed to work with. 'The best course would been to have built a completely new car round the new 1400 hp Napier engine.' But the money was not endless and 'Campbell was determined to go to Daytona the following January.' They had to rebuild the old stager which had been in existence since 1925; but not before Railton had thrown out as much of it as he could, leaving, in the end, the front axle, some brakes, some bits of steering and the two outsized girders which made up the sides of the chassis.

After Segrave's accident on Lake Windermere, though, why did Campbell bother to carry on? Segrave was dead, Parry

Thomas was dead, Frank Lockhart was dead. Even Ray Keech, the last American holder of the LSR, had been killed in a ten-car pile-up at the Altoona Speedway, Pennsylvania, in mid-1929. All the serious opposition was gone. Wasn't there something onanistic about Campbell's now quite solitary struggle for more speed? Surely, frivolous pursuits like the LSR were no longer going to find quite such an easy purchase in the Depression years? As the 17th Earl of Derby – the 'King of Lancashire' – argued with rough intelligibility at the centenary pageant of the Liverpool and Manchester Railway in September 1930, those caught up by the present 'craze for speed . . . were trying to do rather more than they ought to do, while, perhaps, not doing what they might do as thoroughly as they should. The craze for speed was not good for the community at large, and was certainly bad for the individual.' Or, as Max Beerbohm subsequently expressed it, 'The main root of the mischief is that great fetish of ours – speed.' And anyway the Americans would surely have lost interest.

Well, no. The Sunbeam Car Company, slowly beginning its terminal slide into unprofitability, had determined to make a comeback for the LSR, in order to give its image a lift. Louis Coatalen therefore designed a tremendous showpiece record car, thirty-one feet long, containing two colossal purpose-built engines (no whoring after aeroplane motors for him), shaped like a cigar tube and flagrantly named the *Silver Bullet*. The driver was a well-known Brooklands figure, Kaye Don – a moustachioed speed king despite his feminine name – who had been serially successful in a number of Sunbeam racers, as well as at the wheel of Captain Alistair Miller's Wolseley-Viper. His career would end abruptly in the mid-thirties, when he was jailed for the manslaughter of his mechanic after an accident on the Isle of Man. But at the start of 1930 he was a star turn (Castrol was still paying him £2000 a year in endorsement fees) and the authorities at Daytona welcomed him as warmly as they had Segrave, Campbell, Keech and Lockhart.

The way things turned out, the Sunbeam challenge was a fiasco, in which the engines simply failed to deliver and Don was reduced to trudging up and down Daytona Beach in the *Silver Bullet* at 168 mph. Nevertheless, the principle was clear. Daytona was open for business, and there were still candidates for the LSR title, however ineffectual.

Besides, what else was there for Campbell to do with his life? His main business interests, insurance (he was still a member of Lloyd's) and motor cars, carried on almost without his intervention. Indeed, the less he had to do with them, the more profitable they were, given that, as an entrepreneur, he tended to bring the same hectic imprecision to his business innovations as he did to his hobbies. Leaning heavily on another of his maxims, 'Never trade with your own money. Always use that of others', he had got involved early on in the establishment of Europe's biggest and most advanced garage, the Bluebird garage in London's King's Road. Designed by the architect Robert Sharp, this opened in 1923 as the last word in car care for the smart set, with its spacious forecourt and its discreet lounges for lady passengers and their besmirched drivers. By 1925 it was an established landmark and Campbell had acquired the London agency for Chrysler cars. By 1927 it had gone bust and the shareholders (among whom Campbell was not included) lost their entire investment.

Unable to leave well alone, at the start of the thirties he mixed himself up with a high-tone garage in St James's. This had the right address but none of the right facilities, or even space to do anything except show the cars off in museum conditions, and duly went under. The backers lost around £25,000; Campbell, sapiently, lost nothing. With the active encouragement of the Brooklands management, he had opened his own Campbell Shed, beside the paddock, in 1926, from which he traded sports and racing cars. Modifications continued to this wooden structure, on and off, until 1931, by which time it was big enough to host a barn dance. But he got bored even with that and perfunctorily handed it on to Thomson & Taylor.

Gradually, as his personal fame grew, he scaled down his business ambitions, contenting himself with a ragbag of directorships (Ford Motor Company, Zurich General Accident), harmless sinecures (motoring editor of *The Daily Mail*; motoring correspondent of *The Field*; editor of *British Movietone News* – a titular appointment, as the job effectively remained in the hands of the previous editor, Gerald Sanger) and product endorsements for anything from Moseley 'Float-On-Air' Upholstery; to Rolex Watches ('I have now been using my Rolex Watch for some little while, and it is keeping perfect time under somewhat strenuous conditions . . . A very first-class watch, suitable for really rough treatment'); to Grape-Nuts ('Living at high speed! We all do it today! And we all need this grand food to help us along! Keep up your energy with Grape-Nuts – it helps you stay the pace!').

Speed record breaking was Campbell's life: it created about the only social environment in which he felt properly comfortable; and was the professional – or semi-professional – activity to which his diffuse, superabundant energies were best fitted. It was, consequently, a highly nervous and critical Campbell who inspected the new-look *Blue Bird* towards the end of 1930. Not only did he need to recapture the LSR; he needed to confirm his own sense of destiny as a speed king; and he needed to overcome the ghost of Segrave – who, now dead, was doubly glorious, a figure of imperishable gallantry. An awful lot depended on Reid Railton's engineering talent.

By the time Railton had finished with *Blue Bird* it had grown some six feet in length and now was twenty-five feet long. It was also half as heavy again as the 1929 version, weighing in at four tons (of which three-quarters of a ton was lead ballast under the seat to keep the back wheels on the ground). And it had a seven-foot-long tail fin, big enough for an advertising hoarding. 'Actually,' Railton later wrote, 'I am doubtful whether this fin does any good at all.' Each wheel weighed two hundred-weight and had to be lifted on and off by a team of three men. When Campbell sat in the driver's seat he became almost completely obscured. The car had become a monument to brute energy every bit as implacable as J.M. White's *Triplex* or a King Class steam locomotive. Except that *Blue Bird* was not only huge and confrontational, but also purposefully coherent in a way it had never managed before.

Clever Railton had managed to lower the whole machine by resiting the gears and drivetrain, allowing Campbell to sit down inside the car, rather than on top of it. He had also made a Plasticine model of the bodywork and spent weeks tinkering with it in the Vickers wind-tunnel, with Chief Designer R.K. Pierson's help. Suave fairings had grown around the wheels and the radiator at the front now had a compelling, predatory look to it. When it was all ready, save the bodywork and the radiator, it was photographed at the Thomson & Taylor work-shops, with nine of the key protagonists – among them Campbell, Railton, Ken Thomson, Ken Taylor and Leo Villa – leaning against a workbench behind the car. In the picture Campbell stares furiously out at the camera, his arms folded tight across his chest. Railton slouches next to him, gazing at the machinery, a look of baffled regret playing across his face. Villa echoes his master's combative stare. All the rest seem to be enjoying a private joke.

Once the Chelsea-based coachbuilding firm of Gurney Nutting had fabricated the bodywork (none too meticulously, in thirty-six hectic days and nights) and ten coats of blue paint had been sprayed on, the beast was transported on the night of 6 January 1931 to the Rootes showrooms in Piccadilly. There it was displayed for three days to passing crowds, who brought the traffic to a halt. On 13 January it was hoisted on board the White Star liner *Homeric*, along with its team of acolytes and the usual armoury of spares. Napier & Son lent

Joe Coe; while Dunlop provided Dunlop Mac *and* Big Mac, to look after the tyres.

(Since these three were regular employees of their own companies, they could easily have been provided with living expenses directly from Head Office. But Campbell, always conscious of the value of money, paid their expenses out of his own pocket and then claimed them back from Dunlop and Napier at the end of the trip, almost certainly adding his own small mark-up for the trouble. In fact, Leo Villa was put in charge of doling out the spending money, like a knight's man-ciple: he was entrusted with some $4500 plus £60 sterling.)

A momentary snag: just as the *Homeric* was about to sail, Campbell received a cable from the American Automobile Association, panicking about the financial arrangements. 'Daytona refuses to advance over four thousand dollars,' it read. 'Expecting you to put up the remainder, and has not asked for sanction. Believe this entirely inadequate. Advised your American manager repeatedly against you sailing under such conditions unless your backers prepared to underwrite your remaining expenses.' It was a second-hand ransom note, in other words, from the financially pressed City authorities. Showing remarkable cool, Campbell at once sent a reply: 'Sailing today with car and mechanics. If any difficulties USA shall proceed New Zealand.' This resolute stance (coupled with the curious menace of 'New Zealand' – why? what was there?) worked.

When he reached New York Campbell found a sprawl of eager telegrams from Florida waiting for him. One read, 'Florida National Guard welcomes you to Daytona Beach. Special ring-side section reserved for yourself and party for every fight staged in local Armoury during your visit. May we expect you at Armory fights next Monday night? I prepared Beach for your trials here in 1928, under Mayor Armstrong. Yours to command if I or National Guard can be of service in any way. Capt. John O. McNamara.' Another: 'Daytona Beach Chamber of Commerce welcomes you to our Country, our State and our City. If we can be of service, you have but to command us.' The Mayor himself had sent the following message: 'City of Daytona extends you a most cordial welcome and best wishes for your success'. And there was a terse submission from the event organisers: 'Final proposition as follows: City police beach, unload and reload car, furnish garage and watchmen, service car to beach. Timing wires and telephone service on beach. Time limit for trials fifteen days.'

Money was at the heart of it all. The Great Depression in the States was taking a temporary break in its headlong career, before accelerating again in the spring of 1931; but February could be a slow month for tourism and Campbell was as welcome as any freak show, especially now that he had given *Blue Bird* a new and promotable look. Nevertheless, momentarily frightened by the expense of setting up the beach, marshalling the crowds and promoting the record bid, Daytona had decided to put the bite on Campbell. But at the same time they knew that his non-appearance would have been worse, financially speaking, than any short-term dip in the City's funds. Campbell knew this too. Despite his desperate need to get on with the LSR, he was still rational enough to haggle.

The only question was, would he make a mess of it? Kaye Don had failed dismally the year before; and it was Campbell's speciality to stumble towards failure, only to triumph at the last and, by this drama, enlarge the scope of his achievement. Not that he'd managed anything like that in South Africa. That had all been disastrous, and monotonously so. On the other hand, viewed structurally, it at least had the potential to be turned into a kind of feint or diversionary ploy, so that a triumph now, two years on, would appear all the more unexpectedly brilliant.

Having installed his team and set up the car, Campbell made several test attempts, nearly crushing to death hundreds of spectators at the end of one run. This occurred after he had raced off into the haze from his start line. Minutes went by; Campbell was miles off in the distance; people moved on to the beach, gathering in a crowd behind his starting point. Behind them stood a knot of parked cars. After a time he began his run back, but had difficulty telling exactly how far along the beach he was. Abruptly, the crowd appeared out of the mist. He was travelling (he claimed) at nearly 200 mph. He 'stood on the brakes', only to find that, like Segrave's brakes in the Slug, they packed up under the strain, 'while blue smoke came from the drums'.

Campbell wondered if the gawping onlookers might simply run away. 'Then I remembered the cars packed solidly behind the spectators; even if the people ran, I should crash into the standing machines. My only hope of stopping *Blue Bird* was to change into second gear.' This he did, coming to a halt about 100 yards from the frightened mob. A few days later he gave himself another scare when the car jumped out of gear at around 250 mph and nearly blew the engine to pieces.

And when he came to attack the record, on 5 February 1931, his principal drama came in the shape of a motorcycle cop who strayed on to the course in the middle of a thick sea mist, Campbell approaching him at nearly 240 mph. For a split second it looked as if one of Daytona's finest was about to be annihilated, causing *Blue Bird* to spin off into the crowd, explode and kill scores. As it was, the cop skidded off out of harm's way and Campbell carried on to the end of the course.

This unintended near-catastrophe was – of course – a fortuitous addition to the spectacle. Without it, and the other mishaps in practice, Campbell would have been going through the motions. With it, he was attempting a flirtation with disaster – in sharp contradistinction to Segrave's striving for chilly professionalism.

Indeed, Campbell experienced each drive as a profound encounter with life and death. While Segrave was describing the blurred, onrushing scenery in the most quotidian language – 'One straight line drawn on a piece of typewriting paper' – Campbell was aiming for something elemental. The new, beefed-up engine and the new, beefed-up *Blue Bird* brought back 'that strange exhilaration which I had experienced on former occasions', while at the same time countering the state of shrill anxiety which always accompanied his record attempts. Dorothy Campbell was sure that 'He was attracted by what is known as the ecstasy of fear . . . whenever he embarked upon one of his record-breaking exploits he was for weeks beforehand in a state of acute nervous tension. There is no doubt – there never was in my mind – he was afraid and really enjoyed the sensation.'

Perversely thrilled by the dread of what was to come, when it came to the moment at which he pushed down the accelerator pedal and drove off into the mist, towards the red square which marked the start of the measured mile, then he achieved that annihilation of the Self which high-adrenalin sports enthusiasts look for. 'That feeling was wonderful,' he gushed after his final run, talking of the moment when he shifted into top gear and vanquished his dread, experiencing 'a most wonderful sensation, as the car carried me away with it in that tremendous burst of speed'.

In fact, everything was going about as well as it possibly could. The rebuilt car was a success; there had been enough moments of crisis to keep everyone on edge; and, in a triumphant conclusion to the narrative, he managed an average run of nearly 246 mph along the measured mile, taking the LSR by a comfortable margin of nearly 15 mph. Campbell was so happy that when the timekeepers gave him the figures, he grabbed Harry Leech and hugged him.

And it was – still – something for the crowds on the Daytona Beach sand dunes to see. In the chill of early February tens of thousands stood in hats and overcoats in the brilliant white sunlight of the east coast, waiting for this great blue beast – as big as the *Golden Arrow* and half as heavy again – to thunder down the sands not fifty yards from where they were standing, with a noise like a military fly-past and the sharp, hostile smell of aviation fuel and burnt Castrol in its back-wash. There was even a wall-of-death feel to it: loud, simplistic, the lone human trapped in the awful machinery, to touch their atavistic selves. They were present and alive at the very moment when someone travelled faster across the ground than anyone had ever managed before.

'Whoo!' an onlooker yelled as he shot past. 'That's history!' When Campbell struggled out of the car at the end and light-headedly gave in to the vernacular, declaring how he was 'Sure proud of all my mechanics who've helped me to register this speed today on the old *Blue Bird*,' the cheering that greeted him (from a crowd which had to be held back by uniformed guards) was full-throated, mixed with whistles, screams and whoops. *Four miles a minute!* It *was* quite something.

The *New York Times*, it must be said, kept up the note of jealous disapproval it had sounded after Segrave's 1929 success, demanding to know, 'Why should it be Englishmen who go in for tremendous speed? The Campbell car, at her maximum speed, could cover the tight little island from Land's End to John o'Groats in about two hours. It cannot be that British men are in so great a hurry as all that.' But after Campbell had been 'fêted to an embarrassing extent' in Florida, President Hoover conspicuously paid the *New York Times* no heed and took time off from the problems of the US economy to greet Campbell in the White House on 11 February. In the presence of the British Ambassador, Sir Ronald Lindsay, the two men chatted for several minutes, 'And the President warmly congratulated Campbell on his feat.' A day or so later and the *New York Times*, too, had capitulated, printing a long description of *Blue Bird* and calling it both 'an engineering feat' and a 'scientific task'. *Blue Bird* then went on to the British Empire Exhibition at Buenos Aires, where it was put on public display for the next three weeks.

*   *   *

On board that 'Grand Old Lady' the *Mauretania*, coming back
to England, Campbell found himself in the company of Charlie
Chaplin, who was making a sentimental journey home. The
two were photographed together on deck, nonpareils in the
world of sporting records and entertainment. Chaplin got off
the boat at Plymouth – either so as not to get in the way of
Campbell's triumph, or because he knew somehow what was
going to happen over the next few hours: a typically Campbell
encounter with the bathetic.

First, a passenger fell overboard while the liner was anchored
in the harbour at Cherbourg, just across the Channel from its
final destination. Brave Captain Campbell, who was on the
boat deck, jumped to the rails, snatched up a lifebelt and
hurled it to the drowning man, who was then rescued by one
of the liner's own boats. But perhaps the *Mauretania*'s captain
and crew were a little disordered by the experience, for, having
sailed across the Channel on 19 February, and up the Western
Solent towards Southampton – greeted by a flight of RAF
aircraft dipping their wings in salute – they ran the ship aground
on the notorious Bramble Bank, where it stuck fast.

Waiting for Campbell at the *Mauretania*'s berth in
Southampton were a brass band, scores of friends and motoring big shots (seated on a specially erected platform), the
Mayor of Southampton, several newsreel teams accompanied
by banks of powerful arc lights, and representatives of the
BBC, for whom Campbell was due to make a live broadcast to
the nation. They sat and waited. Four tugs were sent out to the
Bramble Bank, to try to tow the liner off on the rising tide.
No luck. Three hours went by. It was now getting on for half-
past nine in the evening. Campbell was due to have been
enjoying his reception at around 7 p.m., while making his BBC
broadcast at 9.20 p.m. to a nation whose radios were powered
both by battery and, increasingly, by mains electricity. A tender
arrived. Campbell went over the side of the boat into the vessel
and set off up Southampton Water. He needn't have bothered.

A few minutes later the *Mauretania* refloated and followed him, *Blue Bird* in its hold.

The moment of triumphal return unravelled further. While still in the tender, travelling up the cold, choppy flood tide towards Southampton, Campbell was handed a telegram. It was too dark to read it. There was no torch on board. Someone fidgeted around for a box of matches. At last, in a trembling match-lit glow, Campbell read the telegram. It was from the Prime Minister, Ramsay MacDonald, and read: 'I am glad to inform you that His Majesty has been pleased to approve that the honour of knighthood be conferred upon you.' Campbell carried on up the darkling Southampton Water, on the brink of greatness, but helpless in his little barque.

Charlie Chaplin was not only in London by now, but had already been mobbed several times by adoring crowds. Waiting for Campbell, on the other hand, when he at last reached land at 10.15 p.m., were no crowds at all – only his wife, the Mayor of Southampton and a couple of friends. Everyone else had left: the band, the movie crews, the motoring fraternity grandees. Striving to salvage the greatness of the moment, Campbell insisted on making his BBC broadcast from his hotel room in Southampton. He began speaking at 10.35, by which time most of his audience had gone to bed.

But things improved. The following day, while condemned to follow the pattern first set by Sir Henry Segrave, he was at least given the treatment unstintingly. What's more, while Segrave was always made uncomfortable by the attention focused on him, Campbell delightedly accepted it as his due tribute. A renamed train – the *Blue Bird Special* – took him up to Waterloo. From there it was into the heart of London in an open Rolls-Royce in the rain and cold of late February. At the boundary to Westminster, Campbell and his wife – travelling with him, her knees shrouded by a heavy rug – clambered out of the car, shook hands with Captain J.F.C. Bennett, the Mayor of Westminster, and then clambered back in

(Campbell making great play of arranging the travel rug on his wife's lap) to drive on to Westminster Hall for speeches and public acclaim. Crowds lined the route, and mounted policemen trotted alongside the cavalcade.

Inside the Hall it was still cold enough for everyone to keep their coats on. Campbell's mother was on the platform, along with Jean; Donald was ill in bed with the flu. Herbert Morrison, Minister of Transport, and Mr G.M. Gillett, Secretary of the Department of Overseas Trade, were on hand to speechify.

Amid loud, ragged cheering from the audience, Morrison and Gillett rehearsed the usual sentiments: 'Outstanding tribute to the efficiency of British engineering . . . some who regarded the pre-eminence of this country as a thing of the past . . . served to enhance British prestige generally . . . proved once more that when the Old Country set itself the task of accomplishing some great feat, it still had an abundance of skill, courage and determination . . . can find expression in the touring car of tomorrow . . .' Campbell replied, praising 'this wonderful and historical building – a building that is wrapped up in all the important history of our great country'. He then swept out again, to continue his progress through the nation's expressions of gratitude.

On to the RAC, where Sir Arthur Stanley presented Campbell with a gold cigarette box and proposed a toast 'To Sir Malcolm and Lady Campbell'. More cheers rang out, then a chorus of *For He's a Jolly Good Fellow*, then three cheers more, then a genteel mobbing of the hero by scores of middle-aged men, murmuring 'Damn fine show, Campbell', 'Damn good' and 'All the very best.'

Campbell was pinned against a wall, his Florida tan contrasting strongly with his gleaming white smile and the pallid complexions around him. He was looking more relaxed than he had done at Westminster Hall, but his body language was still tense. As ever in public, he tended to bow his head, turning it away from a full engagement with his audience; before reminding himself of his position and visibly squaring up to meet the onlookers with a full-frontal glare or grin. When speech-making, he would twist himself away from the microphone or the camera until he was almost in profile, before swivelling back to bear down on the medium he was addressing. At such times he looked small, hunted, like a schoolboy being forced to give an account of his actions.

The luncheon at the RAC was followed in the evening by a white-tie dinner at the May Fair Hotel. This was the site of Segrave's homecoming in 1929. Lady Segrave was invited, but only managed to send a mournful refusal: 'You will understand why I do not feel quite up to mixing with people at such a banquet'. Fortunately, the American Ambassador in London – now Mr Charles G. Dawes, the former United States Vice-President – was able to attend. Better yet, he picked up the theme dear to Campbell's heart. Following the strategy his predecessor had adopted for Segrave's celebrations, Dawes began with a joke. 'Captain Campbell's achievement is primarily a British achievement. But anyway, America furnished the beach!' Indulgent laughter and applause, and then the words Campbell himself might have wanted to utter: 'The performance of Captain Campbell has done more to cement good feeling between the English-speaking people than a dozen ambassadors and fifty thousand politicians.' And then, swept away by his own rhetoric, 'Mrs Campbell is a heroine!'

It was exactly what Campbell had in mind: a larger role – the cementing of good feeling between the English-speaking people – an ambassadorial presence, a fit position for a man of his talents, a way of finally surpassing Sir Henry Segrave. He had even touched upon this a few days earlier, while still on board the *Mauretania* and yet to land. In his usual laboured way he had declared that 'People are very inclined to be continually asking, "What is the use of these attempts on the world record?"' To which the answer was, 'Very valuable lessons are learnt in the question of design. But apart from that, there's another most important aspect to it: an attempt on the record of this sort appeals very greatly indeed to the sporting element in America.'

After a succession of fluffs and stammers he declared that he had 'no hesitation in saying that these trials help cement the *very great feeling of friendship* which exists between the United States of America and Great Britain'. Hence the American Ambassador's fine words were as stirring as Joynson-Hicks's claim, back in 1928, that Campbell was a 'lineal descendant of the great men of the past . . . Drake, Frobisher and Raleigh'. 'More than a dozen ambassadors': even allowing for hyperbole, the phrase painted Campbell as no mere hobbyist but a figure of international importance. It suited him down to the ground.

While *Blue Bird* went on display in Gamage's department store in Holborn, two more things happened. Campbell arranged to record his LSR experiences for the Filmophone Flexible Records company in Camden Town; and he was knighted, on 21 February 1931. The ceremony took forty minutes. Said the new Sir Malcolm, 'The King asked me almost every conceivable kind of question about the great engine of *Blue Bird* – questions about revolutions per minute, about petrol consumption, and so on.' According to Lady Campbell, George V, a keen stamp collector, seemed uncertain as to the point of it all. He kept asking Campbell why he was 'so keen on risking his life in these record attempts and precisely what good was achieved by them when he succeeded in adding a few miles an hour to the existing figures?' To which Campbell naturally countered with the stock responses concerning national prestige and the value of the LSR to motor engineering at all levels. Which résumé was nearer to the truth?

After all, there was a certain inexplicability lurking behind Campbell's knighthood. Segrave – young, dashing, iconic – had been knighted in a moment of tremulous national optimism, his success providing a focus for the expectation that the troubles of the 1920s had been overcome, and that a bright new dispensation awaited Great Britain. Now Segrave was dead and the dream had failed to come true. In the circumstances of the early 1930s, and in comparison with the spontaneity surrounding Segrave, the tribute being paid to Malcolm Campbell seems less an upwelling of national pride and more an attempt to bring back the ambience of past success.

But there was more to it than that. Campbell did not simply walk into the space conveniently vacated by Segrave. It was not just a question of inheritance, as later record breakers would discover. If the 1920s had been plagued by nebulous anxieties concerning Britain's decline in the world, then the early 1930s were focused more sharply on the prospect of immediate national collapse. The mood had worsened but the need for a champion persisted. Campbell's constant trumpeting of the virtues of British craftsmanship and expertise and, more importantly, his doggedness, his refusal to give in, his determination to overcome – these fitted the times every bit as well as Segrave's matinee-idol glamour had suited the twenties.

And it was important that he should be a figurehead for motoring and the possibilities of the automobile. However commonplace the motor car was becoming on the roads of Britain, the fact remained that the car still spoke of modernity and progress – of an increasingly ambiguous future (filled with road accidents, exhaust fumes and traffic jams); but a future nonetheless. The economics of the Depression reflected this. The worst privations were felt in the old, quintessentially Victorian industries of the north: shipbuilding, coal, textiles. In the Midlands and the south of England, however, the new businesses turning out consumer electrical goods and motor cars were highly profitable. Ford's vast car plant at Dagenham was just opening its doors on one side of London; and a year later the magnificent Hoover factory would appear on the opposite side of town, on Western Avenue. (Tobacco products were important, too: by the second half of the 1920s Britons were the greatest *per capita* consumers of tobacco in the world; the great Art Deco Carreras Cigarette Factory opened near Euston in 1928.)

If there was to be a way out of the economic darkness, then these industries would provide it. It was the story of twentieth-century Britain: Campbell was lucky enough to have attached himself to the lively rather than to the exhausted.

Then there was the press. The great mass-circulation daily newspapers of the 1930s – the *Express*, the *Mail* and the *Herald* – still look suspiciously contemporary in their mixture of lively graphic illustrations, news reporting, trivia, periodic apocalypse and lunatic opinionising. As now, their job was alternately to appal and uplift their readerships. And when the press wanted uplift, stories built around celebrities like Campbell were ideal; or, 'We must sell speed'. They looked to Campbell to generate headlines: 'All-British Triumph' and 'How I Beat The Record'. Campbell, said a press report, had to be one of 'Our two great ambassadors of commerce', along with the Prince of Wales. Utterly at home with publicity, Campbell would obligingly 'laugh' and hold out his hand after a record run, 'to show it was steady'. He generated good copy.

And if anyone had any doubts as to the admiration Campbell commanded at this time, they only had to consider the events that unfolded barely three weeks after the King's sword had lifted from his shoulders. A by-election had been called in the St George's division of Westminster in March 1931: a two-party fight, as it turned out, between the Conservative, Duff Cooper; and Sir Ernest Petter, an Independent running on the Empire Free Trade ticket.

The svelte Alfred Duff Cooper was an ambitious Tory who, having represented Oldham for five years before being thrown out in the 1929 Election, was keen to regain a seat in Parliament. In later years he would become the Secretary for War under Baldwin, Minister of Information under Churchill and finally Ambassador to France, ending his days as the 1st Viscount

Norwich, married to Lady Diana Cooper and epitomising the high culture of the British Establishment. He had a streak of thoroughbred viciousness, too: during the Second War he helped defame P.G. Wodehouse after the latter had made his ill-advised broadcasts from occupied France. His Ministry of Information, meanwhile, with its 'Cooper's Snoopers' was the supposed inspiration for George Orwell's Ministry of Truth in *1984*.

Sir Ernest Petter, on the other hand, was a successful industrialist who made diesel engines and had fallen prey to the monocular zealotry that characterised most of the Empire Free Trade movement. This latter was a protectionist bandwagon whose desperation was an index of how far and how fast Britain's international economic position had collapsed. It urged Britain and the Empire to form a globalised trading bloc which would see the mother country through the Depression that was now blighting it. A retired vice-admiral had won the Paddington South seat for the Empire Free Trade movement in a by-election at the end of 1930. The two biggest daily papers – the *Mail* and the *Express* – were enthusiastically in favour of this unworkable scheme. So was Sir Malcolm Campbell.

While his public pronouncements were, in the convention of the time, relatively self-effacing, quick to share credit for any achievement, eager to promote the idea of British supremacy, in private Campbell would gladly contemplate his position as one of the Olympians, one of the very greatest of the great. Segrave's egotism was that of the perfectionist, a self-absorption in pursuit of a goal. Campbell's ego was the kind that demanded recognition and acclaim. And now, freshly knighted, he felt like trying out a new role: he wanted to occupy a bigger stage than even being the Fastest Man on Earth afforded. 'Jix' had called him the 'lineal descendant of the great men of the past'; the US Ambassador had described him as worth 'more than a dozen ambassadors'. In his own mind he felt certain that this was the time to expand his sphere of influence.

So he had written to Lord Beaverbrook – galvanic proprietor of the *Express* – stating his conviction that a courageous
Empire policy was essential for the prosperity of the nation –
a policy of courage, determination and action. 'We surely want
Unionism in the best sense of the word,' he asseverated, 'rather
than the mentality of Conservatism which has so unfortunately
in recent years become associated with vacillation and
hesitation. It is thus that I offer my good wishes to Sir Ernest
Petter.' The *Express* lapped this up, putting him on the front
page – 'Sir Malcolm Campbell's Political Appeal' – plus a photo.
Campbell himself was clearly comfortable with the centrality of
Empire to the new political platform; just as he was with
Protectionism, which the United States had, after all, embraced
in the form of the Smoot-Hawley Tariff, the radically destructive protectionist legislation signed by President Hoover in 1930,
which raised US import duties by as much as 50 per cent. He
was feeling his way towards a new public persona; and this was
as good an ideology as any with which to start the process.

Duff Cooper had been making heavy weather of his by-
election bid and fell on the Campbell letter at once. Making
a stump speech on the evening of 12 March at St Gabriel's
Mission Hall – in a working-class area of the constituency –
he lashed out at the titled owners of the *Express* and *Mail*: 'If
those two peers' – Lord Beaverbrook of the *Express*, Lord
Rothermere of the *Mail* – 'who have never been loyal
Conservatives, and who change their policies as rapidly as they
change the headlines in their newspapers, are allowed to win
the election, democracy in England will be at an end.' This
was a terrible cry of rage and impotence: they had used
Campbell's letter of support for Sir Ernest Petter to further
their own Empire Trade policies. Bad enough to be facing the
Big Two on the newsstands; but to have Sir Malcolm Campbell
as an opponent was too much. Cooper called the publication
of Sir Malcolm's letter 'a vile, dirty and disgusting thing', going
on to assert that 'they have got hold of Sir Malcolm Campbell'

and that they had persuaded 'a man who does one thing well to the admiration of his fellow-countrymen to pronounce his views on politics *and by means of which I have no knowledge*'.

These last words proved seriously miscalculated, sounding as they did like an imputation of venality on Campbell's part, a suggestion that he was in the pay of the news barons. An *Express* hack, lurking in the audience, jumped up and objected to the slander on Campbell and his newspaper. Uproar followed. Then Cooper said, 'The *Daily Express* has no right to buy his opinion!' This was worse; this was positively fatal. With Campbell's popularity at its absolute height, Cooper had as good as called him a paid lackey. The meeting broke up in disorder. Realising what he had done, Cooper knew he had to act fast, before the Big Two denounced him as slanderous, unpatriotic, Campbell-hating. He found himself back in his house in Gower Street, the same night of the St Gabriel's Hall meeting, hurriedly composing an open letter to Sir Malcolm.

'It is alleged,' he wrote, 'that this evening, in reply to hecklers at a public meeting, I suggested that your support of Sir Ernest Petter had been bought by the papers that uphold him. As soon as the allegation was brought to my notice I emphatically denied it, but if,' he went on humbly, 'unwittingly and unintentionally any words of mine conveyed such an impression to my audience, I, of course, not only withdraw them but regret deeply that such a misunderstanding should have arisen.' The next morning, however, he was met by the following front-page headline in the *Express*: 'Mr Duff Cooper attacks Sir Malcolm Campbell's Honour', followed by a detailed account of the previous night's activities.

Cooper set off again to try to smother the Campbell issue; this time at St Michael's School, Ebury Square, frankly confessing to his own frailty in dragging Campbell into the dirt of politics. 'When you realise the unfairness and the power at the same time of the tremendous press combination,' he complained, 'it is enough to make a man angry, and I do not think sincere anger is a thing one needs to be ashamed of, although it is very often a thing one regrets.' One could scarcely blame him for articulating his frustration. Even Stanley Baldwin, leader of the Conservatives, was moved to denounce Lords Beaverbrook and Rothermere for grasping at power without responsibility – 'the prerogative,' as he put it, borrowing from Kipling, 'of the harlot throughout the ages'.

To Campbell all this was intoxicating. His vision and his tenacity had seen him go in two years from one of the worst points in his life to this golden apogee. He was impatient to capitalise on it. At the same time as Cooper was prostrating himself in Ebury Square, Campbell had decided to make an appearance not far away, in Caxton Hall, to state his case amid 'wild scenes'. A crowd of around three thousand people turned up, hundreds of whom were refused admission. Lord Beaverbrook was also present, and Sir Ernest Petter, who arrived late, needed an escort to force a way through.

Campbell led off, his speech beginning: 'This is the first time I have ever been on a political platform, and it requires more courage than getting into a motor car and travelling at 240 miles an hour!' He had to pause here, to let the cheering and applause subside. 'There is no getting away from the fact that as a nation we are in an awful mess, and something has got to be done. Our unemployment is increasing daily and our business is falling away. But thank God our credit is still good and so long as it remains so we can do something.'

So far, so good. But Campbell was neither a politician nor a rhetorician. As always, when left to assemble his own prose, he was unable to prevent his themes from disintegrating, even as he spoke. 'Frankly,' he went on, 'it is no use dilly-dallying any longer. Surely we should regard our Dominions as our kith and kin and children. We should be generous with our children, and in my opinion this Empire Free Trade is the only way to deal with them.'

Here he changed tack, in order to deal specifically with the

Duff Cooper question. 'Personally, I do not believe he made that allegation.' A woman's voice cried out, 'He didn't!' Another voice added, 'It was the *Daily Express*.' Composing himself, Campbell went on, 'If he did make it, I believe he made it in the heat of the moment, and I am sure he would be the first to take it back. I have never met him, but I should like to do so. As to the question whether I have been bought, I have never been paid, and never shall be.' More stirring verities followed; then the plea, 'Why cannot these political fights be carried on with fair play and in a sporting way, without person-alities? Why should the parties get down to the gutter to pick up mud to sling at their opponents?' Cheering greeted this point. In conclusion, Campbell got a grip and veered back to his original theme, which was, 'What we want to do is to make this country a really fit place for our children. So we must do something that will put this country on its feet once more in the sun. Where it has always been up to now.'

The people were duly satisfied and cheered again, lustily, as he closed. He then had to go out on to the balcony overhanging the entrance hall and do his speech all over again, for the benefit of the crowds who had been unable to get in for the first performance. Lord Beaverbrook and Sir Ernest Petter were left to pick up what crumbs he had left them. 'Famous Speed King's Stirring Speech,' duly appeared on the front pages; along with 'Refutation of Slanderous Attack,' and a letter from Lady Somerleyton of Suffolk, who wrote, 'As one who knows the intrepid sportsman and gentleman, Sir Malcolm Campbell, well, I wish to protest most strongly against Mr Duff Cooper's endeavour to besmirch the honour of a man whom to know is to respect.'

Four days later Campbell was at it again, this time at the Victoria Palace Theatre. Now, though, it was not enough simply to appear and acknowledge the crowd's devotion. He may have been called 'the D'Artagnan of modern days' by the *Daily Express* that very morning, but the rules of public self-disclosure obliged him to account for the fact that he was making his second major public appearance in a week, on an issue of national importance. The Duff Cooper question had been left to answer itself for the time being. Campbell's own motives required closer inspection.

'If I had followed my own inclinations,' he declared, trimming his position from that of the bold adventurer of a few days earlier, 'I would not have become involved in this by-election.' Nevertheless, 'I felt it was my bounden duty to come forward.' Declaring himself an 'ardent' believer in the cause of Empire Free Trade, he outlined the necessity of 'assisting our Colonies and ourselves by putting up a tariff and protecting our much-harassed manufacturers'. He found himself having to gloss his earlier interventions. Before, he had been a vocal celebrity; now he was an active participant and was feeling the effects. People had asked, 'Why do I not keep to the racing track and leave politics alone.' The answer? 'Racing is merely a hobby, and I have been a businessman all my life. I am surely entitled to my views – and at any rate, I have the courage of my convictions!' Skimpy though this defence may have been, it worked. Cheers rang, predictably, through the building.

Two days after this speech, on 19 March, the by-election was held. Duff Cooper won the seat for the Conservatives, with a majority of 5710 over Sir Ernest Petter. This was well down from 16,154 at the previous election, but evidently not the deafening victory Beaverbrook and Rothermere had hoped for. The Empire Free Trade movement went into a sharp decline shortly after and never really resurfaced. Campbell, on the other hand, took the result as a promising testimonial to his own demagogic powers.

12

Birkin's Lament

⟪◉ ◉⟫

In the meantime, in this increasingly dislocated age, what was happening to the fast set at Brooklands? After all, as the twenties became the thirties, so began Brooklands' long moment of critical self-improvement. Nineteen-thirty was the year in which the ladies' lounge, bijou golf course, Members' Lounge Grand Staircase and so on were added. A bathroom and changing rooms were tacked on to the Gents' cloakrooms, while the *Autocar* put up a board in the paddock displaying the names of holders of the LSR. Newspaper ads were subtly doctored in search of a less cliquish tone: 'A Jolly Crowd – but no crowding!' they promised, as well as an 'Old Crocks Race' on the 1930 August Bank Holiday and a reduced admission price of 2/6d. For a time it worked: that same year saw sixty-seven world records taken at Brooklands, as well as – following a rejigging of the events calendar – an improvement in attendance figures.

In 1931, though, a mere fifteen records were taken at Brooklands, as Montlhéry – a svelte little oval French autodrome built in 1924 by M. Alexandre Lamblin, just to the south of Paris, expressly for the purpose of record breaking –

made its presence increasingly felt. And while Montlhéry became known as 'the French Brooklands', the original Brooklands was losing business. Even fewer records were set there in 1932. The venue was being squeezed both by the general economic shrinkages of the 1930s (Bentley Motors had gone symptomatically bust in the early summer of 1931, its remains being consumed by Rolls-Royce) and by the slow but relentless arrival of alternative racetracks.

Quite apart from Montlhéry and all the other Continental circuits, Donington Park, in Derbyshire, was about to offer car racing; while the streets of the Isle of Man had been used as a racetrack since 1904 and were still going strong. A few more years would go by and a new purpose-built circuit would open at Crystal Palace, in south London. Britain's concept of motor sport was maturing. When Grand Prix racing finally returned to Britain, in 1935, it was at Donington, not Weybridge. Brooklands' frivolous, DIY-inspired glory days had long gone. Companies such as Riley, Austin and MG were now turning out small, neat, efficient, businesslike cars. Pre-war lash-ups and aero monsters were either progressively uncompetitive or banned as unsafe. Locke King's concrete extravagance was appearing in an increasingly unsympathetic light. And then, in 1932, Tim Birkin blurted out his secret agony in *Full Throttle*.

Thirty-six-year-old Sir Henry 'Tim' Birkin, Bt., was one of the biggest stars at Brooklands. Indeed, for many he was the biggest star: Le Mans winner of 1929 and 1931, famed for his strenuous, no-holds-barred driving technique, often at the wheel of a Bentley – which, much as it delighted the crowds, caused anguish to W.O. Bentley himself. According to Bentley, 'Tim's weaknesses were his love of playing to the gallery and his complete ruthlessness with his cars. I know of nobody before or since who could tear up a piece of machinery so swiftly and completely as Tim.' Campbell, too, was an unregenerate car-mangler ('At times he was pushing the floorboards out of the car,' Villa complained. 'It was useless to explain to him that a

throttle could only open fully; after that, if you kept pressing
your foot down, something had to give. And in fact I collected
quite a variety of badly bent throttle pedals, rods and levers
as a result.'). But even Campbell had to yield place to Birkin.
Moustachioed, clad in impeccable white overalls, a trademark
spotted scarf round his neck and a triple-buckled kidney protec-
tor round his abdomen, Birkin was emblematic of a type: slightly
built withal, yet careless, swashbuckling, motor racing's Errol
Flynn, every bit as celebrated in the motor-racing world as
Segrave and Campbell, Kidston and Dunfee.

The savagery of his driving was equalled only by the zeal
with which he managed to construct a more or less wholly
unsatisfactory life away from the track. He sank much of his
fortune (inherited from the family lace business) into running
a stable of Bentleys. His other great pastime was philander-
ing. His wife finally divorced him after discovering one of his
more outrageous infidelities in the Blakeney Hotel, Norfolk,
where they had previously spent their honeymoon.

Later on he threw his resources into tuning sports cars,
developing a tractor with self-cleaning wheels, and starting up
a franchised slot-car business, for use by fairground operators.
In its made-to-measure domestic version, the Brooklands Race
Game was a sophisticated proto-Scalextric whose cars were
realistic, had to have their tyres changed after a few hours'
wear and had their laps ticked off by an automated lap counter.
The funfair version was operated by carneys who would
guarantee the winner a first prize of twenty Players cigarettes
in exchange for an entrance fee of sixpence. By the expedient
of lying to Birkin about their takings, they drove his firm,
Miniature Speedways Ltd, out of business.

At around the same time he lost the financial support which
had up until then been provided by the ineffable millionairess
the Hon. Dorothy Paget. Paget's main interests in life were
racing and women – rather like Birkin himself – and yet it was
rumoured that Birkin was the only man she had ever loved. It

was this infatuation which allowed her to spend thousands of pounds supporting his obsession with Bentley racers. But when Bentley Motors of Cricklewood went under, so did her enthusiasm for the sport. The cash dried up and Birkin was left merely with the fag-end of his inheritance. Deliverance finally came in the form of septicaemia which he contracted in 1933 after touching a hot exhaust pipe in Tripoli, and which soon after killed him. Paget's enormous weight gain in later life (she weighed well over twenty stone) was provoked, they said, by despair on his death; a despair which left her obese and reclusive in Chalfont St Giles, so vast that she was unable to get into her own car.

Most of *Full Throttle* is a straightforward and convention- ally polite enumeration of successes and failures, war service in the RFC, cars bought and sold. Birkin takes us into his confidence by announcing at one point, 'If my younger read- ers had pictured me as tall and broad and clear-cut, barking out instructions in a voice like a knife, I am heartily sorry; I am quite small and I do stammer.' He then ups his plaus- ibility by sharing with us the ennui of demobbed employment, complaining that his life 'was bounded by the four walls of an office' in which 'each day would seem more vapid and tedious than the last'. Fortunately for him, he had enough money 'to look around for an occupation, and not accept the first that offered' – at which point, the legend of road and track is born and we go behind the scenes with daring Tim Birkin, the Bentley butcher.

All of which makes his attack on Brooklands, several pages later, the more startling. After his pleasantly orthodox start, Tim Birkin, playboy star of the circuit, suddenly rounds on the cradle of his fame in language which – especially compared with the normal banalities of such books – looks amazingly intemperate. He excoriates the track, arguing that 'It has only kept its importance so long, because it has never had a rival in England since its creation. I say frankly that it could not have existed for more than a season in America or on the Continent, while we have been perforce satisfied with it for 20 years.' In fact, it is 'without exception, the most out-of-date, inadequate and dangerous track in the world'. He goes on to insist that 'meetings at Brooklands can only be considered as a joke, if jokes may be combined with such attendant perils.' One might point out that in its twenty-six years of active life, twenty-one people (spectators and competitors) died at Brooklands. This was not bad by the standards of the day.

But Birkin had bigger fish to fry: 'It is amusing to have a race or two, as long as they are not to be taken too seriously. But otherwise the place has become a farce.' The worst of it? Probably not the super-specific monotony of the circuit's shape, but, of course, the handicapping. 'A system of handicapping has been made essential, which affords the ludicrous sight of a car capable of 135 mph chasing round after a midget with a maximum of 105.'

Much of Birkin's fury must have stemmed from the fact that even as he threw his dwindling finances into providing himself with competitive cars (in particular a fierce red single-seater supercharged four-and-a-half-litre Bentley), so the Brooklands management fixed the odds against him, merely in order to generate spuriously close finishes. But then everyone knew this already. As was pointed out on the BARC race cards, 'Prize winners of any previous Handicap at this meeting may be re-handicapped at the discretion of the Handicappers.' In other words, there was a positive disincentive to do well in an early race because of what might happen to your chances in a subsequent race. Or, as fellow Brooklands celebrity Charles Brackenbury observed, 'Fast cars tend to be handicapped right out of it. If you want to win races, use a slow one.' Meanwhile, Birkin's diatribe had provoked so many hurt and baffled rebuttals from Brooklands diehards that he felt obliged to insert an apology in later editions – partly out of embarrassment, partly so as not to harm sales.

Where had all this rage come from? Failure animated his attack. There was the failure of Brooklands to provide a world-class racetrack on which he could hone his skills. There was his own failure to capitalise on these skills, whatever the opportunities. The parochialism of Brooklands and the way it ran its races had left Birkin, and those like him, in an amateurs' limbo, a realm where significant improvement was impossible. And, somewhere in there, was his failure relative to that other Brooklands doyen, Sir Malcolm Campbell.

After all, he, 'Tim' Birkin, was without a doubt the better, more daring, more naturally talented driver. He was the more committed sportsman. He had won Le Mans, twice, and had driven in proper, full-blooded Grands Prix all over Europe: real racing, rather than simply driving fast in a straight line. He was also an entrepreneur like Campbell, although without any of the latter's instinct for hanging on to his own money. And, like Campbell, he was an energetic womaniser. If anyone should have been the talk of the town, it should have been him. And yet here was the freshly minted Sir Malcolm, smug, middle-aged, unnecessarily well-heeled, relishing the acclaim and the knighthood and the opportunities for extending his wealth ('Can you tell me how I can make £10,000 as quickly and easily?' Campbell is reputed to have said around this time, with respect to the rewards that came with the LSR. 'If you can, then I'll drop the whole business.') After all, what was Campbell *for*? How had his success become so eclipsing? Somehow he seemed to have turned himself into that thirties phenomenon the Man of Destiny, without evincing any special skill or talent other than a capacity for sheer persistence. It seemed so unfair.

Of course, Brooklands was one of the last places where one might have hoped to get away from Campbell's overweening presence. Unlike Birkin or, for that matter, Segrave, Campbell liked the place so much that he became one of a handful of drivers to race there in all three decades of its active existence. Even when busy with his LSR attempts, he would still find time to come down for two or three races on a weekend in the season. Certainly he did well there, frequently winning or at least coming in the top three. The mean-minded would argue that Campbell was so attached to Brooklands because what successes he enjoyed were the result of his knowing the track back to front and being rich enough to be able to afford the latest cars.

He also aroused a degree of animosity by using the place as a formal and informal car brokerage – buying an expensive new Sunbeam or Bugatti, displaying it to advantage in competition and then selling it on, often at a profit, to some guileless acquaintance eager to succeed. And he could capitalise on the certainty that whereas in polite society he would have been regarded as no more than a twitchy, egotistical *arriviste* (and never as dazzling a personality as Glen Kidston or Woolf Barnato), here in the context of Brooklands he could legitimately hold his own with the likes of Earl Howe and the Duke of Richmond and Gordon.

On the other hand, Brooklands enjoyed at least some reciprocity in its relationship with Campbell: as his fame grew, Brooklands benefited. As long as Campbell the LSR hero was keen to keep chasing down to the track, then he was welcome as an attraction in his own right, something to add to the golf course and ladies' lounge. He maintained his large and prominent Campbell Shed for five years. He paraded the various manifestations of *Blue Bird* (with all their historical intimations of Parry Thomas's *Babs* and Zborowski's *Chitties*) both in the paddock and on the track.

Brooklands encouraged his sponsoring companies to put up hoardings with his name and face on them. It inaugurated a Campbell Trophy Race, run on a little circuit within the main circuit, built in the latter half of the 1930s. This was, of course, known as the Campbell Circuit: just over two miles long, laid out by Campbell (whose experience of racetracks other than Brooklands was not huge, and was a decade out of touch, besides) and with a corner fawningly named after Earl Howe. And, at the very end of the track's life, Campbell even cornered the shares in Brooklands (Weybridge) Ltd, the company which took over the running of the place in the second half of the thirties.

And yet, however willingly Howe put up with Campbell's ego (as did the sycophantic P.J. Wallace: 'He was a most likeable person and the friend of everybody who raced at Brooklands'), there were others who wouldn't. Brooklands diehard Charles Brackenbury, for one, found Campbell deeply annoying, and let his irritation show. Brackenbury was, in any event, known around the place as a prankster, a 'devil' for tricks and jokes. But he was especially antagonistic to Campbell, whose surface charm at Brooklands was increasingly being replaced by his overwhelming sense of his own importance.

During the 1930s Castrol used a large billboard by the main entrance to the track for its poster campaigns. Shortly before one of the big race meetings, Castrol put up a head-and-shoulders poster of Campbell, promoting the firm's oil products. The sight of Campbell's enormous face was too much for Brackenbury, who, according to Norton Bracey, an old Brooklands hand, said, the night before the meeting, '"Look, I'm going to paint a moustache on it." And he got some brown paint and a ladder and he painted a moustache on Campbell.' The effect of this iconoclasm? 'Campbell went round the bend, and there was a hell of a row.' Not content with that, Brackenbury 'was always doing things to Campbell's car. He'd put bangers on the damn thing, which he'd got from America. And as soon as Campbell started the car up, the thing went up in smoke and with a hell of a bang.' This was even more gratifying: 'Campbell would come rushing up to the clubhouse saying, "I know who's done this! It's you, Charles! It's you!"'

If Brackenbury was the most active and enthusiastic tormentor of Campbell, there were plenty of others who simply failed to get on with him. The Hon. Brian Lewis was still around Brooklands, but scarcely a friend of Campbell's on account of his adulterous liaison with Lady Campbell. 'Taso' Mathieson – sporting motorist, writer and Brooklands racer – was no fan, either: 'I did not like him.' Others simply knew him as 'full of himself' or as a 'cad'. One infuriated friend even went on record as saying to Campbell, 'The trouble you are up against is that you have a unique personality. Most of us have a normal line; sometimes we are a bit above that line, and sometimes we are a bit below it. But there is nevertheless a normal line we follow generally. You have *no* normal line. You are either the most charming person one can meet in a day's march; or you are the most perfect son of a bitch it is possible to imagine.'

And then there was John Cobb.

13

Honest John Takes on Sir Malcolm

《@ @》

John Rhodes Cobb was born on 2 December 1899, the third
son of Rhodes Hawtyn Cobb and Florence Harriet Cobb. The
dynastically named Rhodes Hawtyn Cobb's profession has been
described as 'City broker', 'produce merchant', 'Chairman of
the Falkland Islands Company' and latterly, a 'breeder of pedigree Jersey cattle'. What is certain is that he was a wealthy,
upper-middle-class stalwart of the Kingston and Esher area,
south-west of London, and lived in enough style to be able to
afford a substantial red-brick Victorian house – The Grove –
with surrounding land, a complement of servants and five children: Stanley, Olive, Gerard, John and Eileen. The Grove sat
amid low lanes and pastures just north of Esher village. The
same London and South Western railway line which bordered
the Brooklands track passed a quarter of a mile to the south,
on a long, high embankment; the River Mole meandered round
to the north.

In a world of quiet, undemonstrative privilege, young John
Cobb grew up surrounded by under-gardeners, sleeping walls,
gravel drives, the unthreatening manicured suburban countryside of Esher. It was a pleasant existence. There were lanes to

bicycle along; early motor cars to be explored; there were two brothers and two sisters for company; there was a large and apparently stable family headed by Florence Harriet, the Cobb matriarch. From his earliest years John Cobb was a big, shy, boy, the archetypal introvert whose physical scale merely emphasises his reticence. But the family was accommodating; the brothers and sisters – especially his younger sister, Eileen – were close. If Campbell's upbringing was an assault course of vituperations and Segrave's was interrupted by deaths, remarriages and relocations, Cobb's was, in comparison, stolid, respectable and benign.

Things only started to go wrong in the early stages of the First World War, by which time Cobb was a pupil at Eton, in Mr Rayner-Wood's house (overlapping at the school with Segrave for a year). In the summer of 1915 he contracted spinal tuberculosis and spent the next eighteen months flat on his back, in a canvas straitjacket. It should be pointed out that there was nothing particularly extraordinary in this: tuberculosis – pulmonary and skeletal – was at that time the single biggest killer of people of all ages in the West and continued to be so until the 1930s. Treatments ranged from the straightforward (endless bed rest in a sanatorium) to the determinedly sadistic (encasing the patient in plaster of Paris, the patient being hung upside down for the duration of the actual encasement, followed by months of degrading immobility). Being stuck in bed in a confining vest would have been, in a purely medical sense, both normal and acceptable.

It meant, though, that Cobb's liveliest mid-teenage years were spent trapped, unable to move, dependent on his mother and a nurse, and living with the knowledge that he might quite possibly join the millions who had already died as a consequence of the disease. He survived: but he never returned to Eton (where the sum total of his achievements amounted to appearances in the House Junior Cricket Team, the Lower Boys' Gym Competition and the House Fives Competition).

Nor did he add lustre to the family name by fighting in the Great War, being refused by the Army Board as unfit. He went to Cambridge University but did not complete his time there, the next step on the road to self-actualisation. His radically undermined school education left him unable to pass what were known as the Complete Examinations, a generic test taken by all undergraduates in their second term. Having gone up to Trinity Hall in October 1919, he flunked out in the spring of 1920 and never got near to taking his degree. It was five years, in other words, of illness, confinement and wholesale non-achievement.

In the end his parents got him a job with the family firm: Anning & Cobb, a fur brokers' in Lime Street, in the heart of the City of London. His father was one of the company's directors, but the business was effectively run by his uncle, E.R. Cobb. A few years into young John's apprenticeship as a fur broker, the firm decamped to Arthur Street, near the Monument, a staid and dingy thoroughfare. Warehouses on both sides of the Thames held the pelts in storage. Brother Gerard, as it happened, became a director. London was the centre of the world fur trade, and business was brisk but scarcely glamorous – dealing with pelts, furs, skins; brokering from Canada to Russia; reporting to the London Fur Trade Association; and dealing with the minutiae of cat fur (sheared and dyed), bastard chinchilla, jackal, electric musquash, opossum, wombat and beaver.

Cobb continued to live at his parents' home, commuted from Esher every day, took his holidays at a time convenient to the firm, grew from a large, thoughtful, silent, introverted boy into a large, thoughtful, silent, introverted man. If that had been all, then it would have meant a life of undistinguished repression combined with across-the-board conformity, the whole leavened only by the fact that fur brokers between the wars could make a healthy income out of their trade.

Only there were cars as well, to provide a vital squint into another kind of existence. By the age of eight Cobb and his elder brother Gerard – their devilry finding easy purchase in a prosperous and tolerant home life – had made off with a 1904 De Dion belonging to a family friend in order to taste speed for themselves. By the age of eleven John and Gerard had also driven an old Minerva – given to them by an indulgent uncle – around the lanes of Surrey. By the age of twelve the young Cobb had made his way down to the recently opened Brooklands to watch Percy Lambert drive around in his Talbot. Impressed by the weight-saving techniques used on racing cars at that time he went home and drilled plenty of holes in his bicycle. When his father found out, 'The balloon went up,' Cobb said, showing his lifelong talent for periphrasis and litotes, 'in no uncertain manner.'

Cars, speed, motion, all spoke profoundly to the boy, and continued speaking all the way through illness and failure. When Brooklands reopened after the war in 1920, Cobb was back there, monosyllabic and contemplative. The hysterical sense of deliverance felt by the men who had survived the Great War was meaningless to him. He had none of Segrave's zesty ambition, nor Campbell's superabundant nervous energy. The terrors he had faced had centred around illness, boredom, anxiety, loneliness and failure. Getting behind the wheel of a fast car would be, simply, his liberation from the past.

He was not the only one in his family who felt a need to compete. Another uncle, Francis Cobb, supposedly bet that he could cover the Grand National Course at Aintree while wearing a lounge suit, carrying a pair of binoculars over his shoulder and smoking a cigar, on the back of a one-eyed horse. More plausibly, both he and Cobb's father were keen oarsmen. Rhodes Cobb was stroke of the Kingston Rowing Club crew which won the Steward's Cup at the Henley Regatta in 1884. Francis Cobb rowed in the same crew at bow. Rhodes Cobb went on to spend more than twenty years as Vice-President of the Kingston Rowing Club. Both men were not only oarsmen but also notoriously uncommunicative. Large, too – a characteristic, along with the reticence, which found its way into John Cobb, forever a head taller than those around him, bulky-framed, hungry for a form of competition that involved neither excessive teamwork nor agility.

Brooklands was his good fortune, which he exploited with breathtaking slowness. Instead of rushing out and buying himself the first car he could find and driving around in that, he started at the very bottom, finding himself a position as a riding mechanic with a gloomy and sarcastic veteran named R. Warde, who raced a Fiat. The riding mechanic's job, at the start of the 1920s, was to sit in the passenger seat of a racing car and drudge for the driver – by working various manual pumps to keep the car going, and helping with tyre-changing or mechanical repairs whenever the machine came to a halt. Cobb's mute stoicism and willingness to please got him one ride after another. He moved up to work as riding mechanic with Sir Ernest Eldridge, who was racing the giant aero-engined Fiat hybrid *Mephistopheles*. Cobb characterised Eldridge's driving style as 'a bit exciting'.

Then, in 1925, he finally drove Warde's Fiat on his own account, coming third in his first race. This was a good five years after he had begun haunting the track. It had taken Segrave a year to establish himself as a contender. Campbell had been winning at Brooklands as soon as he had thought to race a car there in 1911. Cobb, by comparison, lived in a world so marked by failure and inhibition that, for him, thoroughness became indistinguishable from a desperate desire not to be seen to get anything wrong. So modest was he in his ambitions that he even won the approval of Parry Thomas, at whose workshops the Fiat was kept, and whose normal contumely was kept at bay by Cobb's humility and apparent lack of ego.

Parry Thomas must also have seen something of himself in the large, serious, pear-shaped young man earnestly enquiring about racing techniques and car set-ups. Like Parry Thomas,

Cobb was out of the run of things at Brooklands, being neither smooth, nor loud, nor worryingly plausible. Like Parry Thomas, Cobb evidently saw something more in motor-car racing than simply going round and round a track, then heading off to the bar. For both of them it was a matter of personal necessity, rather than mere recreation.

Cobb was even invited down to Pendine Sands in April 1926, as part of the support team for Parry Thomas's successful LSR bid. This was shortly before an unexpected intervention in the General Strike of May that year, during which he drove a London bus. What possessed Cobb (while Segrave was racing through the dark in a fast car, chasing insurgents) to take action against the evil that was Bolshevism? The innate right-wing responses of anyone living in Esher? Or the desire to drive a large and interesting vehicle – in this case, a London General Omnibus Company B Type bus; the sort with an open top and a staircase curving sinuously up the back? An unlikely moment of glory is supposed to have come when a picket attempted to climb into the cab where Cobb was sitting behind the wheel. Cobb knocked him out with one blow and carried on to collect some passengers.

A few months later, at Whitsun, he found himself driving *Babs* in a race at Brooklands. Cobb struggled round at just over 111 mph, while Parry Thomas managed over 127 mph. Cobb pronounced the car 'horrible'. Still, he had determined that his future lay in the solitary endeavour of driving a car big enough for him to fit into, on a track big enough for the car to fit into. At last he bought himself the huge ex-René Thomas V12 Delage in 1929, winning his first race in it in August of that year, but nearly killing himself. 'Not so good,' he murmured, after almost going over the top of the banking while overtaking another car.

From the start, his devotion to Brooklands was unconditional. The track's privacy – its cordon sanitaire against the rest of the world – its relatively non-judgemental ways, its heterogeneous personality (planes, cars, motorcycles; the rich, the impoverished, the plainly mad) allowed him to lose himself there. It was also just up the road from where he lived at The Grove and not too bad a drive down from his office in the City. He drove a twelve-cylinder Sunbeam in the British Racing Drivers' Club 500-mile race in October, gave himself 'near palpitations' avoiding another large car – apparently out of control on the Members' Banking – came third, and won £50 in prize money. He took a one-hour Class A record in his Delage, on the Outer Circuit. Eventually he decided that, while the Delage was good enough in its way, perhaps he would have a car specially built for him so that he could both race round Brooklands and take some of the duller, more arduous world records. He went to the Thomson & Taylor engineering company and asked if Reid Railton would design him a one-off special.

Cobb had found his place, after an uncertain start: well-heeled London fur broker, nearing thirty, takes his motoring hobby seriously, invests himself in the playground that is Brooklands, centres – indeed, builds – his life round it, having no other real pastimes (squash and golf get a look-over, but only tangentially), no wife, and a family home with all found, just a few miles away.

The threat of melancholy was never entirely far off, though. First, there had been the tribulation of his teenage illness, followed by the failure of his academic career. Then, when he had begun to settle at Brooklands and befriended one of its most celebrated inhabitants, Parry Thomas – this mentor, fifteen years his senior – was killed at Pendine. Having collected himself after that loss, Cobb faced a greater one: his father's suicide in 1930.

Rhodes Cobb was a depressive who, for the seven months prior to his death, had been in and out of a nursing home at Hillingdon, Middlesex, as the result of a nervous breakdown.

According to his physician, a Dr Stillwell, the sixty-eight-year-old Rhodes Cobb 'unnecessarily worried himself about his health'. Nevertheless, he was allowed to come and go as he liked. On the afternoon of 7 August 1930 he had the family chauffeur collect him from Hillingdon and drive him back to The Grove. There he found they had visitors, and having developed an aversion to social contact, decided to go for a walk around the grounds. Later on, a shot was heard. Eventually William Penfold, the gardener, was sent off by one of the maids to look for the unfortunate master of the house. He found Cobb's body, still in a seated position, a shotgun resting against its chest. A length of string attached the trigger of the shotgun to one of his feet. Cobb had turned the gun on himself, fired it by pulling the string and blown part of his head off. The coroner recorded a verdict of suicide while of unsound mind.

Although suicide had been destigmatised to the extent that its victims could now be buried in Church of England cemeteries, the act itself was still a criminal offence (and would remain so until 1961). And however much sympathy was extended to the remaining members of the family, society still took a narrow view of the morality of ending one's own life. Millions had been killed in the war; tens of thousands died of accident and illness each year. Suicide, at this time, whatever one's mental distress, was seen as perilously close to self-indulgence. Rhodes Cobb had written a suicide note; it was not allowed to be read out in court.

John Cobb tried to deal with this disaster by immuring himself further in the world he had safely ordered around himself. Work on his special racer continued. He spent his weekends driving his Delage around Brooklands and living at home with his mother. His father's estate was worth well over a quarter of a million pounds and was divided among the children. The rest of the family had dispersed, but he stayed behind: the youngest son, the one who had endured a near-fatal illness, the one ill at ease in society, he now saw a benefit in remaining at The Grove – a benefit both to himself and to his mother, who would otherwise have become a kind of tragic lay prioress, ministered to by the sisterhood of her maids and cooks. He became even more convinced of the need to impose certainty, order, restraint on his life. The apparent foundations of his bourgeois world were horribly fragile. He would have to move even more cautiously; be even more sure of his ground.

At Brooklands people were unsure what to make of Cobb, even after a decade of regular appearances. Wedded to his deep circumspection and fear of seeming inadequate was a conspicuously English form of withdrawal, which could be read as either simple reserve or taciturnity. Introversion is easily mistaken for mute hostility, especially when found in a large, pensive thirty-year-old whose features naturally tended to settle in an accusatory frown. His silences felt like disapproval and when dressed in his cloth racing helmet (no hard hat for him) and his all-in-one racing suit, he looked like a gigantic surly toddler.

And yet those who got through Cobb's morose-seeming exterior, his aversion to novelty and his horror of being thought a fool, became part of a lively and sustaining coterie. Given the right company, he could emerge from under the cloud of past events. Those who got to know him found him 'delightful, fun, unpretentious'. He enjoyed socialising, being 'reserved when he first met people; but once he warmed to them he was great fun'. Small, understated anecdotes cluster around his friendships; anecdotes providing the most modest frisson imaginable, anecdotes which testify to Cobb's desire to purge his life of undue eventfulness.

There was the time, for instance, he got into a dispute with G.E.T. Eyston. George Eyston – racer, record breaker, pan-enthusiast – was one of Cobb's circle. Following a needle match in the 1932 British Empire Trophy at Brooklands, Eyston found himself just edged into second place by Cobb. Eyston accepted the results without complaint, only for his backers to insist on lodging a protest: Cobb, they claimed, had deliberately obstructed him. The Brooklands stewards convened for two and a half hours, finally awarding Eyston the race and demoting Cobb to second.

Well, Cobb may have been a decent fellow, but he was tenacious, and had a highly durable sense of right and wrong. He insisted on an appeal. The matter took on a life of its own and went to arbitration at the RAC, where both parties were represented by legal counsel and evidence was called. Eventually the RAC found in favour of Cobb and re-awarded him the race. And yet, even after this turgid and potentially rancorous dispute, Cobb's friendship with Eyston remained inviolate. Immediately after the judgement the two disappeared to get drunk together as if the whole event had been some kind of dim charade.

Or again: in a conjunction of the domestic, the social and the timorous, there was the time Cobb and his friend the Hon. Brian Lewis fell asleep while listening to his mother's battery-powered radio. The battery died on them, and when Cobb awoke he was so dismayed by what he'd done that he and Lewis physically fled the house, not to return until his mother had got over the incident. (It was not only his mother who held him in thrall: when Dame Ethel Locke King – as she had become, following her work for the Red Cross – once had him round for an official luncheon, he arrived at the kitchens instead of the reception room – where he remained for some time before being rescued; then hid in the corner of the room he was supposed to be in, in case Dame Ethel caught his eye and made him say something.)

Then there was the time that the incorrigible Charles Brackenbury took Cobb to the motorbikers' café at Brooklands. This place was normally shunned by the car drivers, partly because the bikers were on the margins of society; and partly because, according to the similarly incorrigible Charles

Mortimer, 'The menu was shocking and consisted almost solely of tea, bread and butter, toast and poached eggs. The tables and chairs were dilapidated, there were no tablecloths and the cups were cracked and the saucers and plates chipped.'

The great joke of the day was to flick pats of butter up on to the ceiling, leave them there and, as the heat of the room gradually melted the adhering surface, watch them fall back on the heads of incautious customers sitting beneath. A specially clean table was often laid as a trap under the worst collection of pats. One day Brackenbury – who, as Campbell-baiting practical joker, preferred the cheeky indigence of the bikers' café to the nullities of the Members' restaurant – brought Cobb in. Cobb was fresh from work and immaculate in his business suit. He headed directly for the clean table. 'No, not there,' Brackenbury cried. 'Why not? It's the only one that isn't filthy,' Cobb said. Brackenbury led him to the table where Charles Mortimer and his friends were lounging. They sat down and an 'avalanche of rancid butter' collapsed on to the rogue table. Cobb at last said, 'See what you mean. Glad you told me.' For this quiet appreciation of the joke and a modest refusal to take offence, Cobb was judged sound; his soundness predicated not least on the fact that as a member of the upper crust (Eton, City job, wealth) and Brooklands celebrity, he was displaying a real unpretentiousness in entering the bikers' café in the first place. 'After that, he was a frequent visitor and always welcome.'

Several years later Mortimer had decided to move from motorcycles to motor cars and was desperate to buy an old Sunbeam racer which Cobb wanted to dispose of. The asking price was £500; Mortimer could only raise £250. Nevertheless, a meeting was arranged at Thomson & Taylor. There Cobb said pleasantly to Mortimer, 'Charles [Brackenbury] tells me you're interested in the Sunbeam. Would you like to try it?' At this point Mortimer had to admit that while he thought £500 a reasonable price, he only had half that amount to spend. Had this been Campbell's deal, Mortimer would have been shown the door. But Cobb mused for a while, before saying, 'Well, if that's it and you would enjoy driving it, why not have it?' And Mortimer went off delightedly with his purchase, the generous Cobb thereafter being 'very much on a pedestal as far as I was concerned'.

In most respects he led a life of blameless gratifications, shared with those who understood him. He liked to mix Martini cocktails by substituting dry sherry for the dash of vermouth (a trick he learned in the States). He once feigned drunkenness for a joke. He almost never lost his temper. Intimates often referred to him as 'Honest John'. The one biography written of him, by his friend the Bentley Boy Sammy Davis, is a muted love-letter from one Englishman to another. And there are, effectively, two sorts of photographs of him in existence. The official, posed sort, bring out the worst in him. He scowls, stares at the camera with dead-eyed mistrust. He looks like tough-guy actor William Bendix (star of *The Babe Ruth Story*). But in other, rarer, more spontaneous pictures, he smiles broadly, the epitome of relaxed cordiality. Those with him are often doing the same. Unlike the edgy, self-obsessed Campbell, Cobb was good company.

And in both sorts of photograph what is noticeable is how often those pictured with Cobb are looking at him with a degree of protective concern that might almost be taken for affection. Even Reid Railton, normally an example of the sheerest detachment, seems to respond to him.

Women, on the other hand, were a problem. Back at The Grove, Cobb's world was a markedly feminine one, his mother and the live-in servants, Edith, Mary and another Edith, setting a calm, domesticating tone. At Brooklands, however, women struck a distressingly false note in the otherwise invariant world he had fashioned for himself. And yet, if there was one essential component, one key to the eager toleration of motoring by the smart set, and in particular to the overall likeability of Brooklands, then it was women.

After all, one expects men at a racetrack. Cars in Brooklands' paddock were predictably surrounded by solemn-faced men in hats, tweeds, plus fours, ulsters, cloth caps. The Members' bar was filled with braying masculine voices. The rich drove Bentleys and Alfa Romeos, the poor rode motorcycles and fraternised in their sordid cafeteria downstairs. The rest of the male spectators simply hung around, trying to be part of the Right Crowd.

Only there was more to it than that. In the early days Gargoyle-MobilOil (later Mobil) liked to strike fear in the male motorist by attacking his weakest spot: 'Women drivers,' the company cried. 'Do they realise the relation of engine lubrication to both petty and serious driving problems? More and more men drivers are realising the importance of using the correct oil in their cars. To their wives who drive the car during the week, the importance of scientific lubrication is even greater. Driving problems, troublesome enough for men drivers, become more serious when a woman is at the wheel.'

But at Brooklands women could escape this pervasive bigotry. From the outset they arrived as spectators, as competitors, and, in the cases of Joe Carstairs and the Hon. Dorothy Paget, as unsmiling plutocratic lesbians. The fact that Brooklands was run by a woman from 1926 onwards is happily coincidental (after the death of Hugh Locke King, Dame Ethel became governing director of the Brooklands Estate Company and unchallenged mistress of Brooklands; she could be seen – especially in autumn, after the track had closed – wandering around the estate in tweeds, clutching a garden hoe).

In this Arcadia, according to one account, a male spectator broke into 'A eulogy on the scores of very young and very attractive girls who were watching their favourites skim past them round the track. "You see young women at all these out-of-door things nowadays of course, but racing and greyhounds and the rest of it do not attract so many fresh-looking things as this business does."' A view seconded by the *Morning Post*, which referred to 'those women and girls who seem to equal the number of men in the paddock, if not the other parts.' The Brooklands woman, it went on, 'wears a smart tailored suit, dainty shoes and a chic hat. There is nothing reminiscent of the hardened race-goer about her, except an occasional shooting-stick.'

The *Motor*'s fashion correspondent, 'Anna', in between analyses of crêpe de Chine, the butterfly cloak and the Magyar top, observed a familiar, womanly side to race-going. 'I was amused at the matter-of-fact way in which a little girl in pig-tails kept trotting between her mother's car and one of the blandest of the "bookies". Both mother and daughter took the business very seriously, and I think they had rather a good day, for the little maid was on several occasions one of those invited to come up for their winnings.' Charles Mortimer was more concerned with the predatory habits of his male friends: 'In the Brooklands paddock one could never be sure of retaining the attentions of one's girlfriend unless one actually held on to her.' Having arrived with three female companions on one occasion, 'all these girls were whisked off as if by magic'. The upshot? At the end of the meeting he asked his girlfriend, 'Did you enjoy the racing?' To which she replied, 'Racing? I didn't see any.'

But it went deeper. The tone of Brooklands was not only radically modified by women who came as spectators, intensifying the sexual magnetism of he-men like Glen Kidston and Jack Dunfee; but also by those women who, from the late twenties onwards, came as competitors – and whose handiness behind the wheel provided a critical commentary on the other, male drivers. Competitors such as Kay Petre, Elsie 'Bill' Wisdom, Doreen Evans and Gwenda Hawkes had a more pragmatic approach to the business of driving than their male rivals.

Gwenda Hawkes – only marginally less romantic a figure than Glen Kidston – was the sister of Glubb Pasha of the Arab Legion and educated at Cheltenham Ladies' College. She drove ambulances on the Russian and Romanian fronts during the Great War, was awarded the Cross of St George and the Cross of St Stanislaus, and was mentioned in dispatches. She had the face of a wind-burnt imp and married three times, working her way through Mr Janson and Mr Stewart before ending up with Douglas Hawkes, who also prepared her cars. All her husbands were lieutenant colonels. She held the Ladies' Outer Circuit record at Brooklands (just under 136 mph) and insisted that her mechanics turn out in spotless white overalls. She paid the laundry bills herself. And she argued that the reason she so enjoyed record breaking (her forte) was because 'no driving skill was required'. Douglas got the car ready, she turned up, drove it and went home, having earned herself a useful fee for the minimum expenditure of time. Later she took to sailing, retrospectively scorning cars altogether: 'The sea is infinitely superior in every way . . . looking back I didn't really enjoy any of it very much. The sea is much better.'

Kay Petre was a tiny, sweetly pretty Canadian, the fastest-ever woman to win a race at Brooklands, fearless, always dressed in powder-blue overalls embroidered with her initials, prone to keeping a lipstick and some cigarettes under the (specially made, tiny) seat of her supercharged Bugatti. In 1934 she drove Cobb's old twelve-cylinder Delage (by then owned by barrister Oliver Bertram) in order to set a new lap record: 'It wasn't difficult to drive; just big.' They attached wooden blocks to the pedals so that she could reach them. A pipe burst in one race and sprayed her with hot oil: 'I looked like a fried potato.' But after crashing at 110 mph in 1937 and spending three weeks unconscious in hospital, then being chased by a burning car at Brooklands in 1938, she calmly turned her back on motor racing and became a journalist.

No tormenting nostalgia for her. Nor for Barbara Cartland,

who, in a moment when she wasn't being ravished by Glen
Kidston, organised a highly publicised three-lap motor race for
ladies only. The Hon. Mrs Chetwynd had raced before and
ought to have won ('You can imagine my rage and despair as
I realized what a farce the whole thing was'), but Princess
George Imeretinsky came in first, with Lady de Clifford as her
mechanic. (The princess later became the fourth wife of Ernest
Simpson, Wallis's ex.) 'I had an awful job to find ten women
who *could* race,' said Miss Cartland.

   All in all, this was lamentably un-male, non-obsessional
behaviour. Several of the men competitors were deeply
concerned by it. But what could they do? That was the ethos
of the place. For Cobb, though, it represented more than just
that intrusive femininity which Englishmen have always found
hard to deal with. When Elsie Wisdom (with co-driver Joan
Richmond) won the Junior Car Club's 1000-mile race in 1932,
Cobb spent days afterwards wandering around muttering,
'Can't think how she does it.' Kay Petre's record attempt in
the vast Delage was worse. 'You should stop her,' he groaned.
'She'll kill herself; or the crowd.' It wasn't just that she was
female (hence unpredictable, skittish, sexual), but that her
success was symptomatic of a world he knew he would have
difficulty inhabiting – the newly arriving world of smaller, neater
machines; of efficient little cars which even little women could
drive successfully. The end, in other words, for big men like
him, driving big blunderbuss-like machines around the only
track capable of supporting them.

   Not that he didn't try to come to terms with the new machinery: 'I don't like small cars,' he said on one occasion. 'The
only time I tried a small car was in the 1929 TT, when I drove
a Riley. Unfortunately, I let it go over a hedge with me.'
However, 'the Alfa-Romeo I drove in the JCC International . . .
is a very nice little car, I must admit.' This was an 8C 2300:
a supercharged, eight-cylinder, 100-mph two-seater, weighing
a ton. Nice and little for Cobb, in other words. 'I like the car.'

But the trend was inescapable. It had taken him ten years to get to the point of winning races, and already he was in danger of being left behind by progress, by change, by 'chits of girls'.

Campbell, on the other hand, just irritated him – although, conforming to pattern, Cobb's dislike of the great man was kept within rigorously circumscribed behavioural bounds. A famous picture taken in the 1930s shows Cobb – dressed in his baby-romper outfit, plus helmet – posed in a group with Earl Howe and Sir Malcolm Campbell. Howe has evidently just made one of his droll remarks and smirks quietly to himself. Campbell is writhing with hilarity, beside himself at Howe's wit. Cobb simply stares levelly at the corpsing Campbell, the tiniest half-smile – which may not even be that – on his lips, an absolute denial of Campbell's reaction. Perhaps Howe's joke has been made at Cobb's expense. But even if the joke is at Campbell's expense, Cobb will simply refuse to enjoy himself in his presence.

At other times he made his enmity known in other, small ways. Sometimes he contented himself merely with referring to Campbell as 'that blasted *show-off*'. Sometimes he would take a positive pleasure in one of Campbell's win-at-all-costs tantrums, as when the latter was deprived of a first place thanks to an official mix-up at a race meeting in 1930. Sometimes Cobb would put the hex on Campbell when the latter was making one of his public addresses. Cobb was as tall and burly as Campbell was small and wiry. Even seated, he had presence. He would sit in an audience – usually composed of motor-sport personalities and industry satraps – and allow his features to settle into an unwavering, heavy-lidded stare, directed at the laboriously articulating Campbell.

As Campbell got older he got more professional at speaking in public. But under Cobb's gaze he would invariably trip and stumble, before finishing in a state of flushed confusion. Cobb would shift in his seat and permit himself the minutest smile; the smile of the unconsidered. It was as if Campbell personified, in Cobb's mind, all the worst of the American principle: flashy, self-promoting, ruthless, money-driven; while Cobb took on the mantle of the model Briton: self-effacing, a little bit dull, utterly determined and straight as a die.

But then there would have been a queue of people in London and the Home Counties who felt much the same way. The big difference between the rest of the world and Cobb was that at some time in the early 1930s he decided that he was going to do more than merely object to Campbell's existence. He was going to beat him at his own game. He would take away the title which Campbell had worked so hard to make his own.

14

Malcolm Campbell's Phoney War

((⊙ ⊙))

For Campbell, after the party, came the letdown. Riding his wave of expectation, he had peaked at forty-six and was now in the uncomfortable demotivating netherworld of middle age. As well as suffering from deteriorating eyesight (and ultimately glaucoma) he was going progressively deaf, through years of exposure to racing engines – worse, to open-exhaust aero engines located no more than nine inches from his toes. The lines and cicatrices in his face were becoming more pronounced. He had started to say, 'You know, I'm getting too old for this sort of thing' and, 'It's ruddy costly, ruddy dangerous and I'm getting on.' He was starting to look like a veteran.

And how much life was there left in the Land Speed Record itself? However much he protested that he was principally a businessman who indulged in the pastime of motoring, nevertheless all Campbell's prestige, the position he had engineered for himself in society, was a by-product of the LSR. How much longer would people care? Did he have any rivals, to make the thing more marketable? He may have enduringly commodified himself, his image found on cigarette cards (State Express, Ogden's Cigarettes, Churchman's); his face (clenched or grinning) appearing in advertisements for oil, tyres, Belco car paints; his *Blue Bird* emerging as one of William Britain's die-cast model toys. He may, indeed, have made himself a household name, as familiar as Wallace Beery or Stanley Baldwin; yet the dynamism, the sense of mission which animated the speed kings in the mid-twenties, was starting to flag.

So he went and broke his own record not once more, nor twice, but four more times. For the next four years he was his only rival. Campbell's long Phoney War began here.

This succession of attempts took on something of the quality of a series of unusually gruelling holidays to the same inescapable destination. There were always the same problems: the weather; the state of the beach; the attitudes of the locals; the rockiness of the economy. By the start of 1932, for instance, the Depression was thoroughly established in the United States. The mood at Daytona was more nervous, more fraught than before. The Florida land boom was long vanished and many of the speculative projects of the 1920s had gone bust, leaving tenantless and decaying buildings the length of the beach. Daytona itself was no longer the biggest draw in Florida and the beach itself was slowly degrading, slowly rendering itself less and less suitable for high-speed racers with every storm that arrived, every surge tide.

In the past the hucksters and boosters had found it relatively straightforward to promote Daytona's speed festivals: 'Over a score of the best benzine battlers who ever pushed the throttle of a race car and who are as unfearful of danger as his Satanic Majesty himself, will go out to cop the prizes and risk their necks,' was one inducement. And, 'Ambulances and a first aid tent have been arranged to take care of the spartans of speed who fall by the wayside or go careering through the fence.'

Times being what they were, though, the Mayor of Daytona felt unable to rely solely on old-fashioned ballyhoo; plus the chance appearances of whatever itinerant auto racers felt like turning up for the speed week. He needed to guarantee the presence of his star turn. He seized the initiative in early January, cabling Campbell: 'The City of Daytona Beach invites you and offers every further co-operation to further your attempt to create new world record.' What's more, he offered to extend the course by taking out several piles from the troublesome pier, creating a fifty-foot gap through which *Blue Bird* could pass in its run-up to the measured mile. This was not entirely without drawbacks, as the car would be doing about 150 mph at the moment at which it shot under the pier and would hit it like a high explosive if Campbell misjudged his approach. 'At that speed,' Campbell later complained to Leo Villa, 'I can tell you that gap looks bloody small.' Everyone involved was nonetheless willing to take that risk.

The Mayor's blandishments worked: Campbell loaded *Blue Bird* on to the *Aquitania* and followed it out on the *Berengaria* a few days later. When he got to Daytona, apart from the 'huge crowd' waiting for him at the railroad depot, Campbell found that the city engineers had indeed taken out eight of the massive pier supports and built a triangulated wooden truss above the boardwalk to support the free-floating fifty-foot stretch of pier.

An atmosphere of ferocious levity prevailed. The bathtub hooch flowed as disablingly as it had before, still awaiting the repeal of Prohibition. Bright orange ribbons were issued to Campbell's team. 'Campbell Crew 1932 World's Records,' they said in stern black lettering. Mass prizefights were held to entertain the English visitors. Twelve or more desperate Negro boxers were herded into an outsize boxing ring, where they were told to fight until only one man was left standing. The winner would then be pelted with coins and notes by the enthusiastic white spectators. Sometimes the fights lasted as much as an hour before a ruined victor could be declared. On occasion they made the fights even more chaotic by blindfolding the fighters. Once they even provided the spectators with a boxing glove on the end of long stick, with which to goad on the sweating, bleeding, sightless wretches.

At the north end of the beach, John D. Rockefeller was still
alive. On 19 February Campbell and the ninety-three-year-old
millionaire greeted each other on the Ormond golf links. 'I
am glad to see you,' cried Rockefeller, shaking Campbell's
hand. 'I hope you have success in your trial for a new world
record. I would not drive my car that fast. I would be afraid
of an accident.' Many a chuckle accompanied this pious
aspiration; but then did Rockefeller actually know to whom
he was talking? 'I hope you drive your car like a silver bullet!'
he added, suggesting that so far as he was concerned, Sir
Malcolm Campbell and Kaye Don were pretty much the same
person.

Not that Campbell had much time to reflect on this slight,
because the next thing he knew was that Rockefeller had spotted a Baptist minister in the watching crowd and beckoned
him over. This was the Reverend Dr Arthur T. Brooks, who
had sung the hymn 'Be Not Dismayed, Whate'er Betide' for
Rockefeller (or 'Neighbour John', as he was known) the previous day. Rockefeller had formed a special fondness for this
song, as being appropriate for the troubled times in which
Americans currently lived. He asked Brooks to sing it again,
which he did. Then he asked the entire crowd to join in another
hymn, 'Passing By'. Quite suddenly Campbell – whom
Rockefeller would have regarded, at the very least, as a super-
stitious libertine, had he known him better – found himself
trapped in the middle of a revivalist meeting out on a Florida
golf course with no means of escape. It was intolerable: but
out here among the palms and the American Evangelists, faced
with one of the richest men in the entire world, the great Sir
Malcolm Campbell had no purchase. He had to put up with
whatever Rockefeller felt like insisting on.

Eventually the singing died down and Campbell and
Rockefeller sat on a bench, where Campbell did his best to
steer the old man away from thoughts of the eternal. 'How
do you find business conditions here in this country?' he asked.

Rockefeller smiled and raised his lizard eyes to Heaven. 'We are hoping, hoping, hoping,' he said. 'We are not dismayed. God is above, watching over us and we are hoping.'

Much of this hanging around, watching boxing matches between slaves and being subjected to Rockefeller's downhome pieties, was occasioned by the weather. The wind blew for days on end, making it impossible to drive the car at all quickly, and crumpling the sands. Rain fell and the mists descended so that it was impossible to see more than a few yards in any direction. The only good news was that this hiatus did allow a couple of no-hoper rivals to come into the frame, phoney foils to Campbell's endeavour, and proof that, despite *The Times*'s cavils ('At a later period he had a close competitor in Sir Henry Segrave, but now he appears to be no one's rival but his own') there were claims on the LSR which came from farther afield than the garage at Povey Cross.

Norman 'Wizard' Smith was a brick-chinned Australian speed king who at one stage in the early thirties held no fewer than fifty-one of the world's lesser speed records. His first record car was called the *Anzac* and was made of a Rolls-Royce aero engine bolted to an old Cadillac chassis. This worked well enough in its way, but 'Wizard' wanted more. There was a fantastically long, straight beach, some 250 miles north of Auckland, on New Zealand's North Island. It was known, reasonably, as Ninety-Mile Beach, and would have been perfect for both long-distance and flying mile record attempts, bar the fact that it was narrow, wet and covered in sharp toheroa shells ('the aristocrat of New Zealand shellfish'). This was the destination that Campbell had in mind when he threatened the Daytona authorities with his non-appearance back in 1931. Sensitive to the accusation that the *Anzac* was just a huge old bus, Smith had a proper LSR machine built for his Ninety-Mile Beach attempt. This car (named the *Fred H. Stewart Enterprise*, like a ship) turned out to be an extremely close copy of Segrave's *Golden Arrow*, and 'Wizard' reckoned it good for 250 mph.

Campbell sent him one of his disingenuous good-luck telegrams before Smith's big push in February 1932.

It didn't work out. 'Wizard' got into a protracted fight with the *Fred H. Stewart Enterprise*'s designer, who then quit. Following this, the streamlining went to pieces when 'Wizard' insisted on bolting an enormous radiator shaped like a beer crate on to the front of the car. Then it turned out that the surface of Ninety-Mile Beach was so bad that the timers gave up and went home. Then the car's engine caught fire. At last 'Wizard' himself gave up and went back to Sydney.

On the other side of the world, another implausible foreigner was also laying down his challenge to Campbell. Barney Oldfield, fifty-three-year-old retired racing showman and 'the Dean of American race cars' declared that he had already drawn up plans for an LSR machine powered by two sixteen-cylinder engines set in a chassis 'designed to resemble an inverted canoe'. He had not raced professionally since 1918, but 'felt better than at any time in the past ten years'. Surprisingly, his announcement was taken at face value and even though nothing was ever seen of the car, the Oldfield story ran quite health-ily for a year or so.

This was fine, either way. Campbell needed the illusion of international challenge every bit as much as the challengers thought they needed to confront him. It all made a useful season-ing for the 1932 bid itself, which dragged on throughout February until, on the 24th, the beach at Daytona was quiet enough for him to make a practice run – which turned into the actual LSR attempt, when he found that his practice was going so briskly that he might as well turn it into the real thing. Taking the time-keepers by surprise, he set a new world record of nearly 254 mph, trailing in his wake a lexicon of worthy self-punishment: 'I shot between the piles and the open beach showed ahead . . . Because of the roughness of the beach, it required all my strength to hold the wheel.' This was 'kicking under my hands all the time' and consequently 'blistered my palms badly'.

And it ought to have been enough. The newspapers and copywriters certainly found the big 250 an adequately resonant figure: 'Sir Malcolm Campbell's New World Record'; 'Mobbed by Women'; '"I Was Terribly Afraid" – Lady Campbell's Relief'; 'He was greeted by the largest crowd that had ever congregated on the sands'; 'Amazing Dash On Daytona Beach'; 'Faster than the most devastating hurricane, Sir Malcolm Campbell sweeps over the sands of Daytona Beach'; 'Shattered! The World's Land Speed Record again falls to Sir Malcolm Campbell again using Wakefield Castrol Motor Oil'. But Campbell was full of protestations afterwards: 'I am not elated. I am very very disappointed. I had hoped to do 260 mph.'

So furious was he at the shortfall that he tried to go out again the next day, despite the thick blanket of rain and fog which lay over the beach. The moment it looked as if the weather was clearing he announced that he was going to take *Blue Bird* to the start line. At which the Mayor of Daytona, terrified lest his biggest low-season tourist attraction might kill himself, declared that if Campbell insisted on going for the record, he, the Mayor, would order the timing equipment to be pulled out of the ground. Campbell gave in, piqued; then went out the next day to set some non-inspirational five- and ten-kilometre records, plus one over five miles. 'I might have put up some real marks if the wind had not been against me on both days,' he said.

With that, he packed away the car and returned to England, where George Moore, the celebrated author of *Hail and Farewell* and *The Brook Kerith*, was enjoying his eightieth birthday by fulminating against the modern world: 'The making of records, now, and, idiotic but apparently inevitable consequence, the breaking of records – what is effected by all this speed? Speed is unimportant. Why this craze for speed?' To which Campbell might have replied that, if nothing else, it earned him another £1000 from Lord Wakefield.

*   *   *

In 1933 Campbell once again stepped off the *Aquitania*. This time he looked 'pale and drawn' following an attack of flu in mid-Atlantic. By the time he got to the beach he discovered that two whole miles of the course had vanished, eaten away by severe winter storms, and that the surface of the sand was as lumpy as a ploughed field in places.

Blue Bird itself was also showing its age, despite the insertion of a new, furiously powerful Rolls-Royce aero engine. This engine was already so celebrated on its own account (having powered the Supermarine S6.B which won the Schneider Trophy for Britain in perpetuity, and been in the stern of Segrave's *Miss England II*) that Lord Wakefield later exhibited, not a real one, but a replica, at the Motor Show at Olympia at the end of 1933. 'Of the size only of an office desk,' gasped the press, 'this 12-cylinder supercharged racing engine is more powerful than an express locomotive. Its design is stated to be so valuable that it is still on the Government's secret list.'

But the thrilling newness of the engine pointed up the senescence of the rest of the car. When Campbell had first put *Blue Bird* together in the mid-twenties, its rivals were Parry Thomas and his *Babs* improvised from cast-offs; the ironmonger's delight which was the Sunbeam Slug; J.M. White's *Triplex*, 'The Spirit of Elkdom'. When it started out, 150 mph was the figure to beat. Now, however much Reid Railton stretched it and remodelled it and crammed it full of Rolls-Royce, it was still the product of a decade-old philosophy, which left it barely able to use the power generated by its fabulous engine. And its target was now 300 mph.

Anxious once again to make sure that Campbell would come that year, and that the beach would be ready for him, the Daytona city authorities expended huge energies to secure the marker flags, electrical timing equipment and other peripherals needed for the record attempt. Rather than attempt to raid the municipal funds, they set up lemonade stands, sold *Blue Bird* lapel badges, promoted more of their own brand of animalistic boxing matches, raffled a car.

When Campbell arrived on 2 February, not only was he now an Honorary Citizen of Daytona Beach, but also the recipient of the biggest official welcome that had ever been staged for him. Having nothing better to do, more people came to the railway station than had ever turned out for a visiting speed king. The American Legion Drum and Bugle Corps led the procession from the station to the hotel, with city, police and Racing Association officials surrounding Campbell in a kind of royal progress. Once he reached his hotel room, Campbell opened the door to find that the space was entirely filled with hundreds of flowers, sent by well-wishers. He then collapsed with post-infective exhaustion and went to bed.

From then on the trip turned into the usual litany of frights and frustrations. After waiting nearly a fortnight for the weather to clear, Campbell at last took the car out. It was not the debut he had hoped for. He was choked by exhaust gases from the huge new engine, which were dragged into his cockpit by the slipstream over the barely aerodynamic bodywork. Every time the car hit a bump, the wheels skidded, and Campbell lost traction and speed. He also tore a group of muscles in his left arm trying to change gear, which left him the job of steering the five-ton car with his right arm alone.

His account of the ordeal is a dispatch from the front line of human endurance: 'Wrenching muscles and tendons all the way up my forearm . . . fumes came into the cockpit . . . visibility was not very good . . . I was so shaken and jarred in the cockpit that it was not easy to keep my foot on the accelerator pedal . . . my left arm was very painful and I felt all in . . . *Blue Bird* began the second run. At once, the weakness of my left hand became evident, while, for some reason, the car "snaked" more than before. Again and again the machine swung out of the straight as speed mounted, so that I had to fight for control . . . it was painful to hold anything in my left

hand, and I could not have gripped the steering wheel properly
. . .' After that he wanted to go out again to set a higher speed,
but his doctor said no. 'He warned me that further strain might
result in further injury.'

Even allowing for Campbell's propensity to exaggerate, this
must have been a particularly frightening ride. The beach was
every bit as narrow as in 1927, when Segrave had used it for
the first time, as well as shorter; the crowds in the sand dunes
were intimidatingly dense, reaching an estimated fifty thousand
people on the day of the record run. There was still spray and
standing water; still the lack of beach on which to come to a
halt. And now this under-rehearsed monster smashing from
bump to bump at over 250 mph, its pilot baked in burnt
aviation fuel, hanging on to the huge steering wheel with one
hand, wrestling with the gear lever, his vision no more than a
blurred mess – this was more vividly dreadful than even
Campbell could have hoped for.

'The worst ride I have ever had,' he announced. 'I thought
I was done for.' And, 'I hope never to make such a run.' Having
told *The Times* that 'If the car had not responded so magnif-
icently to my touch I should have landed either among the
sand dunes or in the ocean,' to Leo Villa he confided, in the
language of men at arms together, 'I'm having one hell of a
job to hold the bitch on her course.'

Hitting a new record of 272 mph was no consolation at all.
This was still well below the 300 mph he had in mind and
meant that more work would have to be done to *Blue Bird*,
more money spent, more time lost. 'I am very disappointed
over the record,' Campbell confessed, 'but feel fortunate in
escaping with my life under treacherous conditions that made
the ride terrible.' A journalist prompted him, 'You must be
pretty tired. Off to bed?' Campbell brightened a little. 'I am
tired . . . but I'm not going to bed – there are too many of
my good friends in Daytona here. But I must get some food.
I'm jolly hungry.' As a codicil, he praised his absent wife for

not making a fuss about her own flu, back in England: 'It was fine of her to keep it quiet. Give her my love.'

But then? Campbell was still trapped in this purgatory, which centred around Daytona Beach. He kept going back, inching up the record, coming home again to readjust *Blue Bird*, not reaching the 300-mph mark. Even he had to admit that he was only battling against the failure of self-will and the arrival of premature old age. The enhancement of national prestige was becoming less tenable each time he marginally broke his own record, no matter how many speculative contenders came forward.

Yes, Commodore Gar Wood had loaned some of his vast speedboat engines to a young chancer named Billy Arnold in order to create 'one of the largest speed mammoths ever to skim Daytona sands, if built'. J.M. White, of the notorious *Triplex*, had announced that after all, his plans were not shelved and that he was working on a four-wheel-drive machine capable of 500 mph, to be ready in early 1934. And Barney Oldfield was still touting his monster supercar, now reputed to have a 'glass enclosed cockpit' and three superchargers. 'The Dean of American race cars' had even, it was said, acknowledged the impossible physical demands of trying to drive such a creation and given the pilot's job to a younger man: 'Stubby' Stubblefield, of California. The problem was that none of these challenges came to anything and Campbell's isolation grew with every fantasist's botched attempt.

Reid Railton had, meanwhile, been sounding off about the limitations of *Blue Bird* – including the brakes, the fact that it was rear-wheel drive (rather than all-wheel drive), that it had a great big radiator in the front, just like any raddled Brooklands sports car. Of course, all these things could be changed, if only there were an enlightened enough patron willing to go all the way for the sake of the LSR. Radiators, for instance, could be made in all sorts of novel and unfamiliar ways, 'But the amount of experimental work required weighed against their adoption on *Blue Bird*.' This inhibition was at the heart of everything, furnishing 'the death-warrant of ninety-five per cent of the brain-waves that one would like to try out'.

When one bore in mind that 'The driver may have to wait for days or weeks until the Beach is in a suitable condition for even a trial run, and that he may want to go for the record half an hour afterwards in case the Beach is never right again,' well then, 'The need for eliminating any experimental element becomes obvious.' Railton's peroration was turning into both a lament and a yelp of frustration. 'When once one is reasonably confident that the car is sufficiently fast to beat the record, any further alteration is frowned upon, even if it is likely to give another 20 mph, so long as it contains an experimental element which might require three or four trial runs to perfect.' Worst of all, 'Anything which by its nature is likely to need much trial and adjustment is avoided like the plague.'

As so often in these things, Railton the designer perceived himself to be not much more than the handmaiden to a rich, purblind obsessive. Everything was done piecemeal. There was no theoretical elegance anywhere. Years later he heaped scorn on the whole *Blue Bird* project, in an essay for the Institute of Mechanical Engineers, claiming that he was 'not sure that the subject is of sufficient technical importance to warrant the Institution's time and stationery . . . The intrinsic value of these world's record attempts . . . being entirely incommensurate with the publicity they sometimes receive in the lay press.'

But by 1934 Campbell was in too much of a state to let Railton off the hook. He had left the record at 272 mph. He had to raise the speed by about 30 mph – roughly the margin by which Segrave had so airily dispossessed him of his title back in 1927. He had to do a Segrave on himself, using a modified version of the very car which Segrave had trounced six years before. Was this the destiny prefigured for him in Maeterlinck's *The Blue Bird*? That the more he toiled towards his dream, the less chance he stood of realising it? The corollary to this – Maeterlinck's wisdom that the Blue Bird of happiness is within our grasp the moment we give up the egotistical struggle and accept some deeper truth about the world's harmony – would have been meaningless to Campbell in 1910; and was now quite beyond his comprehension.

So, nearly fifty years old, Campbell wound his courage up, took *Blue Bird*, the greatest of all the Brooklands monsters, and submitted it to the biggest rebuilding of its life. Brooklands had grown from a spartan Edwardian curiosity into a bustling and well-appointed recreational fixture, which was, nonetheless, like a seaside resort just past its best, touched by decline. *Blue Bird*, likewise, was now full of differently aged strata of development, full of the kind of compromises detested by Railton, still gamely pressing on before the end came.

Off it went to Thomson & Taylor to have everything stripped down, the precious, over-powerful Rolls-Royce engine serviced, a new bodywork designed. By mid-1934 it was ready to have its new coachwork applied by a team of panel beaters (led by a man named Piercy), before going back to Daytona at the start of 1935. True to form, Campbell couldn't bring himself to be present at this, one of the key junctures of his life. Instead, at the start of the great *Blue Bird* rebuilding, he handed Leo Villa a book of post-dated cheques with which to pay for the work and disappeared off to Namaqualand in the Northern Cape province of western South Africa. Diamonds had been found in this beautiful but desperately arid part of the world. Campbell was convinced that he would discover treasure there. 'Keep the lads at it, old boy,' he said to Villa, and left.

There was, of course, no treasure in Namaqualand, and Piercy had to be sacked for dilatoriness. On the other hand, when the rebuilt *Blue Bird* was wheeled out before the press in January 1935, it did look terrifically striking. Campbell, nonchalant in a muffler and plus fours, leaned against the huge machine, parked outside his old Campbell Shed at Brooklands and discoursed on the advantages of the new-look, old-concept car. He was absorbing the novel air of confidence – 'the winning look that weapons have' – now radiated by the car.

Railton had gone to town. This *Blue Bird* was no longer merely an engorged single-seater racer with a hypertrophied fin at the back. Indeed, the fin, that object of Railton's scorn, had slimmed down to something more like the flight of an arrow, or a dart. No, the machine was now wide and low and massively imposing, with two muscular bulges rising over the top of the engine. It was a fraction longer than before, at just over twenty-eight feet, the spaces between the wheels cleverly filled in with sleek blue-painted metal and a broad, sardonic slot – like the mouth of an enormous blue catfish – stretched across the radiator. It had something of Segrave's Deco *Golden Arrow* about it; but also plenty of the overblown, declaratory and incontestably phallic elements that had cheered *Blue Bird* supporters since 1926. It even had two extra wheels at the back in order to master the urges of the Rolls-Royce motor.

The fact that it was a masterpiece of inefficiency (a Mercedes, one-sixth *Blue Bird*'s weight and with an engine one-ninth as big, had managed to hit nearly 200 mph the year before) was immaterial. This was the *Blue Bird* which hundreds of school-boys bought in toy car form. This was the *Blue Bird* which was so sleek yet so brutish that the Americans called it a 'Thunderwagon'. This was the *Blue Bird* which had been sculpted into what Campbell self-deludingly called 'a really efficient streamlined body'.

It was also the *Blue Bird* which failed majestically, out on Daytona Beach on 7 March 1935, raising the record by not quite 4.5 mph and leaving Campbell with another 25 mph to find. The organisers had produced a splendid thirty-two-page *International Speed Trials* official commemorative programme (sponsored by Bell Bakeries Inc.), showing *Blue Bird* on the cover and with a Hollywood-style studio portrait of Campbell in helmet and goggles inside, as if confident that this would be the record to make history. Their optimism was misguided. Two years, thousands of pounds, thousands of hours of work: an increase amounting to walking pace.

There were plenty of reasons why. The weather was awful as usual, making Campbell wait around for five weeks before he took his chances with the record. The beach had been pared away so thoroughly in places by the Atlantic that Campbell had to have a thick black line painted in old engine oil on the sand so that he could see where to drive. Worms had made the sand lumpy and the beach was so badly corrugated that he had to wear two safety straps to keep him from being thrown out of the car. He had a fight with the Mayor of Daytona, again, after the Mayor refused to let him make an attempt in a near-gale. Fumes came into the cockpit. Campbell's goggles got blown off when he went over a bump and caught his face in the slipstream, just like in the old days back at Pendine. He nearly crashed into the pier at 200 mph. He had his tyres explode under him.

On the actual record run Dorothy Campbell, weeping uncontrollably, sat in the timer's box with Odis Porter of the AAA. Surprisingly, Campbell's mother, who had been content up until this point to be no more than a useful crowd-sweller at homecomings and receptions, found herself articulating something of the world's greater frustration. 'If he were to abandon the attempt now,' she said, 'I know only too well that he would be off at the earliest opportunity to try again. He has set his heart on that 300 miles an hour and he will not rest until he gets it.' This is the authentic voice of a woman who has nearly reached the end of her tether. 'Therefore I feel it is better for him to do his best now – reach the 300 mark – and then rest content with that.'

Everyone was beginning to feel something of the exhaustion felt at the end of a sustained, virtuoso musical performance, in which the player simply will not finish his encores, but insists on impressing the crowd long after they've started to get up and go home. 'The sands of time,' said the *Washington Post*, 'were swept away by a thundering demon.' But, said Dorothy Campbell, 'By this time it seemed that public interest was waning somewhat.'

For every trip out to Daytona, there was, of course, a celebratory aftermath. And these too devolved into a standardised rodeo of dinners, speeches, awards and encomia. In 1935 alone – perhaps conscious that they wouldn't have many more occasions on which to do these things – there was a presentation on the Senate Steps of the Capitol by Vice-President John Nance Garner of an engraved commemorative plaque, two-thirds as big as Campbell himself, from the People of Daytona Beach. There was a eulogy delivered by Senator Fletcher of Florida. At Gainesville, a city eighty miles away from Daytona Beach, the city fathers declared 13 March 'Sir Malcolm Campbell Day': more than seven thousand people turned up to celebrate this event at the University of Florida Stadium. And the junior members of the Peninsula Club of Daytona threw a party for eleven-year-old Jean Campbell.

Whatever the year, on his return to Southampton Docks, Campbell knew that he could expect to find the Mayor of Southampton, plus Earl Howe and perhaps Lady and Donald Campbell, waiting for him. In 1933 his ship had been met in mid-Solent by an armada of speedboats, led by three fast motor-cruisers, as used by the RAF. This was the brainwave of the fearless Mr Hubert Scott-Paine, powerboat designer, friend of Lawrence of Arabia, and man of action, who was piloting one of the motor-cruisers, with Lady Campbell and Donald in the back. As soon as they hit the wash of the *Aquitania*, on which Campbell was travelling, their boat sprang into the air and Lady Campbell was almost thrown overboard.

Once ashore, whether heralded by Scott-Paine or not, Campbell would pose for the cameras, shaking hands mightily with the Mayor of Southampton, then go on to deliver an address on the BBC. The next day dinner would take place at the Grosvenor House, the RAC in Pall Mall or the Dorchester Hotel. Lord Wakefield would give him the Wakefield Trophy, as holder of the World's Land Speed Record, plus a reward of £1000, plus (in 1933) a huge gold cup surmounted by a blue-bird in blue enamel.

For his part, Campbell took each fresh burst of limelight as an opportunity to sell himself as a transatlantic statesman-in-waiting. Grosvenor House, in 1932, saw Mr Ray Atherton, American Chargé d'Affaires in London, making a standard speech of praise, answered by Campbell with the tumultuous assertion that 'Had the United States and Great Britain been cemented together as one nation, the Great War would never have taken place.' A year later, having just taken the LSR off himself again, he announced that, proud as he was of his car's British workmanship and design, he was just as proud of 'the fact that I made the record on American sands and' – which was perfectly correct – 'on Washington's birthday'. It was sheer coincidence that the weather had cleared enough for him to try for the record on 22 February. But he was not going to let the symbolism go by.

Indeed, he had already rehearsed a sermon on the state of relations with the United States on the deck of the *Aquitania* a few days earlier: 'I would like to say how kind everybody was – not only to myself but to my little staff while we were over in America. They've always been awfully good to us and nothing has ever been too much trouble. I was very sorry indeed – just as we left, the economic depression got a bit worse.'

This was a level of understatement that even John Cobb would have been comfortable with. By early 1933 US manu-facturing output had virtually halved from its 1929 level; the collapse of the banking system had seen 11,000 of the nation's 25,000 banks fail. This was when people were lining the streets of Manhattan, trying to sell apples; on the Chicago Stock Exchange, 'It was so quiet you could hear a certificate drop';

the terrible American Dust Bowl was starting to gather momentum. It was Steinbeck's *The Grapes of Wrath* and Studs Terkel's *Hard Times.*

'And moreover,' Campbell went on, 'I know that they have the sympathy of everybody in this country' – a Great Britain, in other words, which may have become decadent and whose Empire was mere dead weight, but which at least had avoided the cinematically vivid tragedy now settling on the United States. A Great Britain which, for this moment, could condescend to oblige its cousins with a little sympathy. And again, in 1935: having been described as 'Britain's ambassador of goodwill' in the States, he replied by noting the 'extraordinary feeling of friendship between the United States and Great Britain', and went on to insist that it was 'the duty of everyone to do all they could to foster this friendship,' as it was his belief that 'such a bond between the United States and Great Britain was the future salvation of civilisation'.

When not trumpeting the strength of the ties between the US and Great Britain, he would drift into any other area that looked profitable. Nineteen thirty-four saw him deliver a far-sighted speech about the need for road and rail transport to co-operate: 'It would be much better for road and rail transport to work together in harmony.' After all, 'there are some forms of railway traffic against which road transport cannot possibly compete, such as the distribution of the country's coal and the undertaking of mass passenger traffic at great events like a Cup Final at Wembley'.

The following year he became Chairman of the Road Fellowship League and was helping to launch the National Safety First Association's travelling safety-first information van. This was set up to tour the country dispensing advice on road safety by means of specially made gramophone records. On the side of the van it announced that in the preceding eighteen weeks 444 fewer people had been killed on the roads and 7307 fewer injured than in the corresponding period in the previous year. The Minister for Transport, Mr Hore-Belisha, gave Campbell a brief lesson in oratory by pointing at the figures and bellowing, '*That's what can be done! That's what's GOT to be done!*' Campbell then nervously asked him to be the first person to sign the Road Fellowship Roll and pinned a badge on his lapel. Campbell was believed to get his cigarettes free from W.D. & H.O. Wills as part of a sponsorship deal: they issued road-safety cigarette cards to tie in with the scheme.

Then there was the writing. Over the years, Campbell generated a steady landslide of books, pamphlets and articles, all delivered as part of the strategy to keep him in the public eye. The list of Sir Malcolm Campbell's published hardbacks alone is striking: *The Romantic Story of Motor Racing; Speed on Wheels; The Roads and their History; Key to Motoring; The Life of Sir Henry Segrave; Thunder Ahead; Salute to the Gods; The Roads and the Problem of their Safety; My Thirty Years of Speed; The Peril of the Air; Drifting to War; My Greatest Adventure.*

At least, it would be striking if Campbell had written these books himself. He certainly had plenty to say, but, as his speeches suggest, his prose lacked tautness. Also, he was too busy – or too distracted – to devote himself to the long hours of solitary introspection needed for, say, an 80,000-word biography. So he got someone else to do the writing for him.

There was no great shame in this. Segrave had got J. Wentworth Day to ghost *The Lure of Speed*, and so it was not unreasonable for Campbell to get the same writer in for *The Life of Sir Henry Segrave*, whose authorship would be attributed jointly to Captain Malcolm Campbell and J. Wentworth Day. The problem, so far as Wentworth Day was concerned, was the way Campbell exploited him in the process. As he complained years later, 'Campbell did not write the book himself, but he did not hesitate to hypnotise me into giving him half the royalties . . . Campbell did not hesitate to capitalise on the book on every possible occasion. He took credit for it at public functions, in newspapers, at private parties and elsewhere.' Actually this deal was about par for the course for a ghostwritten biography. The real problems were in Day's attitude to and relationship with Campbell; which was not improved when the book was a best-seller and Campbell, who had written no more than his signature on a publisher's contract, began to rake in the proceeds.

Worse was to come when Campbell subsequently asked Wentworth Day to ghost *My Greatest Adventure*, an account of Campbell's failed 1925 trip to the island of Cocos. Wentworth Day accepted the commission and duly turned the book out. Several months later he went to stay with Campbell and his family at Povey Cross. He, Campbell and young Donald were sitting at the breakfast table one morning, when a bundle of the new books arrived. Donald grabbed a copy, started thumbing through it, turned to its true author and said, 'This is Daddy's latest book. Have you read it? He wrote every word of it with his own hand. Didn't you, Daddy? You told me so.' Wentworth Day, feeling himself bound not to reveal the facts of the case to Donald, struggled for a reply, bitterly remarking how 'Campbell did not answer. He went stolidly through his eggs and bacon . . .'

James Wentworth Day, it must be said, was a man of strange and antic fixations – a *Blut und Boden* kind of atavistic conservative who was for several years the amanuensis and personal assistant to Lady Lucy Houston, DBE, the besottedly far-right Woman of Destiny who helped bankroll the Vickers Supermarine seaplane and spent tens of thousands of pounds in the 1930s trying to overthrow the Government. He was also plainly infatuated with Segrave, whose patrician style caused him to sigh over the way, on the occasion of their first meeting, 'A tall slim quietly spoken man with an athletic figure and the unmistakable air of a gentleman rose from his seat and held out his hand.'

Campbell, by contrast, was an unscrupulous parvenu with none of Segrave's address – even though Wentworth Day merely got a flat fee of £500 for doing Segrave's book, as opposed to a cut of the royalties. Wentworth Day also liked to remind people of what happened when Campbell tried to touch Lady Houston for £10,000 for *Blue Bird* – a not entirely irrational request, given that she spent £100,000 on the Supermarine Seaplane and another £100,000 on helping Lord Clydesdale to fly over Mount Everest: 'If your friend Malcolm Campbell wants someone to pay for his death he must go elsewhere,' she said. 'His father left him plenty of money. Why doesn't he use that? He talks glibly about "Doing something for the Old Country." Rubbish! What he really wants is someone who will do something for Campbell the publicity seeker.' Lady Houston delivered this critique while sitting up in bed, draped in a Union Jack and wearing a blonde wig. 'This lioness of a woman disliked Campbell intensely.' So the odds were against him from the start.

Did this animosity find its way into Wentworth Day's prose? *The Times* noted in its review of his 1931 biography, *Speed – The Authentic Life of Sir Malcolm Campbell*, 'Every few pages throughout this book the reader assists in imagination at the removal of the mangled body of one of Sir Malcolm's rivals. In his enthusiasm for Sir Malcolm Mr Day is sometimes apt to make claims for him that Sir Malcolm may find embarrassing – as, for instance, that Sir Malcolm, whose age is given as 46, was a pioneer cyclist.'

These frictions aside, what principally strikes one is the profusion of titles that appeared throughout the 1930s, allegedly from Campbell's pen (allowances being made for forewords, which he probably did write, however implausible the book – *Physical Culture Simplified*, published in 1932, being an instance). Once Campbell got hold of the idea that literature – or the appearance of literature – was a useful adjunct to the rest of his activities, he had his name put on anything and everything that looked apt. As motoring editor of the *Daily Mail* his byline (on oddly drab topics: driving safely, the importance of regular maintenance) became a regular feature – even though these simple homilies were worked up for him by someone on the paper's staff. Most presumptuous of all, he allowed himself to be thought of as a novelist, ostensibly turning out an entertainment for adolescent boys, *Thunder Ahead* (1934), followed by something for a more mature market, *Salute to the Gods* (1935).

Thunder Ahead is not without a certain forensic interest, if only because, in its cheerfully gross romanticising and mainstream prejudices, it reveals how Campbell saw himself and his team. And because it offers a manifesto for record breaking, in which the key requirements are a huge car driven by an equally huge engine (or engines) placed in front of the driver, this behemoth to be sustained by a small, dedicated squad, led by a charismatic warrior-figure. In this case the warrior-figure is Dan Duncan, whose 'eyes glinted as the light from the windows caught them, so that in that moment, he appeared daring and almost reckless.' The enemy is embodied jointly by a foreigner, a driver named Zarra ('half English and half Spanish, a strange man with a strange name'); and by 'grim watchful Ben Gannet', who heads a rival firm of carmakers – an amalgam of Sunbeam and the *Golden Arrow* team – better funded and comfortably able to dream the biggest dreams. Dan Duncan's secret weapon (apart from the way his name is a flagrant variation on 'Malcolm Campbell') is his patriotism. 'We may only be a little firm – but we're British, and we want to let them all see that we do things properly!' The team's ultimate ambition? To reach 300 mph. This they do.

(The simplicity of *Thunder Ahead* gets lost in *Salute to the Gods*, which has trouble deciding whether it's a simple-minded thriller or a romance built around a surprisingly intrusive framework of fatal car accidents. 'Gipsy' Perrugi fills in the Zarra part – 'Driving like the devil he was' – while straight man Jerry Ross quizzes love-interest Evelyn: 'Why did he keep looking at my eyes?' Her answer? '"Doctors do queer things sometimes," she replied evasively.')

This blizzard of activity, by its very randomness, tended to prompt the question: was Campbell right to expect some larger function in public life; or should it have been enough for him simply to *be*? Even the *Daily Express*, normally an obsequious chronicler of Campbell's doings, struck a perplexed note in its profile of Campbell the man: 'A Gambler In Split Seconds'. Having observed him at a public function where he ate almost nothing, drank a solitary glass of champagne, and kept himself going with half a pack of cigarettes, the *Express* found him 'quiet, even a little shy. Hint of immense reserves of nervous strength . . .' The piece went on to juggle with the usual repertoire of attributes, trying to pin down Campbell's fugitive essence – 'quickness of reaction . . . paradoxical combination of caution and daring . . . balance . . . technical skill . . .' before admitting to 'something difficult to describe, a sort of reservoir of effort . . . all the vital forces . . . nerve, energy'.

And, however much it tried to dress him in the garb of a warrior, the *Express* couldn't help but equivocate when faced with Campbell's lacklustre after-dinner oratory: 'He is scarcely Sir Malcolm Campbell when he is making a big speed effort. He is certainly remote from the rather anguished man who gets up at the subsequent banquet and makes his modest speech . . .' A Parthian shot closes the piece, just to redress the balance – 'He is a sort of human bomb, a terrific detonation of human energy' – but the conviction is somehow lacking.

The *Daily Mail* squared up to this problem by comparing speed kings from more than one discipline to see if the magic personal ingredient revealed itself by adjacency. On his return from his 1933 LSR success, Campbell found himself at a function at the Dorchester Hotel in the company of Flight Lieutenant Stainforth (World Air Speed Holder), Flight

Lieutenant Unwins (World Altitude Record Holder) and
members of the 1931 Schneider Trophy-winning Royal Air
Force team. The *Mail* crossed its fingers and noted that one
common characteristic was 'light coloured eyes, generally light
blue'. This was all well and Aryan, but there was more. 'One
noticed in all, the hair thinning on the temples and brushed
well back, a prominent jaw, wrinkles at the side of the forehead
and always the intent eyes of men who have stared into the
distance amid terrific winds. This was very noticeable – none
of them blinked in the arc lights which glowed terrifically while
Sir Malcolm was speaking.'

The *New York Times*, having already declared that 'He is
47, looks 35, and says that he will be driving racing cars until
he is 70,' took another go at the problem. 'He retains the devil-
may-care attitude of a much younger man,' it said, tentatively.
'Of medium height and trim of build, in appearance as well
as manner he is the typical Englishman. Deep clefts in his
cheeks and a bronzed complexion tell of an outdoor life . . .'

But none of these approaches got very far. Heroes of the
1930s, by definition, defied scrutiny. That was part of their
contract with society. The most anyone could expect was to
take their greatness at face value and rejoice in Campbell's
refusal to age gracefully. Campbell received a hearty slap on
the back from the *Express* editorial team: 'They said Sir
Malcolm Campbell was too old – at forty-seven. They said
that at 253 miles an hour, the speed record which he set up
himself, the driver's muscles could not respond swiftly enough
to the orders telegraphed to them by his brain – at forty-seven.
Yesterday Campbell travelled at the rate of 272 mph and
smashed the land speed record to pieces. After Campbell's showing on the racetrack at Daytona . . . it is plain that no man is
too old for the greatest physical feats while he is still on the
sunny side of fifty.'

A note of puzzlement underlay this, and puzzlement,
however benign, is only two steps away from mockery. What's

incomprehensible soon enough starts to look unjustifiable; and anything unjustifiable – especially on the scale of *Blue Bird* – is in danger of appearing an affectation, and so, an apt subject for derision. After all, even at the height of Campbell's glory in 1931, the *Motor* had printed a borderline-affectionate cartoon of a deaf, balding, greybeard Campbell as imagined in the year 1971, clambering out of his motorised bathchair in order to take one last crack at the Land Speed Record in a rocket-shaped *Blue Bird*. 'What did you say – I've got to beat 545.73? Right!' says the beaky grotesque. 'The Campbell Still Coming,' it reads along the bottom.

As *The Times* had noted, by 1932 Campbell's only competitor was himself. The same year Prince George, Duke of Kent, patron of the British Racing Drivers' Club, murmured at a dinner given on 23 March in honour of Sir Malcolm, that it had got to the stage where 'It takes a Campbell to beat a Campbell' – a head-scratching circularity prefigured in Mr Ernest Instone's address at an RAC event ten days earlier. 'There was a time,' said Instone, 'when Sir Malcolm put up records with fairly lengthy intervals in between. Now, however, it has become an obsession with him. He makes a habit of disappearing into the blue and coming back with a new record.'

Come 7 June, and Campbell was being entertained at dinner by the Junior Aero Club, who were clearly in a mood to take things a stage further by being both frivolous and determinedly condescending. Having had their meal and passed the port, they entertained themselves with a mock trial, in which Campbell was accused of loitering on Daytona Beach at a speed of 254 mph. The chief witness for the prosecution was Flight Lieutenant George H. Stainforth, who, pointedly, had taken the World Air Speed Record in September 1931, at 407.5 mph. Stainforth gave evidence that he had been obstructed by the defendant (Campbell), having given audible warning of his desire to pass. After Campbell failed to secure an acquittal on the grounds that his speed had been wrongly given in the charge, he was found guilty: the sentence passed on him that he should be reduced to the ranks and invested by the gaoler with the jacket, cap and badge of a taxicab driver. But release beckoned. The defendant sought leave to appeal against the verdict. His appeal, heard by the women members of the jury, was allowed and Campbell's dignity was more or less restored.

As an assertion of the primacy of air over land, this was certainly one way of going about it. After all, what had Campbell's *Blue Bird* ever done but leech off aeronautical engineering and practices, merely in order to go slower than an aeroplane? Who were the real trailblazers now? His success, the aviators wanted to remind him, was a lot more contingent than he would have had the world believe.

Another telling moment – this time from Campbell's celebration dinner at the May Fair Hotel in February 1931, the month of his knighthood. Even as the party surged on past midnight, and Dorothy Campbell danced with the American Ambassador, Campbell himself slipped away to another part of the hotel, where the Hon. Mrs Victor Bruce, daredevil aviatrix, was being fêted after her successful solo round-the-world flight.

Worryingly for Campbell, Mrs Bruce was a figure of proportions almost as heroic as he believed his own to be. In 1927 she had driven single-handedly in a blizzard from the northern tip of Scotland to Monte Carlo in order to take part in the famous motor rally. In 1929 she had used a motor boat called *Snotty* to set a speed record for crossing the English Channel. Then, in 1930, she bought herself a tiny biplane with folding wings from Selfridges department store. Unable actually to fly her new purchase, she went down to the flying school at Brooklands and demanded to be taught to fly in two weeks. She got her pilot's licence and took off in September of the same year. Her trip turned into a mixture of off-the-cuff navigation over land; and journeys by boat across the oceans, with her aeroplane folded up in the hold. In the end, though, she could claim to have completed the world's longest flight by a woman – however interrupted – in a light aircraft: 20,000 miles.

The British Hospitality Association and the Women's Automobile and Sports Association (Viscountess Ellbank presiding) had organised her homecoming dinner at the May Fair Hotel. Campbell accosted Mrs Bruce in a quiet corner and toasted her success. She returned the compliment. Her aeroplane was called *Bluebird*.

She was one among many. Whereas the LSR only ever attracted a handful of diehards, aviation teemed with potential champions. There was, of course, Charles Lindbergh, who flew solo across the Atlantic in 1927; there was Alan Cobham, who had flown London–Cape Town and London–Melbourne in the second half of the twenties; Jean Batten, the great aviatrix who made the first flight from England to New Zealand; Amelia Earhart, the first woman to fly the Atlantic; Bert Hinkler, who flew solo from England to Australia in record time; Amy Johnson, the nation's sweetheart; Charles Kingsford-Smith, who led the first flight across the Pacific; Wiley Post, who, with navigator Harold Gatty, flew round the world in just over eight days in 1931; Glen Kidston; C.W.A. Scott; Squadron Leader Gayford . . .

Not that every one of these pioneers was overjoyed by their experience. When H.L. Brooke broke the Australia–England air record in 1935, he claimed there was 'nothing in it' and that he was 'almost bored'. When H.F. Broadbent broke Brooke's record a couple of years later, he said to the *Daily Herald*, on arriving at Lympne Aerodrome, 'I wouldn't do it again for worlds; it's so silly. I don't get anything out of it; it worries my wife; and nobody cares, anyway. I only did it because I told some friends in Australia that I would. It is uncomfortable; it is dangerous; and it is quite useless.'

But the one thing these adventurers could claim was utility. Every new record helped limn a world in which the old network of interminable sea communications was replaced by a new one built around rapid air transport. And with the R101 crash signalling the decline of serious interest in airships, the growing importance of heavier-than-air flying machines for imperial, military and civil purposes was unquestionable. The Hon. Mrs Victor Bruce's four-month odyssey was both a stunt and a small moment in man's conquest of the planet. Campbell's 246 mph at Daytona Beach seemed dangerously nugatory in comparison.

So it was a stung Campbell who found himself, a week after his teasing by the Junior Aero Club, addressing a dinner of the Royal Naval Volunteer Reserve Auxiliary Patrol. He had to inject new seriousness and urgency into the LSR programme. First, he announced that he had 'one great ambition now, and that is to reach 300 miles an hour.' Well, that sounded impressive all right, even if it was still 100 mph short of the Air Speed Record. But there was more. 'Next year there will be serious opposition from the Americans.' The evidence for this? 'Last Sunday I was rung up on the telephone from New York and told that it was no use going to Daytona next year unless I could do something in the region of 300 mph. The Americans are preparing a car of 3000 horse power' – this, presumably, a reference to Barney Oldfield's fantastical two-engined record breaker shaped like a canoe – 'and will do all they can to raise the record figure.'

That was 1932. Three years later he was still well short of his 300 mph target. There were no American challengers. Daytona was finished. *Blue Bird* had simply got too big and fast for the beach. Campbell wondered about Africa again, some high, flat desert somewhere. His LSR attempts were turning into a sporting semi-fixture, events already becoming tarnished by familiarity. He was now fifty and he had had enough.

15

Utah

$\langle\!\langle\mathbb{Q}\ \mathfrak{D}\rangle\!\rangle$

Then, against expectation, John Cobb showed Campbell the way by suggesting a trip to the end of the world, to a place for the crazy and the fixated, to the last place he could ever want to be.

Just as Campbell came back to England after the Daytona attempt of 1935, Cobb set off to the States to attempt some long-distance records in his new car, the *Napier Railton*. This was not a Land Speed Record car *per se*, but the car before the LSR car, a kind of super-evolved dinosaur, a car not built to stagger the world, but a car almost perfectly adapted to a highly localised, doomed environment. It had been designed by Reid Railton as exclusively for Cobb as if it were a tailor-made suit and it represented another of Cobb's painstaking, patiently modulated steps towards the ultimate goal. It was, in fact, a very large single-seater racer, powered by an elderly Napier Lion aero engine and clad in an imposingly businesslike silver bodywork.

On paper the whole affair was a throwback to the post-war days of Brooklands, to the follies that were L.C.G.M. le Champion's Isotta-Maybach, Count Zborowski's *Chitty-Chitty-*

Bang-Bangs. But it was in no sense a Brooklands lash-up, as these monsters had been. It was, instead, a model of rationality. The huge engine, for instance, was just right for the endless expanses of Brooklands, or the endless revolutions of long-distance record breaking, where it never had to work too hard, and where, as a consequence, it never broke down.

Everything else apart from the engine had been designed from the ground up and meticulously put together by Thomson & Taylor, with both comfort and durability in mind. The enormous back axle alone cost £400 – approximately the average annual wage. The petrol tank held sixty-five gallons of regular pump petrol and took ten minutes to fill. In motion it resembled – and still does – a cross between an aeroplane and a locomotive. It would never have worked on a more modern racetrack; but down in Weybridge it could gallop around the Outer Circuit with imperious swiftness, bearing down on smaller, slower cars like a tuna eating an anchovy. Cobb identified completely with the machine, which provided the tangible embodiment of his closeness to the track. Sometimes he could be found stroking the car and talking to it in a low voice.

But it was, despite everything, a contemporary antique. This is obvious if one considers that at the same time as the *Napier Railton* emerged in 1933, Mercedes and Auto-Union were unveiling a new generation of wildly complex and powerful Grand Prix cars with which to terrify the international motor-racing world into submission. At Hitler's instigation these two firms had turned out rival racing cars, both of which were built of advanced lightweight metals, used the latest stream-lining and enjoyed the most cunning engine technology. The Mercedes engine alone was one-seventh the size of the *Napier Railton*'s, but two-thirds as powerful. Both teams also used specially compounded fuels; so toxic that bystanders who breathed in the fumes suffered from headaches, eye trouble and nausea. Between them, Auto-Union and Mercedes annihilated the opposition, right up until the outbreak of the Second World War. They were, in short, the future.

But Cobb was only concerned with the rock pool of his own obsessions. Avant-garde engineering was no use to him. He just wanted to use the car at Brooklands for racing and for setting new lap records; achieving a very local kind of glory. Over the next four years, as well as winning the fastest short and the fastest long-distance races held at Brooklands, his *Napier Railton* also set the highest absolute speed officially measured there: nearly 152 mph. Occasionally he would go out in between the real races and flog the car round the track on his own until he had set a new lap time; as on the cold, gusty, positively dangerous Easter Monday of 1934, after which he had to have his fingers prised from the steering wheel ('That was a mistake, of course. It wasn't the day for it at all . . . Only everyone was counting on me to have a go').

In some ways these lap-record performances were mere stunts to entertain the crowd. But they were also expressions of his innermost longings, his need to possess the circuit; and he strove to make the Outer Circuit Lap Record his personal property. Other drivers took it off him from time to time – Oliver Bertram, for instance, in a Bentley in 1935 – but Cobb's willingness both to fetishise a number and sacrifice himself (if necessary) to the Brooklands track meant that he always forced himself to reclaim what he regarded as his; subject to his control.

The *Daily Herald* (oddly enough, in this moneyed context, a staunch supporter of the Labour Party and decades later, father of the *Sun* newspaper) donated a trophy in 1930 to be awarded to whoever held the fastest Outer Circuit lap time. In the end Cobb held the lap record – this one number for this one section of this one circuit – in perpetuity. The speed was 143.44 mph, set in October 1935. Years later, in contra-distinction to Campbell's groaning (and eventually mutilated) trophy cabinet, Cobb had only three trophies on show in the sitting room of his home. Pride of place over the mantelpiece went, not even to the real thing, but to a scale model of the *Daily Herald* trophy.

Cobb's descriptions of what it was like to punish oneself by driving the *Napier Railton* around the ageing Brooklands concrete centred less on the obliterating discomfort (which he would have taken for granted) and more on the way it threatened a final irresistible gravitational pull towards oblivion, as in Segrave's awareness of 'the whole thing gradually getting little by little above human control'. Cobb observed that 'An attempt on the lap record was very similar to seeing how far one could lean out of a window without falling out.' Or again, the queasy motion at high speed round the curved sections of the track: 'The top of the banking seems very near. It is almost like falling upward, if you can imagine it' – a dreamlike, rarefied analogy, given that his machine weighed as much as a limousine and had no front brakes.

He also tried to take some arduous and powerfully boring long-distance records in 1934, at Montlhéry, with cheeky Charles Brackenbury in the team. His first attempt at this track had been the year before; but the tyres failed and the radiator sprang a leak. This time he was better prepared and was certain he could circulate the Montlhéry loop for twenty-four hours. But problems cropped up again. One of the other drivers, Freddie Dixon, was too small to fit comfortably in Cobb's king-sized bucket seat and kept being hurled around inside the cockpit. Yet another driver, Cyril Paul, collapsed with acute appendicitis and was pulled from the car in agony. Then the track started to come to pieces under the strain. It rained.

Finally Dixon crashed the car into a ditch in the track's infield. A breakdown lorry tried to pull it out and failed. They sent for a tank from a French Army division based nearby in Paris. The tank arrived, attached itself to the *Napier Railton* by a chain and started to pull it out. But Cobb's machine was so heavy and so trapped in the mud that one of the tracks on the tank snapped and fell off. They replaced the track, tried again and pulled out the *Napier Railton* and an entire bank of earth. The car itself was only lightly damaged.

So where did Cobb go to repeat this exercise in more reliable conditions? He went, in mid-1935, to one of the most taxing places in the world: the Bonneville Salt Flats, in Utah. There he drove round and round a ten-mile circle on the baked pan of a dried Pleistocene-era lake, taking a mass of records at 3000 miles, six hours, 500 kilometres and so forth. 'Nightmare Race On Salt Flats,' said the papers, hailing an impressive, if senseless feat of endurance. 'We were absolutely roasted,' said Cobb, his face heavily coated in protective grease. 'As the course became cut up, the salt was thrown up more and more and when we finished, the car was covered with a solid coating of white which was baked very hard. It looked like a giant sugar model.'

Dreadful though it was, and miles from anywhere, Bonneville's virtues were nonetheless that it offered an enormous area of hard, flat whiteness to drive around on, with no distractions, no Atlantic breakers, no threatening sand dunes, no river estuary, no City Mayor alternately glad-handing you and threatening to pull your timing equipment out of the ground. 'Every time a coconut!' said Cobb in his suburban way, whenever a record fell. It all offered a kind of perfection; but at a price.

And this was where he thought Campbell ought to take *Blue Bird* – even venturing to play some mind games on him, telling the *New York Times* that in his opinion Campbell would have 'no difficulty in reaching his goal of 300 miles an hour on the Bonneville Salts'. With a straight course, 'Nothing should prevent Sir Malcolm from driving 300 miles an hour, or even 400, if his car is mechanically equal to the task. Steering,' he goaded, 'will offer no problem whatever.'

Actually Campbell knew perfectly well about the Bonneville Salt Flats; he just didn't want to go there. Back in 1933 he had professed himself 'much amused' by a rumour to the effect that he was going to try for a new LSR in Utah. Indeed, he had disdained the whole idea, claiming that two years earlier he had sent a representative to investigate Bonneville, and had been told that 'The sands of the lake bed there were not practicable for record purposes.'

Now, though, Cobb was right: he had nowhere else to go. This time Campbell endured a reduced level of public congratulation when *Blue Bird* was unpacked back in England. Chief guest at a celebratory dinner given for Campbell at the Park Lane Hotel on 30 April was no more glittering a personage than Mr Hore-Belisha. Having studied the magnificent souvenir menu – which showed a smiling Campbell as the sun in the centre of a great wheel of Art Deco rays on a silver background – Belisha cracked a joke about a £1 speeding fine which Campbell had picked up two days before. But almost as soon as the car had been put on display, it was packed up again in August 1935, with its lumber of spare parts and its retinue of mechanics and, rich with foreboding, Campbell and his entourage set off for Utah.

Even today, after seventy years of progress in the richest and most advanced nation in the world, the land around Bonneville, Utah, is bare, terrible and obscurely primitive. Bonneville itself lies a hundred and twenty miles due west of Salt Lake City (the nearest settlement of any size) and three hundred miles east of the gambling bastion of Reno, Nevada. All around are great off-limits blank areas of the map commandeered by the US military for clandestine testing and training. The rainfall in Utah reduces markedly west of Interstate 15, the highway which more or less bisects the state north to south. Hence the air at Bonneville is dry and clear and pitilessly reveals mile after mile of a world both hostile and supremely ugly. The topography consists of high, parched mountains and flat, sterile plains, littered with occasional buttes and warty boulders. If it weren't for the patches of grass and scrub which cling erratically to the surface, crossing the Great Salt Lake Desert and riding on towards the Goshute Mountains would be like traversing the surface of the moon; or visiting a 1950s inter-stellar Hollywood film set.

In the middle of all this lie the Bonneville Salt Flats them-selves. Covering some 30,000 acres, these are the remnants of a body of water which, 15,000 years ago, was the size of Lake Michigan. Over time this inland sea entirely dried out, leaving a cool, hard, flat, white plug at a height of four and a half thousand feet above sea level. So wide and empty are the Flats, it's possible to persuade yourself that you can make out the curvature of the earth as your eyes drift unhindered from east to west. In comparison with the surrounding miles, the Flats themselves were, and are, beautiful, the Silver Island Mountains rising up in the distance (although, thanks to the rarity of the air, appearing much closer), the salt looking like an immense smooth field of snow.

One or two trappers and drifters managed to cross this geographical blank before Joseph Reddeford Walker mapped the area in 1833. Walker's employer – Paris-born frontiersman Captain Benjamin Louis Eulalie de Bonneville, of the United States Army – almost certainly never set foot on the Flats, but gave them his name anyway. Settlers migrating across to California sometimes died horribly in this blanched desert (the Donner-Reed party of 1846 ending their days amid starvation and cannibalism) before, at the start of the twentieth century, the Western Pacific Railroad Company decided to build a line from San Francisco, across Nevada and into Salt Lake City. Just west of the Bonneville Flats they found a freshwater spring in the mountains and piped it down to the track. This led to the construction of a roundhouse, some sidings, the appur-tenances of life. It also led to the gradual emergence, right on the state line between Utah and Nevada, of Wendover, the townlet which neighbours Bonneville and whose latter-day fragile seediness and air of chronic dilapidation led to its being twittingly renamed Bendover and (by Bob Hope) Leftover.

By the mid-1930s Wendover was a ramshackle halt both for the railway and anyone driving east–west on what is now Highway 80. In fact, there were two Wendovers: Utah Wendover, which was dry – not because of any residual government Prohibition, but because of the Mormonism of Utah State – and a sleazier adjoining Nevada Wendover, which sold alcohol. The Utah Wendover had a population of about two hundred and fifty, with some cabins for passers-by to rent. Just the other side of the state line was a sub-hamlet called Cobblestone, which consisted of an inn with a licence to sell booze, a wood and corrugated-iron garage and a dozen more cabins. A mile west of that lay the fully named Wendover, Nevada: a bar, a gas station, a pool hall and six more wood cabins. There was a dump of about fifty derelict cars just to one side of the road. The butcher and baker had to come out from Salt Lake City. The nearest doctor was fifty miles west. There were once three stores, but two of them burned down.

Without a doubt the liveliest place to be, most of the time, was the main roadside garage, which had been supplying gasoline, water and air since the 1920s to anyone mad enough to drive from Salt Lake City through to Sacramento and San Francisco, or the other way. Thus, an average mid-thirties day at the gas pump might see a deracinated farming family heading west from the Badlands in search of a new life, their world lashed to the roof and sides of the car; a bunch of miners in a truck; a pair of New England WASPs with a lapdog and a Duesenberg, touring. Once a motorist came through on the way from London to Australia overland. He had bought a second-hand car in New York and was going to sell it on in San Francisco before catching a steamer south. An extremely tall sheriff called 'High' Elliott (more familiarly known as 'High Pockets') kept watch over the comings and goings. The sun throbbed in the dreadful cobalt sky and the wind blew hot and dusty from the table land to the south. It was a spot which drew the determined and the determinedly unhinged.

The bar at Wendover, Nevada, was run by a cracked escapee from Northumberland. And this was to be Campbell's new home for the months of August and September 1935: in its way, every bit as barbarous and inhospitable as Verneuk Pan, only with stricter interdictions concerning drink.

The earliest speed kings had actually turned up long before the railway. In 1896 William D. Rishel of Cheyenne, Wyoming, was given the job of crossing the Salt Flats on a bicycle by William Randolph Hearst as a publicity stunt. His bike got stuck in the sticky, tar-like mud which lies just below the surface at the damper extremities of the Flats and it took him twenty-two hours to cross. Still, Rishel was excited enough by Bonneville to persuade 'Terrible' Teddy Tetzlaff to run his Benz racer there in 1914. After this the word slowly spread that if anyone was truly committed, they could attack any kind of speed record out there in perfect safety and near-anonymity.

Anyone could try their luck there; but it took a special kind of obsessive to make the place his own. From the 1920s onwards that obsessive was local boy Ab Jenkins. Born in Spanish Fork, Utah, Jenkins was a dedicated Mormon, whose lifelong abstinence – no alcohol, coffee or tobacco – was believed to give him his extraordinary powers of strength and stamina. 'I owe the maintenance of my endurance ability to the observance of the Word of Wisdom of the Mormon Church,' he said, 'which my good mother taught me as a boy.' His first big test came in 1925, when they built a proper road – the Victory Highway – past Bonneville and through Wendover. Driving a Studebaker, Jenkins beat a special excursion train running alongside in a race across the Flats. In 1926 he drove single-handed across the United States in 86 hours and 20 minutes. In 1928 he raced a car (again single-handed) round a track in Atlantic City for twenty-four hours.

By 1932 Jenkins had struck a deal with the Pierce-Arrow car company to drive one of their new sports models round and round for twenty-four hours in a circle on the Bonneville flats. This he managed with ease, writing notes to his team on a pad of paper stuck to the middle of the steering wheel and then hurling them out at 100 mph. The car, dressed up in a special bodywork of rare hideousness, a genuine Batmobile, was called the *Mormon Meteor*.

The next year he did the same again, despite a 60-mph gale. On the last leg of that test the then fifty-year-old Jenkins shaved himself while driving at 125 mph, so as to look presentable for the cameras at the finish. In 1935 he was still out on the Flats in his *Mormon Meteor* when Cobb turned up with the *Napier Railton* to attempt his logbook of endurance records. Ab promptly moved his car and spares out of the little shantytown of tents and free-sided marquees he had built for himself and, in an access of marvellous charity, handed his entire headquarters over to Cobb. 'Cobb is a great fellow,' he declared. 'It was a pleasure to do everything in our power for him.' He then beat the long-distance records which Cobb had just set and a couple of years later was elected Mayor of Salt Lake City.

On Campbell's arrival at the Flats, at the end of August, the temperatures at midday regularly went over 110°F. Under the auspices of the Salt Lake City Junior Chamber of Commerce the salt itself had been scraped smooth of any imperfections and an eight-inch black line of old diesel oil was being painted down the middle of the dead-straight thirteen-mile track, running north-east to south-west, the road and railway line lying east–west along the southern edge of the course. A procession of telegraph poles, stretching north across the track, had to be negotiated in a ghostly reminder of the cramped pier supports at Daytona.

When Campbell fetched *Blue Bird* out of its Wendover shed

and towed it down the road behind a wooden-sided wagon normally used for carrying timber, instead of tens of thousands of cheering Floridians to greet him, there were no more than a few hundred spectators mopping the backs of their necks. Most of them had driven for two hours out of Salt Lake City. Some were just passing through, indifferently stopping to see if there was 'any racing today'. Mirages drifted across the salt as the day grew hotter. Everyone wore white overalls and solar topees. Shoes had to be soled in rubber – the salt crystals ate away leather. The glare was so fierce that Campbell's dark glasses failed to keep out the worst of it and he was forced to squint.

It was not just the absence of comfortable hotels, restaurants, boxing matches, palm trees, dances, welcoming crowds, swimming pools, that pointed up how different the record attempt felt here. Pendine had been raw, amateurish and elementally British; Daytona Beach was a long way away, but at least had straightforward communications and a carnival atmosphere. But Bonneville had removed all playfulness, imposing its own new level of spartan commitment and sucking Campbell into a kind of desperate new professionalism.

At two thousand miles from the harbour at New York, it was over twice as far to travel overland by rail to Bonneville as it had been to get to Jacksonville by steamer. The train carrying *Blue Bird* to Wendover shunted so violently that, even with the car in its packing crate, the motion broke part of the car's steering. An enormously tall semi-indigent named Sam Lamus – 'the Mayor of the Salt Flats' – inhabited a shack on the dried salt bed, the only living creature for miles. Fifteen years of solitary existence in this desert had given him a mass of debatable insights into the conditions of the salt. He shared this knowledge unstintingly with a Campbell who, partly, was interested to know; and, partly, had no way of escaping even if he'd wanted to.

The boys in the team – even Leo Villa – got terribly bored

in the evenings. The only significant pastime, once both Wendovers had been fully explored, was shooting things: duck, coyote, tin cans, advertising hoardings. Fourteen-year-old Donald Campbell came out. This was the first time he had been allowed to participate in one of his father's LSR attempts. He was introduced to the press as 'my wee son'. The local police let him ride around on a motorcycle and drive a police Ford V8 at 100 mph. He was in a state of high agitation and, like Sam Lamus, could not be avoided.

Was anything worth quite this level of tormenting self-denial, if you weren't Ab Jenkins, but instead, a wealthy fifty-year-old from the Home Counties chasing the number which signalled your retirement from competition and your anticipated elevation into the Establishment? It felt as if everything was going into reverse – thanks to Cobb's bright idea – from the comforts of celebrity, into a wasteland. 'I hope to goodness he will get it if he must, and come home,' complained Lady Campbell, voicing the nervous incredulity that everyone felt about the Bonneville attempt. 'If he does not, I suppose he will consider building another car or something and trying again. I should like him to finish with it.'

Days went by, fettling the car and trying out the course. Then, on the morning of 3 September 1935, Campbell did indeed manage to finish with it. After a surprisingly encouraging test run, conditions were right for the 300-mph sprint, the climax to a decade of endeavour. And, in keeping with the mood of finality which had settled over the attempt, Campbell almost killed himself making the record run.

Confusion attended the start, when a spectator drove across the timing wires and the equipment had to be laboriously reset. The timing station for the Contest Board of the AAA was set up mid-way down the course on a rickety wooden platform twelve feet above the ground. A group of about ten officials sat up in this rookery, wearing hats and scratching their cheeks. *Blue Bird* sat in state at the south-western end of the course under an awning, while Villa and the other team members fussed over its tyres and spark plugs. It took them an hour to get the timing gear sorted out, by which time the sun had risen in the sky. Campbell found himself staring obliquely into it as he crouched in his leather bucket seat.

At last they said he could go ('These long waits are to me very reminiscent of the war – waiting for "zero hour",' he assured the *Daily Mail*) and in a thundercloud of filthy black smoke, the great blue five-ton truck that was *Blue Bird*, with the minute figure of Campbell hunched over the wheel, disappeared off into emptiness on its last great run. Everything was going fine up until this point. The salt was relaxingly smooth after Daytona. The specially placed yellow mile marker boards shot past like signs glimpsed from a train. The red board for the start of the measured mile came up. Campbell hauled on a lever in the cockpit, which (a clever novelty, this, from Railton) shut the mouth of the radiator, smoothing off the prow of the car, reducing the wind resistance and giving Campbell some extra miles an hour for the few seconds he was crossing the measured mile.

Only now, oil started to film over the windscreen and fumes were being sucked into the cockpit. With the radiator shut, all the currents of air through the car were thrown into confusion and the filthy exhalations of the Rolls-Royce engine ended up in Campbell's face. He started to pass out with carbon-monoxide poisoning and the track became a greying blur. He could hardly see the black line on the salt. Lengthening moments of semi-consciousness went by. He thought he might be dying.

As the end of the mile came up, Campbell queasily managed to reopen the radiator, and started to work the brakes. At this point the nearside front tyre simply detonated itself. The car thrashed across the desert at 250 mph; the tyre caught fire and shreds of incandescent rubber flew into the air, just like in the old days at the Dunlop test shed. The car was shaking frenziedly, like a cart on a dirt track. Despite nearly a quarter of a century of competitive wheel-wrestling, with all those trials and runs at Pendine and Daytona – the skids, the lurchings, the drenchings, crunchings, near-misses, crack-ups, blow-ups and emergency stops – this could have been the event to finish him off. A flick of the rattling, shuddering, wheel the wrong way, and what was meant to be his last LSR would have indeed been his last ever, with five tons of *Blue Bird* cartwheeling through the empty whiteness and Campbell, strapped to his seat inside, battered and mangled into oblivion, like Parry Thomas, Frank Lockhart and Lee Bible.

But the car stayed on the ground. Campbell blundered on, dazed, before at last crunching to a halt half a mile from where the *Blue Bird* mechanics were waiting for him under an awning. Leo Villa had been chasing after him in a Lincoln at 100 mph, with Donald in the passenger seat. The team dragged the fresh tyres and the rest of the gear needed for the return run the half-mile to Campbell's car, where he was swatting at the still-burning tyre with a Pyrene fire extinguisher. 'Hurry! Hurry!' he cried, grey-faced with fear and gas poisoning. They had just under an hour to make the turn-around. Normally this was plenty of time – only now, they had to wait for the twisted, incandescent wheel to cool off before they could change it. The sun was getting hotter in the sky. Everyone was sweating. Singeing their hands, they forced the burnt wheel off the car and worked a new one on. Then the word came down that there was more trouble with the timing equipment.

For once Campbell made no attempt to appear masterfully serene. He stamped around on the salt, sucking furiously at his cigarette, muttering to Villa, 'I'm not looking forward to this a bit. I had a bloody awful ride down. I was nearly suffocated.' They fixed the problem with the timing equipment. A genuinely frightened Campbell climbed back into his seat, had the immense engine fired up one last time, pulled down his goggles, shunted *Blue Bird* into gear and shot back down the oily line to the start, leaving the problematic radiator shutter open all the way. At last, 'The little man with the boundless courage rode his bumping mount down to a halt' at the end of the course, skidding dramatically at the end, almost out of space. The car was roughcast in salt, as if it had been standing out in a blizzard.

Back at the aerial timing post, the AAA officials were doing their arithmetic to see if Campbell had actually broken 300 mph. What if the timing gear had failed again? What if the car had underperformed after its near-catastrophe on the first run? What if they had to do it all over? Once Donald had returned in the pursuing Lincoln, he burst into tears, flung his arms round his father's neck and started kissing him. The agony increased: it turned out that Campbell had averaged 299.9 mph. Having been nearly asphyxiated and almost smashed to pieces, he was so desperate not to have to repeat the run that his normal reflex – to treat the setback as an opportunity to display his natural iron resolution – deserted him and he asked pathetically, 'Can't you make it a flat 300?' Well, no, they couldn't. 'Damn. I'll have to do it again.' The small waiting crowd was heard to murmur, 'Tough break.'

As soon as the ever-faithful Lord Wakefield learned that Campbell was going to go out again the next morning, he cabled from London, beseeching him not to do so. 'You have nobly upheld the high reputation of British engineering, and earned the admiration of sportsmen of all nations,' he said. 'May I now appeal to you to rest content on your laurels?' There was a feeling that Bonneville was somehow *maudit*; that the intolerable strangeness of the land was a true indication of its deeper characteristics. And 299.9 mph! Was this some kind of ethereal gesturing to Maeterlinck, to the impossibility of obtaining a given happiness by pursuing it?

Almost certainly, for not long after Campbell and the team had started to pack up and tow the salt-caked, smoke-blackened *Blue Bird* back to the Cobblestone Inn, the timekeepers came up, frantic with apology, and announced that the correct time for the second run was 12.08 seconds, not 12.18, the figure they had incorrectly snatched from their instruments. This meant that, overall, Campbell had averaged 301 mph. He exploded with rage: 'To hell with it!' he shouted. 'You have completely spoiled it for me. You have *ruined* what should have been my final and finest achievement!'

Ruined it in more ways than one: British newspapers went to bed on the information that he had just failed to breach 300 – 'Campbell Trying Again'. Only a few managed to squeeze in a paragraph on the Latest News jotter, to the effect that the speed had been officially corrected to 301 mph. By the time the next day's papers were ready, the story had gone cold and was no longer quite as worthy a lead as it was the day before. The BBC compensated by broadcasting a recording of the record bid during its evening sports bulletin on 4 September. And by 9 September film of the record would be shown in London cinemas, having been rushed back across the Atlantic by the liner *Normandie*, holder of the Blue Riband. But for the national press, the timing was all wrong.

Besides, it was now an anti-story, a story in which everything ultimately hinged on the substitution of one small number for another. There was a scent of pedantry hanging over it: which was busily parodied a day later by Beachcomber, the *Daily Express*'s anarchic, scattergun, reactionary resident humorist. Having dealt with the 'Night of agony in every English home', waiting for news of the result and wondering whether there was any truth in the 'Rumour of $301\frac{3}{4}$ miles per hour', Beachcomber let rip, announcing that '$301\frac{2}{19}$ miles per hour was officially denied, confirmed, unofficially denied, officially denied again, and then unofficially confirmed. $299\frac{7}{26}$ was confirmed unofficially, denied officially (twice), reconfirmed, redenied (both officially and unofficially) and finally both denied and confirmed (officially and unofficially). What torture! What suspense! What tedious rot!'

It really was over. A slip of the timekeeper's pencil and Campbell's last great run – despite all its alarms, its true moments of deadly danger – had lapsed into anticlimax.

When he got back to England he lamely submitted – at a dinner given for him at the Dorchester Hotel – that 'I have promised my wife that if I reached the 300 miles an hour mark I would give it up once and for all.' This turned out to be true. He simply lost interest in *Blue Bird*; he had exhausted himself. So much time, money, energy, determination: all spent. Even as American toy manufacturers such as Lindstrom were turning out thousands of *Blue Bird* toy cars, true to its latest incarnation (covered in tiny rivets and with a sweetly realised impression of Campbell apparently lying supine in the cockpit, like a rheumatism patient in a therapy tank), so the real *Blue Bird* disappeared from view. 'Now that I have reached my goal behind the wheel,' he told the *New York Times*, 'perhaps some day I shall go back to look for the treasure of Cocos Island.'

But instead of returning to Cocos, he decided to seek treasure closer to home. The great *Blue Bird* adventure over, he decided to cash in the investment he had made in his own fame and move forward to what he confidently imagined the next phase of his life would be.

The General Election of November 1935 was now due. This, surely, was the moment he had prepared for, for so long: since the clarion summons of Sir William Joynson-Hicks back in 1928, this was the leap from celebrity into authority that he had dreamed of. He had tested himself back in 1931, bloodying the great Duff Cooper. He had caused countless books to be written in his name. He had appeared in newspapers, made radio broadcasts, helped launch the National Safety First Association's road-safety campaign, made speeches, spread himself thoroughly throughout the land. He was a national and international figure. Now, at fifty, he had the presence and the gravitas to become a Member of Parliament and use all his experience and initiative more fully in the service of his country.

The seat he was given to fight as a Unionist candidate was not ideal. It was the hard-nut, run-down, working-class, Thameside constituency of Deptford, south-east London. Formerly home to the Royal Naval Dockyard, the area had spent most of the twentieth century gradually losing its grip on prosperity. By the 1930s many of the light industries which had grown up around Deptford's river and railway links had folded. The Thames was silting up, unemployment was endemic and about the only long-term employers seemed to be the Royal Victoria Victualling Yard and the world's first large-scale power station, up Deptford Creek. The economy, as ever, was heading west, out along the Great West Road. This part of London was now deeply depressed and prey to spasms of political extremism and social unrest.

The surprise was that in the General Election of 1931 Deptford had returned a Unionist candidate with 26,558 votes – a majority of 4314 over the only other rival, the Labour candidate. Perhaps less surprising when one remembers the fissile nature of Ramsay MacDonald's Labour Party and the way that it had more or less destroyed itself in the General Election of that year, winning a mere 52 seats in Parliament, against 473 for the Conservative and Unionist Party. Four years on, and Labour was still in a condition of near-terminal frailty. For someone of Campbell's starchily right-wing temperament, Deptford was clearly an interesting challenge.

And yet, when it came to it, Campbell's oratorical shortcomings and his inability to convey warmth or sincerity at will to the everyday voter slowly but surely dragged him down. He was shy of the general public, lost his audiences and was persistently heckled at his election rallies. One especially determined woman made a point of sitting in the front row, shouting and swearing at him; but she did, at least, give him his best opportunity for spontaneity. Feeling particularly aggrieved one night, she bellowed, 'Sit down, you fucking bastard, sit down,' as Campbell got up to speak. Showing untypical wit (or having successfully worked out a riposte in advance), he called back, 'Oh, Mother! I didn't see you here. But why tell all these people about our shameful secret?' This had the desired effect: the heckler disappeared, ushered out by laughter and abuse, and was never heard from again. It was, however, the high point of the campaign.

Come 15 November, the day of voting, and Campbell's inherited majority was overturned. The Labour candidate got in, with a majority of 6892, in defiance of the country at large, which went solidly, once more, behind Baldwin's Conservatives. Nor did the successful incoming regime offer Campbell an *ex officio* position concerned with transport, as a consolation.

His Christmas card that year was tinged with regret:

Wishing You A Happy Christmas
And, When Past
A 'Blue Bird' Year Unclouded
To The Last

May all our efforts in 1936 be crowned with success.

He consoled himself by moving out of his home at Povey Cross, with its mixture of cod-baronial and *gemütlich*, and translating everything to the Georgian grandeur of Headley Grove, a stuccoed mansion atop Pebble Coombe Hill, near Dorking. This was a place befitting a man of Sir Malcolm's position, even if he had lost the seat at Deptford. Visitors arriving at the front door of Campbell's new seat of power were surprised to be greeted by a liveried footman, dressed in a jacket in *Blue Bird* blue, with crested buttons, a black and white striped waistcoat and black trousers.

Inside, Campbell would be doing his best to keep busy:

brooding on the layout of his latest nine-hole golf course; or working on his next public pronouncement, such as his address to the Over Forty-Fives Association, who were appealing for a capital fund of 100,000 shillings. 'Formerly there was a premium on age,' said Sir Malcolm; 'to-day that position has been reversed and age stands at a discount.' The answer? 'The question has been much exaggerated and the trouble can best be overcome by intensive propaganda.' The engagements kept coming in. At the start of 1937 he was at the London Motorcab Owner-Drivers' Association ('The question of congestion is very serious'). And at the end of the year he joined the London Press Club at its Ladies' Night Dinner, in the presence of Miss Gracie Fields, where he suspected that the Government was soon to introduce safety legislation governing pedestrians: 'In future, the pedestrian might have to carry an "L" on his back until he has passed an examination.'

But was it, honestly, enough for him? Had he been right to turn his back so abruptly on record breaking? He wasn't an MP; he wasn't really anything now, except a wealthy retiree of fifty living in Surrey. Boredom loomed over him. According to Dorothy, he hated staying at other people's houses and didn't like people messing up his place. He gave up socialising at home. He was 'really a bit of a recluse at heart . . . in his private life all he really wanted was to be left alone . . .'

Surely there was something better for him to do? What about taking the mighty Rolls-Royce engine out of his old LSR car and building it into a powerboat in order to take the Water Speed Record off Gar Wood? Water was much more of a mystery than land – an almost infinite mystery, in fact. But that made the challenge all the more worthwhile. And, of course, if no one else took the LSR off him, it would make him that most superb of adventurers – holder of the World Land Speed Record and World Water Speed Record. Shouldn't he complete his decade-long mimicry of Sir Henry Segrave, in fact?

* * *

And *Blue Bird* itself, the repository of all that work and ingenuity and money? It vanished, eventually turning up in 1950, tragically weathered and distressed, in the cluttered yard of a Wembley-based car dealer named Simpson. At that point Donald Campbell got hold of it, swapped it for his father's *Blue Bird* powerboat, which had indeed been built, and, in its turn, ended up with an American auto dealer. The *Blue Bird* LSR car, the most famous of all the speed machines, returned to the States, its ownership gradually subdividing among interested parties as it was moved from one provincial museum to another. Eventually it became a kind of curatorial embarrassment, a throwback to an age so distant and unimaginable to the average American that it might as well have been a hansom cab. At the time of writing it is in Florida.

16

Two Madmen

⟪℮ ℮⟫

As 1936 dawned there remained just two madmen sweating it out in the wastes of Utah for the World Land Speed Record. Not Harlan Fengler, who, at the start of 1936, announced that he was to build a $100,000 two-engined racer, specifically to beat Campbell's 301 mph. Not Bernd Rosemeyer in a Nazi-sanctioned Auto-Union. Not Billy Arnold, using Gar Wood's old engines. And certainly not Barney Oldfield, in his huge device shaped like an inverted canoe. No, the two madmen had to be British, because by now, only the British cared enough.

Captain George Eyston was one; his friend John Cobb, naturally, the other. Stonyhurst-educated Eyston was just two years Cobb's senior. He resembled Cobb in that he was a large, pear-shaped *haut bourgeois*. In all other respects he was a startling exotic, a sprig off a family tree of legendary Catholic recusants (who had maintained a private Catholic chapel at their Oxfordshire home all through the Reformation), a fitness fanatic, hero in the Great War (being awarded the Military Cross), sailor, pilot, engineer, deviser of asbestos overalls (after an MG he had been driving in a record attempt caught fire underneath him), deep-sea angler and powerboat racer.

Eyston made an entire career out of breaking records of different durations in different sizes of car, and had set over two hundred individual records by 1935. Many of these were taken at Montlhéry. Eyston spent so much time there that the French named him 'Le Recordman' and awarded him the Légion d'Honneur. He was also a Sovereign Knight of Malta and his wife was a personal friend of the Hon. Dorothy Paget. More than *haut bourgeois*, frankly: an aristocrat of the Roman Catholic Church, who, when once offered a cigar-cutter by a guest seated beside him at a formal dinner, merely sliced the end off his cigar with a well-tended thumbnail and proclaimed, 'God gave me my cigar-cutter, young man!' He wore tight, owlish spectacles and a modest moustache. In 1935 he organised an all-woman team of six drivers in three MGs at Le Mans. They were known as his 'Dancing Daughters' (among them Doreen Evans), which indicated a sense of humour, as did his taking a number of records in a car with an AEC bus diesel engine.

His motives for racing and record breaking were mixed – even antithetical. By nature he was an enthusiast; but he drove cars for profit. Quite early on he worked out that, much as he enjoyed competing in races (from Brooklands to Spa to Le Mans to the Mille Miglia) the most efficient returns came from record breaking, in as many classes and over as many distances and durations as possible. A successful record could stand for months, even years, and be used and reused in all kinds of advertising promotions. A race win, on the other hand, was only good until the next race; while a race failure, conversely, counted as positively bad publicity. Records were both durable and profitable in comparison. At the start of 1934 alone, he worked out a record-breaking programme involving the car with the AEC bus engine, a Panhard, a Hotchkiss, a Riley, a Delage and two MGs. His arithmetic led him to conclude that he could finish the entire project by Easter, that it would cost £120 plus expenses to set up, and that he would net around £1500 in publicity money.

He was also shrewd enough to see that, however good business was in 1934, the accumulation of endlessly subdividing records and micro-records was no longer a viable end in itself: the idea of mechanised speed was less intrinsically compelling than it used to be. Eyston had decided that in future only the two big ones would carry any commercial promise: the twenty-four-hour record and the World Land Speed Record.

For the twenty-four-hour record, he built a startlingly ugly special called *Speed of the Wind*, based around an old Rolls-Royce aero engine which had previously been used to power a test bed ventilator. This worked perfectly satisfactorily and in early 1936 he raised the outright twenty-four-hour record to a fraction under 150 mph. That done, he determined to build a real monster car as quickly as he possibly could, to take the LSR before it dwindled to a non-event.

This urgency was just as well, when you consider the competition for publicity he had to face from the rest of the world. In 1936 he had ploughed round in circles in his *Speed of the Wind* at Bonneville, taken his bag of twenty-four-hour records and made modest headlines. But in September alone of that year, the hot 'record' stories ran from the newly launched *Queen Mary* taking the transatlantic liners' Blue Riband from the *Normandie*; to a couple of American airmen named Harry Richman and Dick Merrill trying to fly from New York to London and back again in thirty-three hours (they crashed in Newfoundland on the return leg); to Jim Mollison announcing that he was going to fly extremely rapidly from New York to Johannesburg, via Croydon.

Best of all was single mother and 'Society Blonde' Mrs Beryl Markham, who, on 4 and 5 September, flew solo across the Atlantic from east to west – the first solo flight in that direction by a woman. She crash-landed in a peat bog in Nova Scotia, climbed out of the plane and said to two appalled fishermen, 'I'm Mrs Markham. I've just flown from England.' For this she was given a motorcade through New York City, courtesy of Mayor Fiorello LaGuardia, and became a tremendous celebrity back in England, subsequently writing a best-seller: *West with the Night*.

And what, conversely, was there for the regular motorist back at home? What was the state of car culture? Traffic jams were persistent and omnipresent. Road repairs were permanently behind schedule. Bypasses were appearing across the country, traffic lights had been commonplace since the late twenties, Mr Hore-Belisha's beacons were just coming in, and the car driver's world was assuming all the needling banality by which we recognise it today. Banal and yet wildly dangerous for all road users: there were around seven thousand deaths through road accidents every year; Lord Thomas Dewar observing that there were 'Only two classes of pedestrians in these days of reckless motor traffic – the quick, and the dead.' Significantly, the developers of those new suburban tracts which lived and died by the motor car were careful not to let any cars appear in their advertising features.

The trade in automotive glamour was, in other words, increasingly one way: from the elitist to the general; from Bentley to Austin; from Michael Arlen's 1924 best-seller *The Green Hat* (Iris Storm, thwarted in love with Napier Harpenden, suffers two unhappy marriages and a string of affairs, before committing suicide by driving her yellow Hispano-Suiza into a tree); to George Orwell's 1939 *Coming up for Air* (suburbanised insurance salesman George Bowling drives off in search of his lost childhood: 'I switched the engine off and got out. I never like leaving the old car running in neutral, I'm always half afraid she'll shake her mudguards off or something. She's a 1927 model, and she's done a biggish mileage').

Clearly, Eyston would need to work hard to stem this creeping tide of indifference, and restore some of the old allure of the speed kings. His LSR car took him, it is said, six weeks to cobble together, once he had assembled all the parts. His relationship with Rolls-Royce was by now usefully close (they even offered him a job, on the basis of his interventions with *Speed of the Wind*), so he had access to not one but two supercharged Rolls-Royce aero engines, much like the one Campbell had used in the last *Blue Bird*. This was good. An absolutely huge six-wheeled, eight-tyred, seven-ton car then grew around these engines, Eyston himself taking a hand in much of the design, while a French coachbuilder named Jean Andreau sketched out a thirty-six-foot-long bodywork, shaped like a great silver whale, but with a modish Deco octagon for a mouth. An eight-foot-tall fin stood proud at the rear. Eyston drove some 60,000 miles in the space of a few months in a Bentley with an extra-large boot, carrying the bits and pieces of his LSR car up to the grimy Bean engineering works in Staffordshire, where they were assembled.

Naturally, he approached the usual quarters for sponsorship money – Castrol, Dunlop, Esso and so on – only to be turned down. They had extracted all the publicity they wanted from Campbell's last *Blue Bird* attempt. However eccentric and entertaining Eyston was, he had few of Campbell's astonishing gifts for self-advertisement. So Eyston mortgaged his own home to help raise the necessary funds and carried on hurling his machine together. Impressed by this level of commitment, Castrol relented and got behind the project, as did the increasingly long-suffering Dunlop, who had already spent thousands of pounds of their own money, developing tyres which would stay in one piece at 300 mph.

By the late summer of 1937 the great car was done: full of rough edges, bulging rivets, gaps in the bodywork and paint that would start to flake off above 200 mph. Eyston started for the States in high excitement. Arnold Watson, the PR man at Castrol deputed to look after him, was making his farewells at Waterloo Station, when he said to Eyston, 'I must have a name for this car. What do you want to call it?' In the terrible rush, this was the one thing which Eyston had overlooked. 'Call it what you like,' he shouted, as the train began to pull out.

'I'll call it *Thunderbolt*,' Watson yelled.

'That'll do,' Eyston yelled back.

He arrived in the first week in September. It was raining, and he had to wait two weeks before the Flats were dry enough to use. Then the clutches on *Thunderbolt* kept collapsing under the strain of the Rolls-Royces' huge power and had to be flown out to Los Angeles for repairs. Eyston started to go mad with boredom and frustration. Finally brute energy triumphed on 19 November 1937, and Eyston broke Campbell's LSR at a speed of 312 mph. The Americans, seeking usefully to brand him, called him 'the Captain' and 'Heir apparent to the speed throne'. Campbell-style, his goggles had started to come off his head at 300 mph and he had had to wrestle them back on while steering with one hand: 'It was a hell of a run, and I don't mean that profanely.' The rain continued to fall, and that was the end of that year's record breaking.

Having been mauled by photographers and cameramen ('It's worse than breaking the record') after the long-awaited run, he could only think of getting 'these darned overalls off'. After which his plans were 'To celebrate if I get the chance, then to see Piccadilly, Leicester Square and Hyde Park again as soon as possible. By George! I'm homesick.'

Had he actually been at home at that point, he would have been in a position to appreciate that, so far as the mass media were concerned, his story was already having to cede place to that of Betty Kirkby-Green (a '31-year-old blonde bankrupt club hostess', according to the *Daily Express* of 20 November 1937), who had successfully flown a round trip from London to Cape Town and back, exactly one year after taking her first flying lesson. But Eyston was above such things. He had great plans for 1938 and – once he had received his due congratulations, but no knighthood, from King George VI and placed *Thunderbolt* on display at Selfridges – was hard at work on his car, tweaking the shape of its nose and tail for a more deftly penetrative look.

*　*　*

John Cobb had been back to Bonneville in 1936 in his thunderous *Napier Railton*, retaking the twenty-four-hour and 1000-mile records from Eyston and Ab Jenkins. He was now, unofficially, a 'speed ace', a 'hero' and 'perhaps the best track driver in the world', provided 'track' was synonymous with 'Brooklands'. He was also nearing forty, too big and heavy for the most modern racing cars and their attendant sinuous race circuits, yet still needing to possess for himself the fundamental verities of speed. So, in 1938, having thoroughly matured his plans, he decided to unveil possibly the greatest, most perfectly conceived and executed LSR car of all time. The only question was, did anyone care?

Whether they did or not, the record had been on his mind since the early thirties. When the *Motor* interviewed him in 1934, he first of all said, 'You won't put in any silly stuff about me, will you?' Then, after half an hour of matter-of-factness and uncontainable self-effacement, he was asked if he wanted to go in for the LSR.

'Too expensive for me.'

And of course, it was such a big thing to go for, nudged the *Motor*. Cobb thought about this. If you were the appalling Sir Malcolm Campbell, it was the biggest, most hazardous thing anyone could possibly imagine. Cobb's interest flickered for a moment. 'Oh, I don't know,' he said mildly. 'It's just a straight run after all, isn't it?' And then, just in case anyone missed the essential detraction that he was trying to convey, he added: 'Just a matter of keeping going.'

A few years went by, in which time the thought of beating Campbell became increasingly overwhelming. Much as he feared and hated the idea of failing in public, Cobb knew that the Land Speed Record was something he would be good at. He had the money to pursue the ambition. He still had his inward, visceral dislike of Campbell and he very much liked the idea of owning *that* number. He also had the assent of his mother. There was no good reason not to try for it.

Finally he commissioned a car with which to go after the record, much as any wealthy enthusiast might commission a yacht or a country residence. He got Reid Railton to design it, with a view to keeping to a reasonably tight budget: 'Reid's ideas are not only clever but also practical to build and he always considers costs.' It had two engines – but unlike Campbell's or Eyston's last-word Rolls-Royce motors, the best Cobb and Railton could lay their hands on were a pair of superannuated Napier Lion aero engines. These were a good ten years old and had last seen active duty in one of Marian Carstairs's *Estelle* powerboats at the end of the 1920s. The new machine also made do with a mere four wheels (but four-wheel-drive), round which Railton designed a cool, teardrop-shaped body of great elegance and modernity (known by the design team as 'the Bun', in contradistinction to the other shapes tested at the National Physical Laboratory: 'Long Tail' and 'Cigar'). The Thomson & Taylor job code for the car was the enigmatic 'Q.5000'. It cost around £10,000 to build.

And it was – and still is – something of a masterpiece. Cobb's stroke of genius was to leave the entire design to Railton, who, at the age of forty, was at the peak of his abilities. *Blue Bird*, in all its Railton-manipulated forms, still had Campbell's personality stamped through it and was fettered accordingly. Cobb, on the other hand, was like Segrave in that he entrusted the design and engineering to others, saving himself for the driving and the administration. Unlike Segrave, who could be both intrusive and aggressive in order to hurry things along, Cobb left Railton, Thomson and Taylor alone. So far as Railton was concerned, Cobb was the perfect patron; and he lavished on the project all the daring and brilliance which long moments of speculation on the ideal LSR car had invested in him.

Indeed, Cobb approached the project in what looks to have been a startlingly progressive manner. Hindsight gives the impression that, all along, everything was planned, involving a managed progress towards a clearly stated, faintly Utopian end. Cobb's long and wearisome apprenticeship at Brooklands; his first record of any description – the one-hour record for his class in his Delage, in 1929; the building of the *Napier Railton* back in 1933 – all fit a pattern, in which each move is a considered step towards the final goal. It seems a very 1930s scientific approach, logical, democratic, faintly collectivist; as opposed to Campbell's wilful embodiment of that other 1930s type, the Dynamic Individual. Delegating everything to Railton, an absolute technocrat, Cobb got a car which was half as powerful as Eyston's terrifying *Thunderbolt*, but also half the weight, smaller, lower, sleeker (it had no radiators, only iced water) and markedly cleverer.

Cobb even allowed himself to become invisible when actually inside the car. All the way up to the last, biggest *Blue Bird*, Campbell occupied the traditional driver's seat, just astern of the massive engine, wrestling with the elemental force of the machine, exposed to the elements. Originally, back in 1926, his head, arms and torso had all been visible at the wheel; latterly only his tiny head to act as a signifier that he was still there, still exerting his masculinity, enduring. Cobb, on the other hand, sat right inside the nose of what was now being called the *Railton Special*, enclosed by a little aluminium and glass conning tower. All that you could see of him with the lid on were his smoked-glass goggles, peering out. This not only made for better aerodynamics, but enabled Railton to shove all the complex mechanicals away behind the driver's seat in the most space-efficient manner possible.

So relaxed was Cobb about his significance to the venture that he was happy to lose himself inside this curiously sexless, denatured machine – a machine that was halfway to being a flying saucer and which looked like a drop of mercury, skimming across the Salt Flats: the 'Strangest racer ever built,' according to the *Weekly Illustrated*.

And he was patient. He even seemed to like the waiting, the trials, the tests, the endless small rectifications. In the middle of the hour turn-around time allowed during a record attempt, he would say, 'Is there anything I can do to help?' And, on being told that there wasn't (Ken Taylor would be scrambling around the machinery; the increasingly corvine Railton staring at his watch) Cobb would stand aside and clasp his hands behind his back, as if waiting in a queue at the post office. Processes seemed as important to him as the record itself.

But then his whole relationship with the LSR, the big number, was unlike that enjoyed by Segrave or Campbell. He articulated it in a kind of manifesto of record breaking which appeared at around this time. It appeared in *The Romance of Record Breaking*, but was refreshingly unromantic in its approach. 'You might as well ask,' asks Cobb, 'why kick a football around a field, or knock a cricket ball about, or run round and round a stadium, or play games at all for that matter. Why do men climb mountains – there's nothing at the top but a view?' The personal imperative is, of course, what matters: 'Record breaking in motoring is just another outlet for this drive from within to do something nobody else has done, and by that alone, in my view, such things are justified.' What of the furious patriotism of Campbell and Segrave? What of the need to improve the humble passenger car by driving at 300 mph? 'If it amuses a man to drive a car faster than anyone else – or even to try to – then that is enough reason for his trying, so long as his attempt does not bring hardship on anyone else,' is Cobb's private and somewhat Hobbesian answer.

Actually he does end his *tour d'horizon* by paying lip service to the old creed, but not without some struggle: 'Records which tend to perfect the motor car engine and chassis tend also to improve the ordinary car which the customer buys in the shop – although what is learnt in records may not be applied for many years to the touring car.' As for national prestige and the glory which accrues to British industry and workmanship – not a mention.

Cobb actually liked the sheer inaccessibility of Bonneville, quite apart from its spaciousness, as it let him get on with the work in hand, unmolested. He didn't have to make speeches, or wave at the crowds. Before he had left England he had been badgered into saying a few things about the *Railton Special* for the cameras – he was, after all, the owner of what was probably the most complex wheeled motor vehicle in the world; possibly the fastest, too. But while Campbell, chipper in his plus fours and muffler, was happy to launch the last, greatest *Blue Bird* at Thomson & Taylor's – firing the engine up in a barrage of smoke, chatting for the cameras – Cobb had to be loaded into the driver's seat on the bare chassis of the *Railton Special*, where, with a look of furtive horror, he read his address from a sheet of paper stuck to the steering wheel. 'The chief feature of the car is its perfect streamlined form,' he managed to announce.

As well as finding it enormously difficult to speak in public, this speed king reminded the world how far things had changed regarding personal appearance. Segrave had been something of a bald, golden god. Campbell, if not so obviously delicious, was at least lean, crinkly and hawkish. Eyston looked like a powerfully built and mildly unconventional maths teacher. And Cobb, with his broad, flat face, receding hairline and prominent nose; his large, formless body; his expression, both placid and affronted – looked like a bored, wealthy farmer, even dressing like one from time to time, in smart tweeds, flat hat and tent-like topcoat.

Perhaps it was as well that the enterprise now had acquired something of the necessary concealment of one of the big air record bids. Just as Mrs Beryl Markham had disappeared into the gathering dusk over the Atlantic, not to be seen again for another twenty-four hours, so, by August 1938, Cobb had disappeared to a spot which was unknown and unknowable not just to most of the world, but to most Americans as well. Save the occasional presence of the shiftless film crews and pressmen, plus whoever had driven out from Salt Lake City that day, the British driver and his little team of mechanics and assistants were left to themselves.

George Eyston was also in Utah in August 1938. He was there in his rethought *Thunderbolt*, waiting for the rain to stop. He had turned up in midsummer, expecting to set a new record and go home before Cobb arrived. But the Salt Flats were flooded and it took five weeks for the rain to halt, the water to dry off and the salt to harden up. So both parties squeezed into Wendover and fidgeted with their machines. Dunlop Mac had a stash of 100 tyres capable of reaching 400 mph, their surfaces 'almost as smooth as peach skins', as he lovingly recalled. The Utah authorities gave Cobb and the team honorary driving licences and stuck a whimsical Utah number plate on the front of the *Railton Special* chassis. In God-fixated Mormon country, what significance was there in the fact that the number plate ended in 666, the Number of the Beast from the Book of Revelation?

Eyston seemed to be having more problems, overall. At various times in his relationship with *Thunderbolt*, he was blinded and suffocated by smoke when the brakes came on; parboiled in the steam from his cooling system; and wedged so hot and tight in his seat that it took him five minutes to thrash his way out of the car at the end of one run ('I had the devil of a time. The heat of the motors must have swelled my body'). Before long the *Thunderbolt*'s radiator had been blanked off and the engine filled up with iced water; the melodramatic tail fin had been removed, in order to get a few extra miles per hour out of the beast; the cockpit was completely enclosed by a transparent cover.

On 24 August Art Pillsbury, the head AAA timekeeper, urged him on with the words, 'We're all set down here, George. Get it done and make it good.' To which Eyston replied with an absolutely scorching record attempt. The commentator from

KSL Radio News (Utah's premier radio station) described how 'This mad streak of grey is throwing out sand behind it in a mad race for time. This is a time for superlatives! . . . The roar of the motors! There he goes off up toward the north end. He's on his way. Whatever is done now, is done . . .' But the timing equipment had cracked up. Eyston scrambled out of his car, bright with expectation. Pillsbury confessed the AAA's failure and burst into tears. But Eyston, great with Christian forbearance, merely put his arm round Pillsbury and told him not to worry: they would tell the press that it was simply a successful practice and not the real thing. 'Anyone else,' said Pillsbury, 'would have bawled me out good and proper, in front of everybody, but he just lifted that weight off me.'

Cobb and Eyston spent a good deal of time in each other's company. The air of Utah was filled with British voices. When Cobb discovered that the boys in his squad needed some beer money to spend in Nevada, he at once peeled off a handful of dollar notes, and, perhaps thinking ruefully of Campbell's gift with money, declared that 'If anyone tells you a man can get rich out of the LSR, then he's a liar.' Every now and then the *Thunderbolt* or the *Railton Special* would set off in a storm of hysterical noise for a practice run; and the dense black smoke from the exhausts would stream out for two or three miles behind the car in the crystalline Utah air.

Apart from the remoteness of the setting, the mechanical unconventionality of the cars, the insufferable glare of the salt, the absence of vegetation, the heat, the insultingly implausible mirages (of trees, houses, ghost trains, floating rocks), the mountains in the distance and the lonesome bare line of the railway track echoing the black line painted down the speed course, it all resembled, in many ways, Brooklands. After all, there were George Eyston and John Cobb, old friends and competitors, reliving their famous 1932 Empire Trophy battle. There was Dunlop Mac – without the rustic shed in which he normally worked at Brooklands, but still benignly fussing over his tyres. There was Joe Coe, from Napiers. There were Reid Railton and Ken Taylor, from the Thomson & Taylor works.

Even Railton's hard-cover notebook was a repository of Brooklands arcana, dating back to 1917 and the days when he had worked as an assistant to Parry Thomas at Leyland Motors. The back pages carried notes and sketches in Parry Thomas's own hand for an experimental aero engine; the front was full of Railton's more recent postulates and calculations concerning shock absorbers, brakes, gear control (he wrote of the brakes, if they 'will absorb these loads for 30 seconds before coming to rest – OK. Otherwise *NBG*'). As at Brooklands, all these familiar names and faces were contained within a semi-private, enclosed environment, with the Silver Island Mountains and the Great Salt Lake Desert providing the necessary barrier between them and the outside world; and Salt Lake City standing in for Weybridge. In the evenings the teams used to eat together and be British.

For a moment it almost became a proper race, too. Not quite the neck-and-neck thrills once dreamed of by the Mayor of Daytona, back in the twenties, but as close as it was likely to get in the thirties. At the end of August Eyston set up a new LSR of 345.5 mph. A couple of weeks later Cobb went out and beat him at 350.2 mph, making him the first man to reach 350 mph. Eyston then returned to the course *the day after* and did 357.5 mph.

Startled by this relative outbreak of competitiveness, the press immediately cried it up as an 'amazing and expensive duel on the queer salt flats.' This irked Eyston: 'I do not want to talk of any speed battle with John Cobb. The whole thing is distasteful to me.' Choosing to ignore the fact that he and Cobb had been in and out of each other's hair for weeks and that they had had dinner together the night before (at which meal Cobb remarked, humorously, 'I hope it rains like hell'), he went on, 'I don't know anything about Cobb or what he is doing. I have no plans at the moment – but my car will go faster and I have not finished with the world record.'

The problem was that his car wouldn't go very much faster, and he knew it. Cobb, displaying an almost oriental calm, would take out his superstreamlined *Railton Special*, test it, submit it to adjustments and go for a proper run, getting gradually faster all the time. When Eyston bagged his 357.5 mph, taking the record back from Cobb, Cobb affably shook Eyston's hand and said, 'Great work, George. You've got it again! This is becoming amusing!' But Eyston was running out of ideas. 'This is all so confusing,' he said, when he finally retook the LSR on 16 September. 'I am terribly happy to have established a new record . . . my motors did not warm up to their task as quickly as I had hoped, otherwise I might have attained our dream of 360 mph.'

In fact, Eyston's sense of dislocation did more than just express his dizziness at having snatched the record back from Cobb. It was true to the wholly novel experience of driving at more than 350 mph. Sitting under a cockpit bubble like that of a fighter plane, he was no longer caught up in the same buffetings and exterior frictions as his predecessors. On Bonneville Salt Flats he was removed from any conventional relationship with the earth's surface. It felt to him at first as if 'the salt is coming down in front of the car and as though I am going downhill.' Then he 'seemed to be speeding through water'. There was also a 'strange mirage which made it seem as if I were heading straight into a huge lake'. In the end, 'I just seem to be whistling through space.'

Cobb was sitting ahead of the front wheels of the *Railton Special*, rather than behind, as Eyston was in *Thunderbolt*; and much closer to the ground. 'The car,' he said, 'seemed to be trying to run right out from under me.' Despite the fact that 'my vision was blurred. I could hardly see anything at all,' he compared peering through his windscreen with 'standing in front of a window during a tearing gale'. On top of which, he had 'the odd sensation that the line' – the one marked on the salt – 'ran steeply uphill into the sky, which seemed to have gone dark, and I was climbing it'.

The days of sand dunes, corrugated sea mists and crowds of spectators had been replaced by something closer to the unreal world of Flight Test, of the recently established Muroc Air Base, California; or, for that matter, Wendover Air Base, about to be built just down the road by the US Army Air Corps. What elements of showbiz remained were increasingly fortuitous. At the end of Eyston's successful run, both teams called it a day by getting drunk on the Nevada side of Wendover, and singing *Glorious Devon* and *Mad Dogs and Englishmen*.

Eyston's and Cobb's dislocation from the rest of the world was more total than even the normal solipsism of the record breaker would suggest. Even as they struggled through September in the white void, so the Munich Crisis was building up and then fracturing into an uneasy peace. While the press strove to talk Hitler down, the rest of the world contemplated the prospect of its second major conflict in twenty-five years. Churchill's campaign against German aggression was reaching its climax: Munich was a 'total and unmitigated defeat'. Mussolini had consolidated his position at the head of a Fascist Italy and Franco's Nationalists were gaining the upper hand in Spain. All across Europe dreadful history was being made, while the LSR teams fussed and fidgeted in their blinkered isolation.

In order for the technology and performance of the Land Speed Record breakers to improve, they had had to get away from Campbell and his Florida circus, to disengage from the world. But it was Campbell who, by embracing the world, had kept the LSR vital. Who had cared, terribly, whether it was 250 mph, or 270, or 276? What mattered was that it had been Sir Malcolm Campbell in his British institution *Blue Bird*, in a glamorous American setting, fighting a battle with the elements and himself.

Stuck out on his Utah moonscape, Eyston did dent the public's consciousness somewhat; and he did make some money out of endorsements and promotions, as he had hoped: Lodge Spark Plugs, Titan Safety Steering Stabilisers, National Benzole, all chipped in.

Significantly, though, Wakefield Castrol and Dunlop felt that Eyston's name alone (to say nothing of Cobb's) was not enough for their publicity material. To sustain the magic aura, they resorted to retroactively grouping him with Campbell – '"Congratulations Capt. Eyston" – says Sir Malcolm Campbell'; and 'All the Sensational Speed Records Held by John Cobb, Capt. G.E.T. Eyston and Sir Malcolm Campbell Were Achieved on Dunlop!' Mere achievement was no longer enough in itself.

But Cobb was working to a different agenda. His imagination was so comprehensively taken up with getting his *Railton Special* to go faster that he and his team simply ignored the question of commercialism, to say nothing of the arrival of conscription in Great Britain, the annexation of Albania by Italy and Hitler's menaces against Poland; and went back out to Bonneville, in August 1939, to claim the number he knew he was entitled to. In this sense his instincts fitted in with the times. The world was now a dangerous and complicated place. The solitary hero, the glorious futility of the *beau geste*, were no longer meaningful symbols on which to pin one's aspirations. It may be a truism to paint the twenties as frivolous, the thirties as serious, but things could hardly have been more serious than in the late summer of 1939. It was not the time to go in search of fame or column inches. Cobb's reclusiveness was fitting.

Eyston had accepted the inescapable, shelved his LSR plans and sent his *Thunderbolt* off to New Zealand to take part in an exhibition. It would remain there during the war, before accidentally burning down in 1946. No one else was much interested, apart from the Germans, greedy for any opportunity to publicise the forcefulness of Nazism and the supercompetence of German technology. In this, though, the industrial combines of Mercedes and Auto-Union were actually less successful than the British amateurs. The great Grand Prix driver Rudolf Caracciola had nearly killed himself in 1937, driving an imperfectly streamlined Mercedes record car ('unsafe' was his word for it) along the Frankfurt–Darmstadt Reichsautobahn.

The equally great Grand Prix driver Bernd Rosemeyer did kill himself in an aerodynamically dubious Auto-Union, on the same stretch of road the following year. Both drivers hated these high-speed tests on what was, after all, a relatively narrow public highway, and complained that a single record attempt demanded as much concentration as a whole Grand Prix race. So, after two runs in January 1938, Rosemeyer announced, 'I'll only try once again.' On the third run a gust of wind threw him off-course at 270 mph. The car took a quarter of a mile to destroy itself along the surface of the concrete road and in the woodland to its right.

Despite this, in 1939 Daimler-Benz built an excessively advanced aero-engined car, covered in fins and aerodynamic fairings, with a view to seizing the LSR. The Nazis, however, refused to let the car go out to Utah, insisting that it break the world's record on a new seven-mile stretch of autobahn near Dessau. The fact that this, like the previous German autobahn tests, would have been insanely difficult and dangerous made no difference. The attempt only lapsed when it was decided to mine brown coal under where the road ran.

So Cobb – making sure, as usual, that his LSR efforts didn't interfere with the family fur business back at Anning, Chadwick & Kiver, as Anning & Cobb was now known – set his car up and, on 23 August, at dawn, set a new Land Speed Record of very nearly 370 mph. Just to make sure that Campbell was completely expunged from the record books, he also took the five-kilometre and ten-kilometre world records which Campbell had set in 1935. Art Pillsbury increased Cobb's pleasure by recalling Campbell's suffering in his efforts to get to 301 mph, observing that 'If you can't go more than 300 miles an hour now, you're a bum.'

Cobb imprinted his own special reticence on the occasion by observing how it wasn't 'so very frightening' to drive at six miles a minute, and, 'I'm rather happy about it all.' Reid Railton, by now stick-thin and quite unearthly looking in a pair of wraparound black goggles, smirked: an act of silent collusion in Cobb's vision of the world. Was he going to go for one last record attempt, to try to hit the 370 mark? 'Let me digest this one first,' he said comfortably.

At this point the international political situation finally impressed itself even on John Cobb, and he and his team packed up. Ken Taylor took the *Railton Special* off to Canada for safekeeping. A rapid celebration at the Cotton Club in New York for Cobb and his friends Beris Harcourt-Wood (a Bentley driver at Le Mans) and John Dugdale (a journalist) was followed by immediate embarkation on the *Aquitania*, on 30 August. By 3 September they were out in mid-Atlantic when the ship posted a notice that war had been declared. Shortly after that, the *Athenia*, an Atlantic liner of the Donaldson line, was sunk by a German U-boat. Of the 1100 passengers on board, 115 died in the attack.

The *Aquitania* was blacked out and started to head farther south, far away from its normal transatlantic route. It got disturbingly warmer on board. Passengers drifted from deck to deck in a state of growing anxiety. Anti-submarine precautions were taken and hatches were kept shut. Several days later the weather started to cool down again and England came into view.

By the time Cobb had got back to Southampton, shaken the Mayor's hand and been bundled into a car, the Germans were in Poland. And when, in all other circumstances, he might have reasonably expected dinners, presentations and speeches, Cobb found himself buried under the news that Finland had fallen to the Russians and that Stalin had annexed eastern Poland into the Soviet Union. As he worked his way painstakingly towards the most authoritative possible realisation of what it took to achieve the LSR, so the rest of the world at last had something so much bigger to consider that his heroic capture of the record – his, incontrovertibly, in August 1939 – became a dying fall, a perfect irrelevance.

17

Cobb's War

《☬ ☬》

Whereas Cobb could fail to make the headlines even at the height of his powers, Campbell, naturally, could make headlines even when he didn't really mean to. Having turned his back on the LSR, he had indeed built himself a super-fast *Blue Bird* motor boat, round the Rolls-Royce aero engine that served him so well. He took the World Water Speed Record in 1937, 1938 and, with a rebuilt Mk II *Blue Bird*, in 1939. Each occasion was visited by the press and public with slightly less interest than the last, but he had at least trounced Segrave, who had only ever taken the WSR once. Frankly, the main excitement centred around how much his noisy boats irritated the locals – at Coniston Water, and at Lake Geneva, where someone left a note on his *Blue Bird* which read, 'You annoy us with your speed trials.'

The Second World War, though, was not a good time for him. Partly this was because he was now well into his fifties and unable to set any more records in any medium; partly because his marriage to Dorothy had irretrievably collapsed, leading them both into a scandalisingly entertaining and expensive divorce. This took place at the end of April 1940.

Campbell's (and Cobb's) old friend the Hon. Brian Lewis was named as the main party to Lady Campbell's infidelities (going back all those years to 1929); to which Lady Campbell replied with the accusation that Sir Malcolm had been conducting an adulterous liaison with a certain Mrs Atherton. This was thrown out by the judge, as was her argument that Campbell had condoned her adultery in the first place.

She then unveiled a full repertoire of swoonings, collapses and multiple nervous breakdowns, appearing at the steps of the court physically supported by a nurse and her daughter Jean (who herself had been estranged from Campbell for four years). Campbell's counsel complained that up until that point Lady Campbell had 'appeared to be in extremely good health. She has had a nervous breakdown between yesterday and this morning, and I suggest that there might be a series of nervous breakdowns whenever the case comes up.' Lady Campbell's doctor testified to finding her 'lying on the floor, sobbing', but to no avail; the case proceeded. Sir Malcolm retaliated by planting Donald (wearing a Homburg and smoking a pipe) at the back of the court, where he laughed sarcastically at key moments.

Lady Campbell was forced to admit to taking a flat in which she pursued her affair with Lewis. The judge, Mr Justice Hodson, ended by stating that her accusations against Sir Malcolm were both 'wicked and untrue'. Campbell was granted a decree nisi on 29 April. The cost of the case was believed to have run to the astronomical figure of £4500. *Time* magazine claimed that the whole thing 'set a new low in Mayfair muckraking'.

Astonishingly, Campbell committed himself to matrimony for a third time, at the end of the war. He married a Mrs Betty Nicory. 'We have known each other for quite a long time and we are very happy,' he affirmed. But after three months she went on holiday to France and never came back. By then Campbell had sold Headley Grove to the Maharajah of Baroda and moved to Little Gatton, near Reigate. This was a house built by the novelist Sax Rohmer. Lady Campbell found the place 'creepy and redolent of Fu Manchu', Rohmer's famous oriental super-villain. The atmosphere of Little Gatton combined with Campbell's increasingly querulous disposition to drive the third Mrs Campbell into the arms of the Comte André Louis de la Salle in a flat in Sloane Street. She told Campbell that she was 'not the kind of woman he expected he was marrying'. Two years after their marriage they were divorcing.

The war itself found Campbell pursuing various makeweight employments: inventing an armoured car, which he personally demonstrated to King George VI; as well as outboard motors for the Commandos. He reinstated himself as captain with his old company, the Royal West Kent Regiment. Desperate, even at the age of fifty-five, to be useful in the prosecution of the war, he pestered his superiors into letting him accompany a Commando party on one of their raids. Reluctantly consenting, they told him to meet up with his group at Waterloo Station. From there they were to take the train to Southampton and pick up their raiding craft. But even as the train readied to leave, the announcement 'Captain Malcolm Campbell is required at the Station Master's Office' rang out across the Waterloo concourse and Campbell was taken off the mission. His military seniors had lost their nerve: he was too unreliable to let loose again.

Cobb, meanwhile, was displaying his usual adherence to the principle of slow, incremental progress, by joining the General Duties Branch of the Royal Air Force Volunteer Reserve. He had learned to fly at Brooklands (and occasionally landed his plane in the field next to The Grove) but was at first posted to Air Traffic Control. This was both boring (being a ground job) and unnerving (because he was surrounded by WAAFs). The high point of this period of the war came when he acted as a crowd-filler for the 1941 RAF drama documentary *Target for Tonight*. The authentic story of a bombing raid on Germany, filmed with the actual servicemen involved, this won a Special Academy Award for its 'vivid and dramatic presentation of the heroism of the RAF'. 'A direct hit,' said Walter Winchell. Cobb had to stand around silently during a briefing scene, pretending to be an Equipment Officer.

By 1942 he was more actively involved in flying and had moved to the Air Transport Auxiliary, where his job was to ferry RAF aircraft to their bases up and down the country; an echo of Campbell's ferrying duties in the previous war. Campbell was known to be 'ham-handed' as a pilot, whereas Cobb was 'strangely delicate in control for so large a man'. His problem lay in his chronic fear of failing, or appearing to fail. Although he was happy to fly in daylight, night navigation baffled him and he asked for his training to be stopped altogether, convinced that he could never master the skill. So they took him up after dark as a passenger, in order to persuade him it could be done. This ruse, elemental in its simplicity, nonetheless worked and he completed his training.

'His common sense and knowledge of his own limitations made him a reliable and steady ferry pilot,' said one RAF report. He moved to the Air Transport Auxiliary Ferry Pool at White Waltham, Berkshire, where he was described as the 'best possible type of officer and an excellent influence on the Pool'; and ended up as a first officer, based at No. 6 Pool at Ratcliffe, Leicestershire.

Cobb's war concluded with him in his mid-forties, unscathed and preparing to settle back into the fur business. He had expanded somewhat as a human being. At some point in the war he had got used to women and their intrusions into his world; and in early 1947 he actually stopped living with his mother (who had by now moved out of The Grove and taken a house in the middle of Esher) and married Elizabeth Mitchell Smith, an attractive, smiling brunette. 'I've been a bachelor for too long,' he announced.

*   *   *

Campbell's war ended with his ageing rapidly and having trouble with the glaucoma which had been advancing since the 1930s. He then rebuilt the *Blue Bird* powerboat with a de Havilland Goblin jet engine, which he couldn't get to work properly. The last picture taken of him before his death shows him posed in front of this pointless final *Blue Bird*, looking startlingly frail and spindly, lost inside a double-breasted suit which he would have been bursting out of ten years earlier. He stands, memorialised, between Harry Leech and Leo Villa. He and Villa lean towards each other like an old married couple on an outing.

However debilitated he was, he nonetheless managed to deliver a casual parting blow to Cobb, the new global speed king, by selling Brooklands from under his nose. Ethel Locke King had sold off her interest in the track and aviation ground in 1936 to a new company, Brooklands (Weybridge) Ltd. This had taken over the running of the place up to the outbreak of war. The last-ever race there had taken place in August 1939: the Third August Outer Circuit Handicap, won by G.L. Baker, a beaming fifty-seven-year-old in a ten-year-old car. After that Vickers took over the circuit in order to build military aircraft, turning out over 2500 Wellington bombers in the course of the war. They placed sheds and hangars all over the usefully firm, level track and took a section out of the Byfleet Banking in order to extend their runway.

By the end of hostilities Brooklands was overwhelmed with aviation buildings, weeds, saplings and low shrubs. A concrete anti-aircraft battery had been erected on the Members' Hill. Dr Barnes Wallis had taken over the clubhouse in order to design his Tallboy and Grand Slam bombs. The concrete track, never good, was now a shambles. It would have cost a fortune to restore to its pre-war condition and who would have raced there anyway?

Vickers-Armstrong (as they now were) saw their opportunity. Campbell, according to 'Taso' Mathieson, was believed to have cornered the shares in Brooklands Ltd after it was floated in 1936, and promptly flogged the lot when Vickers expressed an interest in taking over the property in 1946. 'Taso', indeed, was one of the handful of people to invest in the scheme: 'When I made the investment,' he wrote, 'my broker was horrified. His warnings came only too true for I never received a dividend and only on the sale of the property to Vickers did any of the shareholders recover their money with a very small gain.' That 'Taso' got anything back at all was mainly due to Campbell 'coming to an agreement' with Vickers in the first place; the track was valueless otherwise. But no one likes being defrauded – least of all Cobb, who was less concerned by Campbell's business cynicism (which he would have taken for granted) than by this ruthless dispatching of his spiritual and emotional home.

When the motoring journalist William Boddy came to write a detailed history of Brooklands a couple of years later, he approached Cobb to write a foreword. This Cobb did, and spent nearly half of his slim, 176-word introduction vilifying a spectral enemy: 'I agree with the author of this book when he says that its' – Brooklands' – 'desecration should be a matter of shame to those responsible. I for one am glad that I have no part in it . . .' And, 'It is sincerely to be hoped that the author will not be long in producing a second volume which will take us up to the time when Brooklands was sold, an event which, in my humble opinion, may well cause a decline in British Motor Racing from which it may never recover.'

This was a sincere, but, in the end, self-deluding response. After all, Brooklands had been slowly yielding to the inexorable force of air power ever since the first biplanes turned up in 1907. The track declined in relevance as the airfield grew. The mighty Vickers sheds beside the Fork were a constant reminder of this truth and had been since 1915, when the company moved in, taking over the old Itala factory. The reliance of the first Brooklands pioneers, and later all the LSR speed kings, on aero engines, showed who was leading the way, all the way, in engineering terms. The absorption of Brooklands into Vickers (and ultimately into British Aerospace) was business Darwinism, not the Gresham's Law Cobb seemed to think it.

But now, at least, Cobb had another riposte to Campbell's shabbiness. He could take out his *Railton Special* once more and do something really dramatic with the World Land Speed Record, make it incontestably his own – as Campbell had tried to do all through the twenties and thirties. He was still just young enough to manage it. The car was still good. He had survived the war, was married, felt ready for the job. And, as it chanced, the authorities at Bonneville were ready to invite him back out there as part of Utah's 1947 centennial celebrations – it having been 1847 when the first Mormon settlers reached what was now Utah and made it their home. They would set everything up for him.

Marriage agreed with Cobb. His face, although hollowed and darkened by age and the exigencies of wartime, had less of its customary expression of affront. Astonishingly, when asked to pose with the dusted-off *Railton Special* for the cameras, he even smiled. Outside Thomson & Taylor's sheds, he sat in the leather bucket seat in the nose of the car and read another script propped up on the steering wheel. Only this time the new Mrs Cobb was also there, summery in hat and floral dress. She darted forward and leaned over him, protectively, while he pretended to explain something about the instrument panel. The cameras filmed this moment of companionability, so useful for filling out Cobb's persona, reassuring the audience that only two years after the war domestic virtues were intact. She smiled warmly; he returned the smile, still shy, but evidently pleased.

Off they went, the *Railton Special* shipped on the *M.V. Georgic* back to Bonneville and Wendover, along with Dunlop Mac, sixty tyres in twenty-six packing cases, the inexhaustible

Ken Taylor, the new Mrs Cobb; and sponsorship from the Mobil Oil Company. The *Railton Special* was now the *Railton Mobil Special* and sported a red Pegasus – the Mobil corporate logo – on either side of its nose. Still daringly sleek, and still the fastest and most advanced motor car in the world, the *Railton Mobil Special*'s looks were only improved by its new fiery aerial mascot: Pegasus, the winged horse that discovered the spring of Hippocrene and carried lightning bolts for Zeus. It was a different kind of *Blue Bird*, validated by the modern authority of commerce. Reid Railton now lived in San Francisco for his health and would fly out to meet them all.

Wendover had also changed, but at a more fundamental level. In 1941 the dusty little airfield to the south of the town had been taken over by the Army Air Corps and enlarged. Duly upgraded, it would have spent the rest of its days as an outpost of the military's training network, but for the arrival of Colonel Paul Tibbets in 1944. Tibbets and his 509th Composite Group saw to it that Wendover Field became a vast, two-runway airbase, housing over 20,000 servicemen at its height, plus several of the latest B-29 Superfortress bombers and a multitude of military and civil technicians. The reason? This was where Tibbets and his team trained to drop their atomic bombs on Hiroshima and Nagasaki, making around 155 test flights over the desert lands to the south, before leaving in spring 1945 for their final outpost on Tinian Island. A city of wood and tarpaper sheds grew up on the Utah side of Wendover, with one especially huge corrugated-metal hangar for the Superfortresses. The rest of Wendover was filled with cheap Government housing, plus an enlarged Cobblestone Inn, which now boasted air-conditioning.

All this, bar the 509th Composite Group, was still in place when Cobb and his team arrived. So far as they were concerned, however, there was no dreadful historical pall hanging over Wendover. They had closed their minds to the brooding presence of Wendover Field; they simply enjoyed the benefits of all this

Government investment: a swimming pool; and a new ramp for unloading large or heavy objects from the railway. They also relished the air-con at the Cobblestone.

For the speed record attempt itself, the Utah authorities produced a handsome and misleading Official Program, announcing that 'Cobb Assaults World Record' and claiming that his car cost 'approximately $100,000' to build. It also noted that Cobb was 'the first Britisher to drive on the Bonneville Salt Flats' and that 'since his student days, Cobb has been interested, from an engineering standpoint, in developing better and better internal combustion engines; the culmination being the engines that power the *Railton Mobil Special* and the car itself'. However inaccurate the content, the tone was what mattered – a generation away from the 'Benzine battlers' whom Daytona used to promote – indicative, in those sober times, of purpose and practicality.

Not that sheer entertainment had been overlooked altogether. For the more frivolous onlooker there was a designated spectator area, along with free parking and a refreshment stand. There was also a space marked out on the salt, called 'Victory Lane, where John Cobb would drive his *Railton Mobil Special* following completion of his run'. The timers' eyrie stood, as ever, at the midpoint of the measured mile, and contained a timing system which weighed three-quarters of a ton and was accurate to half of one-hundredth of a second. The spectators were penned back some two thousand feet from the black centre line of the course. Motor cars and light aircraft stood in neat ranks on the edge of the salt. 'Don't try short cuts,' warns the Official Program. 'The short cut may look safe, but the land surrounding the salt is very treacherous. Stay on the roads and be safe!' Also, 'Not only for your own safety but also for that of Mr Cobb, it is essential that spectators remain within their designated areas at all times.'

Inevitably, things didn't work as well as they might have. The car had been stored in bits in a barn in southern England, with the engines kept at Brooklands, and had had to be cleaned up and reconstituted. The engines were refurbished and various clever improvements were made to satisfy Reid Railton. But it was, however you looked at it, a ten-year-old car (Cobb was going around calling it 'second-hand') with twenty-year-old engines. It needed endless adjustments. Cobb kept calm and the new Mrs Cobb helped to lift the body on and off the chassis.

The team had been at Bonneville since mid-July and it was only by the start of September that they were in a position to try for the record. The smart centennial programme had the event earmarked for August, but there was nothing anyone can do about this slippage. On one occasion the whole vehicle ran into some marshy salt and started sinking. Ken Taylor and the mechanics tried furiously to drag it out. A small crowd gathered, offering divergent advice. Taylor rounded on them, snapping, 'If any of you know a way to get this fucking car out of this trouble, I'll carry out your instructions. If not, stop yammering and help.'

Then a hole burst open in the bodywork at 370 mph. The onlookers asked Cobb, as he walked to the timing stand, 'Are you going for a second run?' He replied, 'It's all off for today. As we seem to be doing this the hard way, another day or two won't matter, I suppose.' Elizabeth, his wife, glossed this quiet moment of deprecation by declaring that 'I was terribly thrilled and terribly nervous. He was nervous too, but he doesn't show it.' Cobb was the only one not to lose his temper over a period of two months.

At last the day came. It was 16 September and a gale had been blowing since before dawn. If they tried to lift the lightweight bodyshell off the chassis, it would blow away. But everything else was ready. Had Campbell been there, this would have provided the foundations for a whole day of hysteria. But Cobb merely wandered around pacifically, while Ken Taylor was convinced that the wind would drop in the evening. This it did. To the satisfaction of the few hundred spectators who had turned up, the run was set, the car was fuelled up and fitted with fresh tyres. The thirteen-mile track ran from the north-east to the south-west, towards the yellow setting sun.

Cobb, wearing his Mobil-embroidered overalls, white cloth helmet and smoked-glass goggles, got into the car. This was not simple. He could not clamber over the bodywork and drop in through the little hatch over his seat: the metal was too thin to take his weight. A Dodge service truck had been loaned for the trials ('John Cobb selects Dodge service truck for dependability,' it read on the side). This had a slim wooden gangplank built out from the back, with a parallel wooden handrail running out above it.

The Dodge backed carefully towards the *Railton Mobil Special*. Cobb climbed on to the truck and stepped out on to the gangplank, holding on to the handrail. A mechanic carefully wiped any debris from the rubber soles of his shoes. Cobb then shuffled along the gangplank until he was over the cockpit and lowered himself into it. The little metal and glass conning tower went on. The Dodge truck from which he had clambered into the *Railton* then came up behind and inserted a special pushing rod into the back of the car. It engaged gear and started to push. The two vehicles slowly moved forward.

After a few seconds the *Railton* fired up; terrible, filthy smoke poured out of the exhausts on the machine's back, as well as those that vented underneath the car. It started to move away under its own power, leaving the pushing rod and the Dodge truck behind. The Napier engines made a harsh, growling sound, rising in pitch as Cobb accelerated. Inside ten seconds he was going at 100 mph and was almost lost to view from the start line. At the end of a minute he was doing well over 200 mph and had vanished altogether. After seventy seconds he was travelling at 300 mph.

Inside his cockpit, his feet some fourteen inches above the salt unreeling at jet speed beneath him, Cobb was hot, sweaty and, despite the plugs in his ears, deafened by the roaring engines just behind him, as well as by the noise of the gale outside. Moreover, every time he blinked he covered a couple of hundred yards and found himself 'driving blind half the time'. The salt lake rose uphill and he accelerated into the darkening sky. On either side of the black guideline a pair of big red boards appeared. A solid black rectangle suddenly over-stamped the salt. These two manifestations indicated the start of the measured mile.

By now Cobb was going not much slower than the fastest piston-engined aeroplane in the world – a Messerschmitt Me209 – and about as fast as the average Supermarine Spitfire. A mass of vicious shakings seized the car for a second as he went over a rough patch of salt. Then he thundered past the next red billboard, over the next black rectangle and through the beam of the electric timing eye to begin his slowdown.

Being Cobb, he managed this without burst tyres, exploding radiators, molten brakes, skids, off-*piste* calamities, fires or poisonous smoke fumes. At the far end, his team hauled off the glossy silver carapace of the *Railton*'s body, changed the tyres, tumbled a barrelful of ice into the cooling system like a delivery of coals, and filled up the petrol tank with a fierce distillate, stronger than the mere aviation fuel used before the war. Cobb clambered back in, and the team lowered the body back over him and clasped it in place. He squirmed in his leather seat, untucking the humid clutch of his overalls, suffered the conning tower to be fitted back on, was pushed off again by the Dodge truck and rocketed back down the black line even faster than before.

A few minutes later he drove the exhaust-blackened *Railton Mobil Special* into Victory Lane, exactly as promised in the prospectus; just a month late. Everyone remarked how docile the machine seemed to be, rumbling into the reception bay like a Sunday tourer. The windscreen came off and Cobb jumped out of the car, assisted by two American officials. The next thing that happened, as the flashbulbs popped and burst in the gathering dusk, was that Elizabeth Cobb, wearing 1940s labourer-chic dungarees and headscarf, hurried forward and embraced him. He smiled down at her, apparently oblivious to the applause and whistling going on around him. He wore an expression of sheer pleasure: that of a man who has come home after a long and arduous, but not especially worrying journey.

Naturally, the Land Speed Record was his, by a grand margin. Indeed, on that run, Cobb became the first man ever to drive a car at over 400 mph – hitting 403 on the return run and still accelerating past the measured mile. The two runs averaged out at a scintilla over 394 mph. Almost as soon as Cobb had finished, the rain started to pour down, flooding the Salt Flats and ending any more record attempts for the year. In the evening Cobb and Ken Taylor took over the Cobblestone Inn and insisted on tipping the contents of a succession of five-gallon milk churns over the floor of the cafeteria and using the resulting mess as a kind of skating rink. Cobb paid. Two days later he was presented with the Utah Centennial Commission Medal of Honour and an official Certificate of Performance from the Contest Board of the AAA, signed by Art Pillsbury, on stiff cream card.

If anything, though, his sense of timing was even worse than it had been in 1939. When he finally returned to England there was no one from any of the British motoring bodies to welcome him. In *The Times*, the most visible acknowledgement of Cobb's triumph was a tiny advertisement for KLG Spark Plugs ('Once Again!') sandwiched between two larger ads, for Cook's 'Sterling' Holidays (in Gibraltar, Uganda, the Channel Isles etc.) and the General Assurance Corporation.

The *Autocar* did its best to recreate the shameless rhetoric of before the war, claiming that 'Here is a magnificent refutation of the challenge that Britain can no longer make it; not only can Britain make it, but also it is obvious that she can make it better than any other country.' The *Daily Mail*, like all other papers, struggling with a vastly reduced supply of newsprint, managed to squeeze him into its four broadsheet pages, which was a tribute of a sort. It even managed to build the *Railton Mobil Special* into a political cartoon, as the *Express* had done nearly twenty years earlier with *Blue Bird*. This time the artful silver *Railton* was realised on a sketchy Bonneville and renamed (in typically Labour-detesting *Daily Mail* style) the *Socialist Special*, rushing headlong across a 'Measured Mile To Disaster'.

Eventually Cobb got his heavily rationed celebration dinners and his round of austerity speech-making; which only emphasised how big a discrepancy there was between his brilliance as an instigator and facilitator and as a self-publicist. In November 1947 the luminaries of motor sport foregathered in what was now known as the Segrave Room of the RAC in Pall Mall. Cobb had to share his glory with another long-standing record breaker: Major Goldie Gardner, OBE, who had set a number of records on a road outside Ostend in a souped-up MG. Lounge suits were worn. Cobb was large and impassive as usual. He made a small, stiff speech. But then, to try to jazz up the experience, he was browbeaten into doing some toneless cross-talk with Goldie:

Cobb: Well, Goldie. What about having a crack at the Land Speed Record?

Gardner: No, John – you've put it up so high I'm going to stay down in the smaller classes, I think.

Cobb (*after a pause*): Well, what do you figure your horse-power is compared to mine?

Gardner: Well, I've got about forty times less than you have. (*Pause*)

Cobb: That's quite a bit, isn't it? And it shows how much power is required to go from a hundred and twenty to four hundred miles an hour.

Gardner (*with relief*): Certainly does.

But then, it was lucky that Cobb got any recognition at all, having set his first great Land Speed Record on the outbreak of the Second World War and his second at a time when the famished gloom of the Peace had fully descended. Campbell was at his height during the Depression; but this was another world. In prefabs and bomb-damaged semis everywhere, a cold, bereaved, half-ruined nation examined its newly intro-duced bread ration, its recently halved bacon ration, its lack of soap, decent clothing, chocolate, beer, stockings, petrol, coal, paper and potatoes. In the autumn budget of 1947 the Chancellor, Hugh Dalton, put the price of twenty cigarettes up to 3/4d. 'Smoke your cigarettes to the butts,' he said. 'It may even be good for your health.' It was not a world with suffi-cient mental latitude to get much satisfaction out of a super-hobbyist's fixation with driving fast.

Besides, the fashion had moved on, ever since the arrival of jet-propelled aircraft, which could do 600 mph without undue effort. Cars and piston engines were *arrière-garde*. And on 14 October 1947 Chuck Yeager broke the sound barrier in his Bell X-1 rocket plane, a scant month after Cobb had taken his record in Utah. Yeager was five hundred miles away from Bonneville, at Muroc Air Base; but he might as well have been on the moon – which destination, in its turn, thieved all the glamour from high-speed, high-altitude aircraft a decade after Yeager's flight.

And yet: *400 mph on land*. Given a moment's reflection, it still has the power to arrest. A commonplace throughout the record-breaking 1920s and '30s was to illustrate the potency of a new record by relating it to everyday experience. At its top speed, George Eyston's *Thunderbolt* could travel from London to Brighton in nine minutes; at 200 mph and given a forty-five-degree ramp, Segrave's Sunbeam Slug could have jumped over the Eiffel Tower. But such relativities were, by and large, unhelpful. Translating something hard to comprehend into something notionally familiar but, in practice, equally hard to comprehend, was self-defeating; and obscurely patronising. It was the sheer weight of the number which created an impression; that, and whatever naked self-advertisement its champion brought to the event. Even now, four hundred sounds big; impossible to gainsay.

Moreover, it took years before anyone else broke Cobb's record. So purposeful and efficient was he that he held his title for nearly a quarter of a century; almost twice as long as the next most durable candidate (Richard Noble, OBE). Yes, this was partly the result of chance. There was an intervening war, followed by a spell of apathy: the 1950s went by without any significant interest in rebreaking the record. But it was also because 394 mph – the LSR proper – was exceedingly difficult to top. He had made it look easy; but it wasn't. And it was this sheer durability, brilliantly contrived and patiently won, which secured Cobb's place in the great trinity of speed kings.

Segrave was the inimitable, restless, glamorous originator; but his records, however dazzling, were made to be broken. Campbell was the most famous, the most commercially successful, the greatest exponent of the LSR as a public event; but his records were almost secondary to the legend he strove to create. Cobb, in the end, was the one who was the most dedicated, made the fewest compromises, who proved the hardest to beat: whose record endured.

18

Crusader *Passes*

In 1948 Elizabeth Mitchell Smith, Cobb's wife of fourteen months, died. Bright's disease, or chronic nephritis – an inflammation of the kidneys more normally found in children and middle-aged men – killed the new Mrs Cobb before the year was halfway through. It looked as if untimely death had decided to make a return to the life that Cobb had so painstakingly crafted for himself. He at once sank into a profound depression. And there were no amusements or distractions left. Brooklands was closed. The Land Speed Record was finished. He couldn't face his friends. He carried on working as Joint Managing Director of Anning, Chadwick & Kiver; and saw a lot of his mother.

Malcolm Campbell died, too, at the end of the year: one of the few external events to penetrate Cobb's gloom. Still possessed of his gift for the dramatic, and having given Leo Villa his last slap on the face, Campbell died of a stroke at the very end of 1948. He was sixty-three. His death was so finely balanced between the stroke of midnight, 31 December and 1 January 1949, that even now the given year of his death varies from one account to another. He had broken the World

Land Speed Record nine times; the World Water Speed Record four times; and still held that record on his death. At his memorial service, in St Margaret's, Westminster (where Segrave had been mourned), the crowd was heavy with dignitaries such as Sir Hartley Shawcross, MP; Air-Vice Marshall Sir Douglas Harries; Lieutenant Colonel Sir Hugh Turnbull; Sir Algernon Guinness. There was a strong sense that they were making their farewells not just to the man, but to an episode in national life.

Campbell left an estate worth over £175,000 and was careful to ensure that his children didn't keep the tokens of his past glory: his *Blue Birds* and *Blue Bird* memorabilia were auctioned off. The Campbell family did get to share out his five hundred-odd trophies. But everything else went under the hammer. The proceeds were then put in trust for his grandchildren. Donald and Jean received interest on the trust, plus a small legacy from their grandfather, William Campbell. Donald was reduced to buying back what mementoes of his father he especially wanted, at valuation prices. Sir Malcolm was buried alongside his parents – two relatives who were in no position to decline his presence – in St Nicholas's churchyard, Chislehurst, Kent.

Cobb slowly began to come out of his depression. He was cheered by the fact that his old *Napier Railton* – the single-seater racer which he had so successfully driven round Brooklands – was taken out of storage in 1950 and recycled in the Anglo-American film *Pandora and the Flying Dutchman*.

No low-budget austerity number, this, but a big, Technicolor piece, staring James Mason and Ava Gardner at her most conspicuously luscious. Mason is the eponymous Dutchman, condemned to drift around a latter-day Mediterranean, searching for true love. Ava Gardner, in a succession of cocktail dresses, falls for him. Nigel Patrick – looking and sounding quite like the late Sir Malcolm Campbell – plays a speed ace with ambitions for the LSR, who is also in love with Ava.

Cobb lent his old *Napier Railton* to play the part of the LSR car. Motoring enthusiasts will especially enjoy the sequences shot at Pendine Sands, where, in a delirious conflation of whimsy and historical fact, Nigel Patrick takes the LSR in John Cobb's old non-LSR car in the manner of Malcolm Campbell's great 1927 *Blue Bird* run. Sand and spray fly everywhere, in authentic Pendine style. The car radiator springs a leak. Nigel Patrick fights his goggles. For a moment, you can believe that this must be how it really was, back in the twenties.

As a film, however, it doesn't come off. Critic Pauline Kael is puzzlingly indulgent in her observation that '[Albert] Lewin's direction is static, yet his staging is so luxuriantly mad that it's easy to get fixated on what, if anything, he could have had in mind.' C.A. Lejeune, on the other hand, calls it 'conspicuous in its confident assumption of scholarship and its utter poverty of imagination and taste.' *Halliwell's Film Guide* is even harder: 'Pretentious, humourless, totally unpersuasive fantasy.' It *is* a terrible film, and over two hours long. But it kept Cobb happy, even when the *Napier Railton* had to be hurled over a cliff as a token of true love.

And then he remarried, in the summer of 1950, finally laying to rest the notion that he was frightened by women other than his mother. His new wife was Vera – or Vicky – Henderson: thirty-two years old, pretty, vivacious, charming. It was clear that Cobb not only preferred to share his life with a member of the opposite sex, but that he actually had an eye for the ladies. It was also clear that women were prepared to look past Cobb's reticent, somewhat slow-moving exterior, in order to reach the gentlemanly decencies within. 'A big man, but he was very gentle, very quiet and thoughtful of others,' Vicky Cobb later observed. Also, 'a relaxed man in company he knew' and, 'he had a very special sense of humour with his friends'.

Cobb and his new wife settled into Cobb's unassertive stockbroker Tudor home at Coombe Park, Kingston, only a few yards from where Segrave and Doris had moved in 1928. He carried on at Anning, Chadwick & Kiver, occasionally taking time out for a promotional trip to the States, where the *Railton Special* was on show as part of an exhibition of British cars in New York; or to write a road test for the *Field*.

Campbell, too, had contributed to this magazine in his day, as part of his long-term media campaign. It was an obscure publication, but nonetheless exuded the right kind of gentrified cachet. Cobb would dutifully turn in his copy, which appeared next to the byline 'John Cobb, Holder of the World Land Speed Record'. Then would follow a tremendously well-mannered description of, say, the Vauxhall Velox: 'An internal heater and ventilator is available as an extra at the very reasonable price of £8 . . . the present-day Vauxhall is the easiest car to drive that I know . . . wonderful value for the very cheap price at which it is sold . . .' Or the new Land-Rover: 'I climbed banks which made me fearful that the vehicle might turn over, but the centre of gravity is low enough to make this virtually impossible . . . the list price is £570, which I think is exceedingly reasonable in view of the variety of tasks it can perform in such an efficient and economical manner.'

In 1951 the *Railton Special* – now in the hands of Dunlop Tyres – was taken out and put on display at the Festival of Britain, parked under the eaves of the Dome of Discovery. It looked as fresh and futuristic as ever, a belated recognition of the fact that Cobb really had taken the Land Speed Record for Britain and himself all those years ago. Optimistically, he and his wife thought about starting a family.

Why, then, did John Cobb allow himself to attempt the World Water Speed Record? He was over fifty; he had made his point; he held the absolute lap record for the now-defunct Brooklands; he was the fastest man on earth. There were furs to be bought and sold, his Chairmanship of the Falkland Islands Company to attend to, friends to share Sunday lunches with in the pubs around Kingston and Esher, a pretty wife. It was, in all respects, a perfectly realised 1950s existence. What was water to him?

Well, the old itches were still there. Segrave had taken the WSR in 1930. Kaye Don, a failure at Daytona Beach, had nevertheless succeeded in Argentina, Italy and Loch Lomond, taking the WSR four times in total, twice in 1931 and twice more in 1932. Campbell had taken it twice in 1937 at Lake Maggiore; again, in 1938, at Lake Hallwil in Switzerland; and finally, in 1939, at Coniston Water. His son was now trying to recover his father's old record from the current holder, an American named Stanley Sayres. It was one of those axiomatic goals. When asked what was the point, Cobb answered, 'And why not? I am not an old man. I like going fast. It gives me a thrill. And if I do break a record I suppose it's a good thing for Britain.'

There was indeed a passing sense that the national mood could be lifted by another pointless appropriation of a number. Numbed and appalled by the Great War, Britain had taken Segrave to its heart as emblematic of a kind of national renewal. Following the even greater destruction and demoralisation of the Second World War and the years immediately after, Cobb could, perhaps, take on the same role. Enough time had passed for the initial shock of conflict to have worn off and for the British to start fretting about their shrunken position in the world; to contemplate internationally resonant gestures (involving jet flight, early computing, the atom bomb) and dream of rebuilding lost prestige. They had dusted off the *Railton Special* and set it prominently on display at the Festival of Britain. They could do much the same with John Cobb, who, with Campbell gone and George Eyston in a more conventional job as Castrol's competitions manager, was the last half-active survivor from the pre-war golden age of the speed kings. The fact that the whole adventure was ill conceived and steadfastly against the grain of everything Cobb had achieved up until that point was lost in typical post-war British desperation to make a statement.

For a start, it was all to do with water and Cobb knew nothing about water. He knew plenty about cars and a bit about aeroplanes, but water is a sinister, inscrutable and disorientating medium of which most land-based creatures are rightly wary. As he observed, the fastest he had ever been on water up until this point was in a boat with an outboard motor at about 45 mph. His plan was to reach 200 mph.

Then there was the absence of that painfully slow incremental acquisition of experience which had been the hallmark of Cobb and his cars. It had taken him eighteen years to work up to his first LSR. His WSR boat appeared on a drawing board in 1949 and was in the water three years later. Reid Railton was, as ever, behind the design; Commander Peter du Cane, of the shipbuilders Vosper, at Portsmouth, oversaw the construction; Castrol put some money in and got George Eyston to organise the teamwork and logistics. Cobb committed £15,000 of his own money right at the start, so keen was he to make progress. But there was no aquatic Brooklands where he could polish his skills; no smaller, slower powerboats leading up to the big one. Segrave had raced *Miss England* several times before killing himself in *Miss England II*. Campbell had spent months fooling around in craft of all sizes and speeds before devoting himself to the first and second *Blue Bird* craft. Gar Wood had spent decades building racing boats, culminating in the gargantuan, four-engined *Miss America X*. Cobb was coming to it cold, and in a hurry.

And there was yet another sharp distinction between pre-war and post-war practice: the technology, this time, was all new. The *Railton Special* was a beautiful, novel and elegant application of already familiar engineering: a fresh take on the present. Cobb's new record boat, on the other hand, would be using an absolutely up-to-the-minute, and still somewhat unpredictable, de Havilland Ghost jet engine (like those used in the doomed Comet jet airliner) to propel it. This was so new that it had to be tricked out of the Ministry of Supply, in much the same way that Campbell had got hold of his Napier and Rolls-Royce engines in the twenties and thirties. No one, not even Reid Railton, knew quite what to expect from it.

What they did know was that Malcolm Campbell had sweated away pointlessly with a de Havilland Goblin jet engine in his last *Blue Bird* boat, only for Donald Campbell to remove the thing in 1949 and reinstall the old Rolls-Royce piston engine, along with a traditional propeller, as part of his first WSR bid. But this precedent would only have increased Cobb's desire to prove Campbell wrong. Besides, he remembered Campbell junior as an irritating child at Brooklands – two decades earlier, he had stolen Cobb's spark plugs immediately before a race and thrown them into a bath of oil – and there'd be no harm in reminding him who took precedence in these things.

Then there was the question of planing. Railton had worked out a way to get Cobb's boat to rise up on three little skids ('like a tricycle with one wheel in front') and effectively ski along at 200 mph. But, of course, no one had put this into practice, except in the form of a two-foot plywood model with a kind of Guy Fawkes rocket stuck to the back, with which Railton and du Cane had experimented at Vosper, before progressing to a five-foot plywood model. Nevertheless, happy enough with these craftlets, they decided to go straight on to the real thing, which was finished in 1952.

The real thing was thirty-one feet long, with the look of an enormous toy about it. A central body, curiously dumpy and truncated, like a sea bream, contained Cobb, sitting almost on top of the jet engine. Two reinforced skis stuck out on either side on outriggers. A three-foot hole at the back let the jet out. Most of the structure, apart from the engine, was wood and aluminium alloy, painted silver and red. It weighed three and a half tons and was called *Crusader*. Cobb claimed that this was because 'In the old days a crusader was a man who liked to get away from his office and have some fun.' Naturally, it helped that *Crusader*, with its Richard the Lionheart, Plantagenet overtones, should also fit in with the fragile sense of national revitalisation surrounding the New Elizabethans.

Cobb was being rediscovered: a minor national treasure, neglected for over a decade, but now invested with some fresh, chivalric significance. And this, too, was out of keeping. All his pre-war adventures were manifestations of his twin private urges to secure numbers for himself and to prove Campbell beatable. The *Crusader* scheme would have started in something of the same vein, a private preoccupation, with Railton using his clever ideas for boat design to draw Cobb out of the depression which had imprisoned him after the death of his first wife. By mid-1952, though, he was fully part of a promotional circus. When the boat was unveiled in bright July sunshine at Vosper's works, it sat on a specially prepared trailer with 'JOHN COBB'S "CRUSADER"' painted down the sides in inescapably large lettering. Photographers went up stepladders and stood on the roofs of their cars to get shots. Cobb had to lean proprietorially against *Crusader*, a can of Castrol oil near his feet.

And then, towards the end of August, the machine was off, in a courtly procession from the bottom of England up to the Scottish Highlands. Loch Ness was the destination: twenty-three miles long, good and straight, a thousand feet deep.

They unloaded the boat and set up base camp at Temple Pier, Drumnadrochit, where steamboats and pleasure cruisers came and went in what passed for summer in the Highlands. The remains of the thirteenth-century Castle Urqhart glowered down on them. Railton was there, along with George Eyston, the mysterious Captain Cronk of Vosper's engineering team, Major F.B. Halford, who designed the engine, Commander du Cane, George Bristow of de Havilland, and Mrs Vicky Cobb. It was a team of thirty, all in all. They set up radio telephone communications along the loch. Tourists and locals alike drove their cars to vantage points in order to see what was going on. Eyston, Railton and Cobb, never the most youthful or youthful-looking of men, were now positively old. White hairs shone among the gloom. Cobb's face was worn, bagged, undermined.

What *was* going on? Cobb was finding the work hard and unfamiliar. Reaching into the same kind of word-hoard as that with which he had described the sensation of disappearing over the top of the banking at Brooklands, he said that trying to pilot *Crusader* was 'like driving a London omnibus without tyres on'. He did his best to stick to his original principles of steady caution by driving the boat at 50 mph, then 100, then 150. It took weeks to get right. September arrived and dragged on. 'He wasn't a man for discussing his problems,' said Vicky. 'I didn't know anything about the mechanical side of things, had no idea about engines, so there wasn't any point in talking about that.'

The famously dreadful Scottish weather sent rain squalls, mists, downpours across the loch, which could be in broad daylight at one end and buried in obscurity at the other. Downpours in the mountains then washed a mass of debris and driftwood into the waters of the loch; all of which had to be mucked out by the team. 'You've got to have patience on a job like this,' Cobb said phlegmatically, trying to quieten the shrill background noise of expectation.

Good manners and a desire not to antagonise the local residents meant that he kept open house around the base camp. Schoolchildren were allowed to come up and inspect *Crusader*. Out of deference to Highland Sabbatarianism, the team did not work on Sundays, and the children of Drumnadrochit made Cobb a keepsake out of cardboard after he had shown them around the boat. The three young sons of the Duke of Gloucester turned up one day in kilts, along with the Duchess of Gloucester. They scrambled over the craft while Cobb, in his tent-like raincoat, forced himself to make conversation with the Duchess. Her Majesty the Queen Mother – as she had recently become – even arrived from Balmoral. Still dressed in black (King George VI having died only in February), she smiled and chatted with Cobb, who struggled to find something to do with his free right hand while bending attentively to her conversation. She came up to just under his armpit.

The last WSR figure Stanley Sayres had set – in July 1952 on Lake Washington – was nearly 179 mph. Halfway through September, Cobb made his first serious attempt at breaking it. He hit 185 mph one way; but it was too breezy to go at anything other than half-throttle on the way back, where he only reached 161 mph. Still, even though the average was still off the record, Cobb did it to see what it felt like; and to give the crowds something to enjoy. 'Cobb fails,' announced the papers.

The twenty-eighth of September arrived, bringing with it perfect conditions. The water was calm and there was no wind. But it was also Sunday. Mindful of the Highlanders' respect for the Sabbath, Cobb decreed that they shouldn't run. Seething, the team sat around at the Drumnadrochit Hotel, smoking and drinking tea. Then, on 29 September, he determined to go out and make one last big push before packing up and returning home. It was plain by now that parts of the boat weren't strong enough to take the sledgehammer punishment of water battering them at nearly 200 mph. The aluminium planing shoe at the front of *Crusader* was looking particularly weak. Commander du Cane wanted to take the whole thing back to Vosper and revise it at the company's expense. Cobb thought it might be worth attempting his two official runs first; and wrote a letter beforehand, formally absolving du Cane of any responsibility in the event of an accident.

Too much was riding on this bid. Back in Utah, it had all been solitary, unbothered, the attempts emerging as semi-abstractions in the press days later. Now he was stuck in front of his home crowd – as when he had taken out the *Napier*

Railton for the first time at Brooklands and nearly killed himself on Easter Monday 1934, setting a new lap record. He didn't want to disappoint people; he didn't want to be seen to fail. Castrol, after all, had specially printed up a batch of postcards – one side showing a photograph of Loch Ness and Castle Urqhart; the other, bearing a printed message, 'I thought you might like to know that today I broke the World's Water Speed Record on Loch Ness Using Castrol. John Cobb.'

After getting up at dawn, only to find that a breeze had sprung up, Cobb and the rest of the team had spent the morning hanging around in the hotel lounge, waiting for the loch to calm down. By lunchtime it had. 'Conditions seem to be quite favourable,' he announced. 'Let's take advantage of it.' Cobb clambered into his jet-age pilot's outfit, pulled on his helmet and headphones, worked his goggles over his eyes. *Crusader* was towed out from the landing stage at Temple Pier. Its engine was started. Its horrible, contemporary, Cold War shriek echoed down the sides of the loch. He set off towards the south-west, a fantail of steam and spray pouring out of the back of the boat.

Along the measured mile, he hit a mind-blowing 206 mph, peaking at one stage at 240. Then the trouble started. A sequence of flabby ripples, left by an errant support boat, set *Crusader*'s nose pitching up and down. Each bounce smashed the water into the aluminium front skid. The skid began to collapse. Spray churned into the jet intakes. Within a couple of seconds the front skid had started to give way completely. The boat buried its nose in the water and instantly ripped itself apart. There was an explosion as the furious, scalding jet plunged downwards. A few seconds after that, all that was left was a dark pool of wavelets, and thousands of shreds of red and silver floating on the loch's surface, 'like confetti'.

His body was found. The cause of death was established as shock. George Eyston had to deal with the aftermath and poor

Vicky Cobb was sent back to London by car. On 1 October Cobb was given a funeral procession through the streets of Inverness; a service was held in the chapel of the Royal Northern Infirmary. 'Rain fell,' wrote Eyston, 'and it was some consolation to walk bareheaded.' Although he didn't break the WSR – having travelled the measured mile in one direction only – the Marine Motoring Association, in charge of the timekeeping, gave Cobb the posthumous consolation prize of having reached 'the fastest speed ever obtained on water'.

And this time he made the headlines that had been denied him for fifteen years: 'How Cobb Died – 3 Ripples May Have Killed Him'; 'Speed Cracked Cobb's Jet Boat'; 'There Was A Puff Of Smoke – And Crusader Was Gone.' The *Express* wanted to know, 'John Cobb – pioneer or playboy?' The answer? 'Let there be no mistake. John Cobb was a pioneer.' The *Daily Mirror* gnomically averred that 'Faster and faster . . . said King Cobb.' The *Mail* wrung its hands in the time-honoured way: 'Another Brave Man has fallen victim to the quest for more and more speed.' Front and back pages were liberally plastered with pictures of Cobb in his boat, Cobb meeting the Queen Mother, *Crusader* thrashing itself into a million pieces. *The Times* ran a gentlemanly 'Mr Cobb Killed On Loch Ness', plus photos; while *Picture Post* launched into a six-page elegy – 'Crusader Passes' – claiming that 'Crusader's loss may not end the story.'

There was no great irony in all this – the spectacularly mistaken appropriation of Cobb's longing for speed as part of the post-war mood; the haste to reclaim an overlooked national figure; the embarrassing 'playboy' tag. For once, Cobb's timing was spot-on, so far as the rest of the world was concerned. His disaster was entirely newsworthy.

His body was later buried at Esher Parish Church, near the graves of his father and his first wife. The memorial service was at the end of October, in St Mary's, Cornhill. Vicky Cobb was too distraught to attend. Reid Railton lost all heart and never worked again on high-speed craft of any kind. The villagers of Drumnadrochit, meanwhile, paid for and erected a stone cairn on the bank of Loch Ness, opposite the point at which Cobb's boat exploded. A year after his death Cobb's sister Eileen unveiled the memorial. 'In memory of a Gallant Gentleman,' reads the bronze plaque affixed to the side facing away from the loch.

Epilogue: The Jet Age

《☾ ☽》

The Americans rediscovered their enthusiasm for the World Land Speed Record at the start of the 1960s. Some racers built themselves piston-engined specials, relying on lighter, more modern engines to deliver the goods. Others followed the tried-and-true path of parasitising aircraft technology for their motive power. Just as the early speed kings had benefited from the leftover aero engines of the First World War, so the 1960s contenders picked up the scrap jet engines of the Cold War and plumbed them into rolling chassis, which they then tried out at Bonneville.

California dragster racer Mickey Thompson started out in pursuit of the LSR in 1958; years went by as he built and rebuilt various hot-rod-engined specials, before he admitted defeat and gave up in 1968. Athol Graham, 'the Mormon Preacher', killed himself in 1960, trying to set a record in a DIY project car filled with a Second World War piston aero engine. In 1962 Dr Nathan Ostich put a turbojet taken from a Boeing B-36 bomber into a wildly jet-age body, and still failed. At around the same time Leopold Schmid, of the Porsche car company, designed a futuristic jet car ('which can travel at speeds in excess of 500 mph over long distances – just as soon as suitable highways have been developed') which was never built. Art Arfons ('the Junkyard Genius') built a vast jet machine called the *Green Monster*, which didn't quite make it. One Glenn Leasher set off in a jet car to take the record, only for it to explode on national TV, killing him outright. Bob Knapp put *two* jet engines into a chassis, while Bill Frederick – a butcher from California – settled for one. Bob Herda, an aero-dynamicist with a helicopter manufacturer, tried using a really large car engine. None of these contenders succeeded.

Eventually, in 1963, Craig Breedlove, in his *Spirit of America* – basically a jet fighter with no wings – unofficially took the record at a speed of 407 mph. Unofficially, because the Fédération Internationale de l'Automobile (which had taken over from the AIACR in 1946) refused to recognise the legitimacy of a record set by a car whose wheels were not driven by its engine. Reid Railton had sneered in 1947 that 'Carried to its ridiculous extreme, nothing will stop a man from claiming the world speed record by running a roller skate tied to a fast aeroplane over the measured mile.' Merely attaching wheels to some kind of rocket or jet power and hoping for the best, was not sufficient.

It fell to Donald Campbell, therefore, to break the LSR correctly in 1964, in his turbojet-powered *Blue Bird*, whose four wheels were driven by an enormous Bristol-Siddeley aero engine: a jet-age reinvention of Cobb's *Railton Special*, in effect. At the awkward and inhospitable Lake Eyre, South Australia – an antipodean version of Sir Malcolm's Verneuk Pan – he managed an average of 403 mph, as opposed to Cobb's one-way 403 mph. Afterwards it turned out that Donald had been mugged in the cockpit by the ghost of his father: 'Well, boy. Now you know how *I* felt that time at Utah when the wheel caught fire,' the spectre is supposed to have said, leaving him helplessly reflecting on his achievement through the distorting lens of his own father. 'There never was anyone like the Old Man, was there?' he asked forlornly on the evening of his triumph.

This 403 was only achieved after endless Campbell-style misjudgements, delays and one enormous crash at Bonneville which fractured Donald's skull. Work actually started on *Blue Bird* back in 1956, and the car rapidly became an overweening showpiece for British know-how and technological skills. It was massively sponsored by the British automotive industry, and by the end was widely held to have cost £1 million to build. Dunlop alone spent £75,000 on a new test rig at Fort Dunlop, in order to supply him with the best tyres; their first high-speed rig having been built in the mid-twenties for almost nothing, using second-hand bits and pieces.

When *Bluebird* first arrived at Bonneville in 1960, the Americans, busy cobbling together their record cars in garages and back yards all over the States, were flabbergasted by the size of the backup team and the amount of *matériel* that came with it. Campbell, who looked like his mother but was as obsessional as his father, complained that 'I never knew what loneliness was until I started this record business' as he gazed at the Bonneville wastes. He then wrecked the machine at 360 mph and it had to be completely rebuilt. There were rumours that Sir Alfred Owen, the industrialist behind much of the *Blue Bird* effort, wanted Campbell out of the driver's seat and a professional put in his place. Four years later, in July 1964, he silenced Sir Alfred's doubts and took the LSR.

Campbell held the record for all of two and a half months, before Tom Green in a jet car called the *Wingfoot Express* hit 413 mph; then Art Arfons finally got the *Green Monster* working properly on 5 October 1964 and imperiously snatched the title from him at a speed of 434 mph. And that really did put an end to Cobb's reign. Campbell gave up on the LSR, went back to the WSR and was killed in 1967 on Coniston Water. The FIA meanwhile bowed to the inevitable, recognised the non-wheel-driven jet car records and within a couple of years the Americans were routinely doing 600 mph at Bonneville. In October 1970 Gary Gabelich, driving the *Blue Flame* (which had a rocket at the back; not even a jet engine) hit a record of 622 mph. There the matter rested, apart from a moment in 1979 when Stan Barrett, a Hollywood stuntman, allowed himself to be strapped to a wheeled rocket (the *Budweiser Rocket*, in fact, after its principal sponsor) and may or may not have broken the sound barrier one-way at Edwards Air Force Base, California.

Then, in October 1983, English businessman Richard Noble took his *Thrust II* jet car out to the Black Rock Desert in Nevada, where he reclaimed the LSR for Britain, at 633 mph. His lineage and his intentions were both impeccable. As a six-year-old boy Noble had been on holiday in the Scottish Highlands at the time when Cobb was grappling with his *Crusader* bid. A trip to Loch Ness, the sight of the jet-powered boat and the presence of the great man were enough to inspire the young Noble with a dream. Years later, after the Americans had held the LSR for a full decade, a lust for adventure and straightforward patriotism – the full mix, as experienced by Segrave and Campbell – set him to work on building a record contender: *Thrust*, followed by *Thrust II*. His success made him famous, won him the Segrave Trophy, the John Cobb Memorial Trophy, the Sir Malcolm Campbell Trophy and the OBE.

One thing led to another: October 1997 saw his monstrous twin-jet-engined *Thrust SSC* break the sound barrier, again at Black Rock, and in the teeth of American competition. This time, though, the machine was piloted by – well, a pilot. It was Noble's car, all right; but the physical and mental qualities needed to sit in it and work the controls were now so rarefied that the job had to be done by an RAF fighter pilot named Andy Green. The elision from motor car to grounded aircraft looked to be more or less complete; while the division of labour – Noble the motivator and organiser; Green the daredevil – would have baffled Sir Malcolm Campbell.

But was this functional separation very much different from, say, that between the *Golden Arrow*'s designer, Captain Irving, and its driver, Captain Segrave? Well, if it had been Irving's idea to go after the glory and construct the car, with Segrave only employed later on to drive it, then no. But the ambition, the essential dynamic, had to come from Segrave for the record to be his. No one expected him to build his own car – he wasn't Parry Thomas – but he had to inspire it and drive it. However amazing *Thrust SSC*'s achievement, whom do we revere at the end of it all? The nerveless Andy Green? Or the indefatigable visionary Richard Noble, OBE? Their relationship recalls that between J.M. White, inventor of the *White Triplex*, and Ray Keech, its fearless driver.

And how do we relate to the incredible speed of 766 mph, which *Thrust SSC* reached? A century earlier, Gaston Chasseloup-Laubat took the LSR at a speed twice as fast as a sprinter could run; only a bit faster than a bicycle could manage, downhill. Thirty years on, and when tens of thousands watched Segrave and Campbell thunder by at over 200 mph, there was still, just, some kind of direct connection between the audience and the event. The speed itself was intelligible. But now, in the Nevada desert, where the record cars are visible only as plumes of dust in the distance, and the speeds are only numbers on a read-out, plus the echoing thunder of the sonic boom, this almost-race has become something else: a near-abstraction, a distant experiment, a dynamic exploration. And when someone manages to travel on land at over 1000 mph, what kind of event will *that* be? What would Sir Henry have said?

Index

Thomas, René, 38
Thompson, Mickey, 327
Thomson & Taylor, 53, 178, 183, 217, 258
Thomson, Major Ken, 42, 178, 183
Thrupp & Maberly, 144
Thunder Ahead, 250
Thunderbolt, 282–3, 289, 294, 312
Thurst II, 330
Thurst SSC, 330
Tibbets, Colonel Paul, 305
Times, 325
Todd, James, 78
Tour de France, 3
Traub, Charles R., 150, 151
Triplex see *White Triplex*
twenty-four-hour record, 280

United States, 88–90, 245–6
  car-minded, 76–7
  and Great Depression, 245–6
  relationship with Britain, 89–91
  and Segrave's LSR, 84–6
Unwins, Flight Lieutenant, 251–2
Utah 262–3 *see also* Bonneville Salt Flats

Vanderbilt Cup, 4
Vanderbilt Jr, William K., 4, 38
Verneuk Pan (South Africa), 131, 132, 138–41, 162–3
Vickers Aviation Ltd, 20, 118, 143, 302
Vickers-Armstrong, 302–3
Villa, Leo, 106–7, 108, 109, 113, 119, 183, 184, 241, 302
Vincent, Colonel C. G., 152
Voiturette Grand Prix (1923), 61
Von Opel, Fritz, 120

Waghorn, Henry, 164
Wakefield, Sir Charles, 43–4, 73, 126, 143, 156, 158, 167, 170, 171, 174, 236, 271

Wakefield Trophy, 158
Wales, Prince of, 156–7
Walker, Joseph Reddeford, 263
Walkerley, Rodney, 62–3
Wallace, P. J., 24
Water Speed Record *see* WSR
Watson, Arnold, 282
Waugh, Evelyn
  Vile Bodies, 22–3
Webster, S. N., 119
White, J. M., 121, 146, 151, 239, 331
White Triplex, 121–2, 146–7, 150–1, 183, 236
Wilkins, Harold T., 136
Willcocks, Michael, 171, 172,173
Windermere, Lake, 169–70
Wingfoot Express, 329
Wisdom, Elsie 'Bill', 224, 226
Wodehouse, P. G., 196
women racing drivers, 224–6
Wood, Commodore Gar, 166, 167, 168, 171, 175, 239, 319
World Air Speed Record *see* Air Speed Record
World Land Speed Record *see* LSR
World Water Speed Record *see* WSR
WSR (Water Speed Record), 166, 167, 276, 323, 329
  Campbell takes (1937–39), 298, 318, 320
  Cobb's attempt (1952), 317–18, 319–24
  Segrave takes (1930), 169–73, 318
  Wood takes (1929), 166, 171

Yeager, Chuck, 312

Zborowski, Count Louis Vorow, 27, 39, 44, 93